music 2.50

THE
BEATLES

Twayne's Music Series

Developed and edited in
cooperation with
Chris Frigon and
Camille Roman

THE
BEATLES
A MUSICAL EVOLUTION

By Terence J. O'Grady

Twayne Publishers

Boston

The Beatles: A Musical Evolution
Twayne's Music Series
Chris Frigon and Camille Roman,
consulting editors

Copyright © 1983 by G. K. Hall & Co.
All rights reserved

Published in 1983 by Twayne Publishers,
A Division of G. K. Hall & Co.
70 Lincoln Street, Boston, Mass. 02111

Printed on permanent/durable
acid-free paper and bound in
the United States of America

First Paperback Edition, August 1984

Book design and production
by Barbara Anderson

Typeset in 10 pt. Optima by Compset, Inc.,
with Baby Teeth display.

**Library of Congress Cataloging in
Publication Data**

O'Grady, Terence J.
The Beatles, a musical evolution.

(Twayne's music series)
Bibliography: p. 201
Discography: p. 193
Includes index.
1. Beatles. I. Title.
ML421.B4035   1983   784.5'4'00922
82-21288
ISBN 0-8057-9453-0
ISBN 0-8057-9469-7 (pbk)

*To the memory of
my mother and father*

Contents

About the Author
Preface
Chronology
Key to Symbols

About the Author

Terence J. O'Grady received his Ph.D. in musicology from the University of Wisconsin–Madison in 1975. He is currently an associate professor in Communication and the Arts at the University of Wisconsin–Green Bay where he teaches courses in music history and music theory, ethnomusicology, and popular music. He has published articles on musicological and aesthetic topics in *The Musical Quarterly, Ethnomusicology,* and the *Journal of Aesthetic Education* among others.

Preface

In the years since the Beatles' first commercial recordings in 1962, the group has become solidly entrenched among the foremost cultural heroes of the 1960s. The extent to which their music has been disseminated and consumed worldwide since that time suggests that the group has also been one of the most significant forces in the history of popular music. The Beatles have become virtually synonymous with the popular music revolution of the mid-1960s, and the many rereleases of their recordings as well as the still frequent imitations of their musical styles bear witness to their continuing popularity and impact.

In the 1960s, the Beatles were examined by journalists and scholars primarily in terms of their sociological significance. Their lifestyles and public images were studied as potential influences on the morals and mores of young people. Their songs were often characterized and evaluated only in respect to the content and merit of their lyrics. Trends were determined not on the basis of musical considerations but rather in terms of the messages and literary postures evident in the song texts. The Beatles themselves were questioned at length in regard to possible interpretations of these texts, and their responses (serious or not) were seized upon as meaningful contributions to the understanding of their songs.

It has become increasingly clear that this somewhat lopsided view ignores much of what is most significant in the Beatles' accomplishments. For it is their success in solving musical problems, rather than their social or literary postures, that has proved to be their most distinctive and lasting contribution to popular music. And yet, this aspect of the Beatles' achievement continues to be neglected by even the most recent studies, most of which remain content to examine their role as mythmakers in contemporary society. It is for this reason that this study will focus on the musical evolution of the Beatles and will analyze their use of melody, harmony, rhythm, form, and instrumentation as it develops from their earliest stages to their final album.

It is reasonable to ask whether it is in any way useful to deal with the Beatles' music in terms of traditional musical analysis. The Beatles in general have not been impressed by such attempts and this is understandable, perhaps even to be expected. At the same time, however, there is evidence to suggest that the Beatles did have a reasonably well developed grasp of the uniqueness of their achievements. These achievements can be best appreciated, perhaps only appreciated, in their rightful stylistic context. It is not certain that this context is, more than ten years after some of the group's most successful recordings, particularly clear to most listeners, if indeed it ever was. And so the Beatles' protestations over analytical examinations of their music are interesting but irrelevant to the value of such an undertaking.

Of course, it is extremely difficult to capture any oral tradition with notated examples (the standard published sources being notoriously inaccurate) and analytical procedures primarily designed for "classical" music. So the reader is urged to become a listener simultaneously and to try to use the comments found here to focus and renew the listening experience, because it is there that the greatest reward resides.

Since parts of this book derive from my 1975 doctoral dissertation at the University of Wisconsin–Madison, I would like to thank my graduate committee members, Dr. Lenore Coral and Dr. Lois Anderson, and especially my advisor, Dr. Lawrence Gushee, for a great deal of assistance.

I would like to express my gratitude to my mother, Isabel Geddes O'Grady, and my brother, William Walsh O'Grady, for their proofreading of the manuscript as well as for their many useful suggestions for its improvement.

I would also like to thank my wife, Judy, for helping me and encouraging me in many ways.

Terence J. O'Grady

University of Wisconsin–Green Bay

Chronology

1940 Birth of Richard Starkey, July 7. Birth of John Winston Lennon, October 9.

1942 Birth of James Paul McCartney, June 18.

1943 Birth of George Harrison, February 25.

1960 Beatles' first appearance at the Indra and Kaiser Keller Clubs in Hamburg, Germany, August.

1961 Beatles begin a series of engagements at the Cavern Club in Liverpool, January. Second trip to Hamburg; engagement at the Top Ten, April. Recording session with singer Tony Sheridan, April. Brian Epstein becomes the Beatles' manager, December 3.

1962 Recording session for Decca Records, January 1. Polydor single release: "My Bonnie" / "The Saints," January 5. Beatles win *Mersey Beat* popularity poll, January. Third trip to Hamburg, April. Audition for George Martin and EMI Records, June 6. Richard Starkey (Ringo) replaces drummer Pete Best, August 16. First recording session at EMI studios with Martin as producer, September 4–11. Parlophone single release: "Love Me Do" / "P.S. I Love You," October 5.

1963 Parlophone single release: "Please Please Me" / "Ask Me Why," January 12. First nationwide British tour with the Helen Shapiro Show, February. Parlophone LP release: *Please Please Me*, March 22. Parlophone single release: "From Me to You" / "Thank You Girl," April 12. Tour with Gerry and the Pacemakers and Roy Orbison, May 18–June 9. Vee Jay LP release: *Introducing the Beatles*, July 22. Parlophone single release: "She Loves You" / "I'll Get You," August 23. Sunday Night at the London Palladium

Concert, October 13. Royal Variety Performance at Prince of Wales Theatre, London, November 4. Parlophone LP release: *With the Beatles,* November 22.

1964 Capitol LP release: *Meet the Beatles!,* January 20. The Beatles' first American tour; two appearances on "The Ed Sullivan Show," February 7 and 21. Publication of Lennon's *In His Own Write,* March 23. Capitol LP release: *The Beatles Second Album,* April 10. Began tour of Hong Kong, Australia, and New Zealand, June 8. United Artists LP release: *A Hard Day's Night,* June 26. World Premiere (London) of film *A Hard Day's Night,* July 6. Five week tour of the United States and Canada, August 19–September 20. Capitol single release: "I Feel Fine" / "She's a Woman," November 23. Parlophone LP release: *Beatles for Sale,* December 4. Capitol LP release: *Beatles '65,* December 15.

1965 Capitol single release: "Eight Days a Week" / "I Don't Want to Spoil the Party," February 15. Capitol LP release: *The Early Beatles,* March 22. Capitol LP release: *Beatles VI,* June 14. Concert tour of France, Italy, and Spain, June 20–July 4. Publication of Lennon's *A Spaniard in the Works,* July 24. World Premiere (London) of United Artists film *Help!,* August 1. Parlophone LP release: *Help!,* August 6. American tour, August 13–September 1. British tour with the Moody Blues, December 3–12. Parlophone LP release: *Rubber Soul.*

1966 Capitol LP release: *"Yesteray"* . . . *And Today,* June 20. Parlophone LP release: *Revolver,* August 5. American tour, August 12–29. World Premier (London) of Warner Brothers film *The Family Way* with music by Paul McCartney, December 18.

1967 Parlophone LP release: *Sergeant Pepper's Lonely Hearts Club Band,* June 1. Beatles attend conference of the Maharishi's Spiritual Regeneration League in Bangor, Wales, August. Manager Brian Epstein dies, August 16. Capitol LP release: *Magical Mystery Tour,* November 27.

1968 The Beatles go to India for a Transcendental Meditation course at the Marharishi's academy. Ringo and Paul re-

turn to England before the course is completed, February
–April. Apple LP release: *Wonderwall Music* (Harrison),
November 1. Apple LP release: *Unfinished Music No.
1–Two Virgins* (Lennon-Ono), November 11. Apple LP
release: *The Beatles,* November 22.

1969 Apple LP release: *Yellow Submarine,* January 13. Zapple
LP release: *Unfinished Music No. 2: Life with the Lions*
(Lennon-Ono), May 9. Zapple LP release: *Electronic
Sound* (Harrison), May 9. World Premiere (London) of
United Artists film *Yellow Submarine,* July 17. Apple LP
release: *Abbey Road,* September 2. Apple LP release: *The
Plastic Ono Band—Live Peace in Toronto 1969*
(Lennon-Ono and the Plastic Ono Band), December 12.

1970 Apple LP release: *Hey Jude* (or *The Beatles Again*), February 26. McCartney announces his decision to leave the
Beatles, April 9. Apple LP release: *Let It Be,* May 8. World
Premiere (New York) of United Artists film *Let It Be,* May
13.

1980 Death of John Lennon, December 8.

Key to Symbols

The notated examples included in this book make use of Roman numerals for chord symbols. Large Roman numerals indicate major chords and small Roman numerals indicate minor chords. For example, typical diatonic and chromatic chords in the key of C would be designated and labelled in the following way: (See Ex. A)

(Ex. A.1 and A.2)

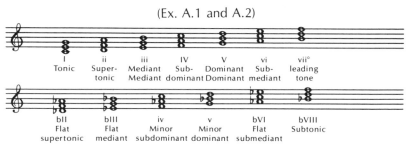

I	ii	iii	IV	V	vi	vii°
Tonic	Super-tonic	Mediant	Sub-Mediant	Dominant	Sub-mediant	leading tone

bII	bIII	iv	v	bVI	bVIII
Flat supertonic	Flat mediant	Minor subdominant	Minor dominant	Flat submediant	Subtonic

The use of a "7" after a chord symbol indicates that a seventh is added to the triad. For example, V7 and IV7 would be designated in the following way: (See Ex. B)

(Ex. B)

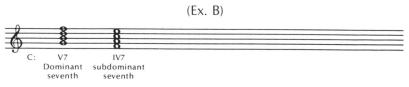

C: V7   IV7
     Dominant   subdominant
     seventh   seventh

If the added seventh is not diatonic in the key, it is designated as b7 or Maj. 7 depending on its type: (See Ex. C)

(Ex. C)

C: Ib7   V Maj. 7

The use of a "9" after a chord symbol indicates that a ninth is added to the seventh chord: (See Ex. D)

(Ex. D)

Diminished triads and augmented triads are designated as follows: (Ex. E)

(Ex. E)

A triad with an added sixth is designated as follows: (See Ex. F)

(Ex. F)

A triad that includes a suspended fourth is designated as follows: (See Ex. G)

(Ex. G)

A triad that has a dominant relationship to the following triad (i.e., a secondary dominant) is designated as follows: (See Ex. H)

(Ex. H).

Unless otherwise indicated, all examples show the vocal melody and accompanying harmony.

The Music of
the Beatles

Any investigation of the musical achievements of the Beatles should begin with an attempt to understand the larger stylistic context for their work. This will involve a stylistic survey of those performers who most influenced the Beatles in their early period and whose work constitutes a mainstream against which the Beatles' innovations and achievements can be measured.

In order to define the scope and parameters of the Beatles' style in a given period, it will be necessary to examine a reasonable sampling of compositions within that period. Such an examination will reveal that the Beatles were actively engaged in enlarging the stylistic boundaries of rock in a variety of genres for several years.

For the most part, these contributions involved techniques relating to melody and harmony and, increasingly, distinctive uses of instrumentation or recording technique. Beginning with the 1965 album *Rubber Soul,* the Beatles began to show a conceptual sophistication which was to revolutionize the format of the rock album. Their next album, *Revolver,* demonstrated not only a series of innovations in melodic-harmonic structure and recording technique, but also a new art-consciousness in the Beatles' lyrics.

The 1967 *Sergeant Pepper's Lonely Hearts Club Band* represented the high point of the Beatles' career in terms of album concept and influence, but it became evident with subsequent albums that the Beatles' musical development was not based merely on a desire to produce innovations for their own sake. The Beatles changed direction without hesitation when they felt that they had reached a creative roadblock. The record-buying public would certainly have welcomed another

Sergeant Pepper, but neither of the next two albums, *Magical Mystery Tour* and *The Beatles* (the "White Album"), seemed designed to exploit their earlier success. In fact, the self-conscious expansion of musical resources that characterized the Beatles' development up to *Sergeant Pepper* clearly begins, with *Magical Mystery Tour,* to be replaced with new creative postures that are fundamentally unconcerned with inno- vation as such.

This period of retrenchment is marked by a return to older styles, both as parody and as a vehicle for serious expression. Neither of the two final Beatle albums, *Let It Be* and *Abbey Road,* explored any new musical ground and, despite noteworthy successes in each album, both can be seen as demonstrative of the Beatles' abdication of leadership in the popular music world in terms of innovation.

Still, this eventual abdication in no way cancels the Beatles' achievement, especially since the source of an innovation is far less important than the use to which it is put, and the Beatles continued to draw on a number of resources with skill and imagination. In general, this ability to take from numerous popular styles while continually contributing their own fresh outlook and the tendency to enlarge the capacities of popular music is unparalleled in the 1960s. It is for this reason that a study of the Beatles' evolution is important: their music can be seen as the ultimate barometer of stylistic change in the popular music of their time.

The Early Years

Because the biographical facts of the Beatles' upbringing and early years have been related many times,[1] only the briefest account will be supplied here. In general, their earliest years seem to be lacking in the sort of dramatic events or circumstances that are so frequently seen in retrospect as indicative of future greatness. In short, the Beatles' youth appears to have been rather conventional in most respects and, in general, similar to that of innumerable other working-class Liverpud- lians involved in popular music in the late 1950s.

John Winston Lennon was born October 9, 1940, into a working-class family beset with domestic problems. He died tragically on December 8, 1980, the victim of a senseless murder. John had first become in- volved with popular music near the end of his high school days when he and four friends had formed the Quarrymen, a skiffle group (the nature of which will be described in chapter two), which Paul McCartney and George Harrison were to join by 1958.

John Paul McCartney was born June 18, 1942, also of working-class parents. Although dabbling initially with piano (his father had played piano with dance bands in his younger years) and trumpet, Paul's interest in popular music blossomed at age twelve upon receiving his first guitar. After a casual encounter with Lennon and the Quarrymen in the summer of 1956 in which Paul had impressed them with his guitar technique, he was invited to join the group. McCartney began composing songs almost immediately with Lennon following suit, and the sort of cooperation which characterized their relationship for several years was underway.

George Harrison was born January 25, 1943, once again of working-class parents. George met Paul at Liverpool Institute (a prestigious high school), joining the Quarrymen at Paul's invitation by 1958, having previously led a similar group, the Rebels.

Ringo Starr (Richard Starkey) was born July 7, 1940 to a working-class couple. Leaving school at fifteen, he tried his hand at several jobs and was an apprentice fitter when he helped organize the other apprentices into a skiffle band. Ringo eventually joined Rory Storme's band, one of the most popular of the Liverpool beat groups, where he came to the attention of the other Beatles and, later, their future producer, George Martin. Ringo finally linked up with the Beatles in 1962 at the request of George Martin.

Meanwhile, the three original Beatles continued to refine their skills. Changing the group's name from Quarrymen to Moondogs and eventually to the Silver Beatles (in emulation of Buddy Holly and the Crickets), the Beatles finally managed a successful audition with a local promoter, earning a two week tour of Scotland as a backing group with the then popular Johnny Gentile. The group used Stuart Sutcliffe, a friend of Lennon's, on bass guitar and another in a series of temporary drummers. Upon returning from this brief tour, the Beatles played several times at the Casbah Club. Here they found a steady drummer in Pete Best, son of the club's owner. Work remained sporadic, however, and the Beatles jumped at the chance offered in 1960 by promoter Alan Williams to go to Hamburg, Germany. George Harrison was out of school by this time and McCartney had just completed his A level exams. Lennon's aunt protested his abandonment of art college, but the call of adventure was too great to be denied.

The Beatles' stay in Hamburg began in the Indra Club. The club closed after two months, and the group began an engagement at the Kaiserkeller. During this period, the Beatles played as long as eight hours and started to emphasize showmanship more than they had in the past. The atmosphere of the clubs, and perhaps the language barrier as well, encouraged a more raucous performance style that employed hard rock more than had been the case back in Liverpool, although recently released recordings from that period show that their song selection was still highly eclectic. (The group's early repertoire will be examined more completely in later chapters.)

After nearly five months, the tour ended somewhat ignominiously when it was discovered that Harrison, under eighteen and without a work or resident permit, would have to leave the country. A few days later, Paul and Pete Best accidentally started a small fire in a new club. They were jailed briefly, then deported. Shortly thereafter, John and Stu Sutcliffe had their work permits revoked. The Beatles straggled back to Liverpool one by one.

The Beatles eventually regrouped and performed once again at the Casbah Club and, on December 27, at the larger Litherland Town Hall, a job booked for them by Bob Wooler, a local disc jockey. The Beatles' raucous style and extroverted performance mannerisms made them a smash hit with an audience more accustomed to blander fare. The result was a near riot and the beginning of the group's almost fanatical following.

Other dates at larger ballrooms followed in 1961, and the Beatles soon became the main attraction at the Cavern, a prestigious jazz club which had turned to rock. They played at the club 292 times from December, 1960 to February 1962,[2] and their following grew steadily. Still, they accepted an opportunity to return to Hamburg in April, 1961, performing at the classier Top Ten Club. The Beatles' distinctive hairstyles stemmed from this visit (encouraged by the German girl friend of Stu Sutcliffe) as well as their first recording session on which they backed Tony Sheridan, a popular singer from the Top Ten Club. (The musical details of this session will be discussed in chapter three.)

The Beatles returned to Liverpool in July, 1961, leaving Stu enrolled in a Hamburg art college. They continued to be greatly sought after although perusal of a pop music newspaper of the period, Mersey Beat, suggests that they were probably third in popularity behind Gerry and the Pacemakers and Rory Storme and the Hurricanes.[3] But an important break for the group came on October 28, 1961, when Brian Epstein, the manager of a local record shop, received a request for a record entitled "My Bonnie" by the Beatles (actually a by-product of the Hamburg recording session with Sheridan doing the vocal).

Discovering that the Beatles were a local group, he sought them out and became interested in them, eventually becoming their manager on

December 3 of that year. Epstein immediately went to work for the Beatles, lining up an audition for them at the Decca recording studios. Decca proved uninterested in the group, but the Beatles' popularity remained undiminished, even winning a *Mersey Beat* popularity poll that month.[4] This was followed by their third trip to Hamburg, this time for an engagement at the Star Club, the biggest club of its type in that city. Meanwhile, Epstein had taken the tapes of the Decca audition to George Martin of Parlophone Records. Martin was interested enough to request a live audition and the Beatles returned to play for Martin in June. (The musical details of this audition are also discussed in chapter three). Martin subsequently offered the Beatles a contract on the condition that drummer Pete Best be replaced by Ringo Starr of Rory Storme's group. Despite vigorous protest from the many fans of Best, the change was made. On September 11, 1961, the Beatles went to London to record their first British record, "Love Me Do" backed with "P.S. I Love You." At this point, the Beatles' history and their music became synonymous.

2

Early Influences
and Recordings

Liverpool's pop music environment in the 1950s and early 1960s was an amazingly rich and varied one. An often quoted remark by Lennon refers to the prominence of country and western music and the enthusiasm for blues:

It [Liverpool] is cosmopolitan, and it's where the sailors would come home with the blues records from America on the ships. There is the biggest country and western following in England in Liverpool, besides London—always besides London, because there is more of it there.

I heard country and western music in Liverpool before I heard rock and roll. The people there—the Irish in Ireland are the same—they take their country and western music very seriously. There's a big heavy following of it. There were established folk, blues and country and western clubs in Liverpool before rock and roll and we were like the new kids coming out.[1]

While specific country and western-oriented performers will be singled out later as likely influences on the Beatles, it can be stated at this point that a taste for country and western was reasonably widespread in Liverpool with many artists ranking high even on the youth-dominated popular record charts. For example, two versions of "Little Bitty Tear" (one by American Burl Ives) were in the *Mersey Beat* Top 20 simultaneously in the week of February 22, 1962,[2] while both Marty Robbins's "Devil Woman" and Johnny Tillotson's "Send Me the Pillow You Dream On" had earned spots on the same list in the week of October 18.[3] Of course, these records had "crossed over" to the pop charts in the United States as well and "hard core" country and western generally remained the province of the older generation in Liverpool. The pop charts also reflect an interest in "rockabilly," a combination of rhythm and blues and country and western music which will be referred to again in connection with specific figures.

In regard to the blues following in Liverpool, Charlie Gillett, in his *The Sound of the City: The Rise of Rock and Roll*, suggests that there existed a definite enthusiasm for "traditional" American folk music and rural blues in England in the 1950s, an enthusiasm focused on the pre-World War II era of acoustically accompanied solo musicians. Gillett reports that even prominent American bluesmen were obliged to play only with acoustical backing in England although held to no such restrictions at home.[4]

The Beatles seem not to have shared this "purist" attitude, generally preferring the electric rhythm and blues tradition:

> You tend to get nationalistic, and we would really laugh at America, except for its music. It was the black music we dug, and over here even the blacks were laughing at people like Chuck Berry and the blues singers; the blacks thought it wasn't sharp to dig the really funky music, and the whites only listened to Jan and Dean and all that. We felt that we had the message which was 'listen to this music.' It was the same in Liverpool, we felt very exclusive and underground in Liverpool, listening to Richie Barret and Barrett Strong, and all those old-time records. Nobody was listening to any of them except Eric Burdon in Newcastle and Mick Jagger in London. It was that lonely, it was fantastic. When we came over here and it was the same—nobody was listening to rock and roll or to black music in America—we felt as though we were coming to the land of its origin but nobody wanted to know about it.[5]

The Beatles' Skiffle Period

The skiffle movement was born in 1955 with Lonnie Donegan's hit single of "Rock Island Line," which featured an accompaniment of only acoustical guitar, string bass, and washboard. Donegan, a refugee from Chris Barber's jazz band, built a reputation with his energetic performances of mostly American folk material and, in 1955, John Lennon joined thousands of his contemporaries in starting his own skiffle group, the "Quarrymen." The group, which McCartney joined the same year, featured two acoustical guitars, banjo, washboard, various drummers, and an occasional "tea chest" bass, and performed a repertoire of folk, country and western, and a handful of simple rock and roll songs.

The change in repertoire from the standard skiffle material of the original Quarrymen to the more current rock and roll songs of the day was brought about by several factors: McCartney's preference for this new style; the addition of George Harrison (formerly the leader of his own skiffle group, the "Rebels"); and the ever-increasing popularity of rock and roll idols Bill Haley and Elvis Presley in England.

Elvis Presley

Although the Beatles' attraction to Bill Haley and the Comets was a fleeting one, their admiration for Elvis Presley was not. His first recording for RCA, "Heartbreak Hotel," showed the blues-based intensity that made him the archetype of the white male rock and roll (or rockabilly) singer and this intensity appealed very much to the young Beatles. Although they made relatively few recordings of his material, his vocal mannerisms were imitated both by Lennon (his aggressive rhythm and blues-cum-rockabilly style) and McCartney (his husky ballad style). It should be noted, however, that Presley's contributions to the British pop market by the early 1960s were mostly commercial ballads (e.g., "Can't Help Falling in Love," and "She's Not You") with an occasional uptempo pop-rock song (e.g., "Return to Sender"); his earlier hard rock style was seldom in evidence.

Little Richard

Another significant influence on the young Beatles was the black rhythm and blues singer Little Richard (Richard Penniman). Due to difficulty in negotiating a British distributor for his American hits, Little Richard's impact on the British scene was delayed until 1957. His influence at that time, however, was strongly felt by the Beatles and Paul McCartney in particular. McCartney's father has stated that although Paul had emulated both Elvis and Little Richard in the 1950s, his best imitation was of Richard:

> I used to think it was awful . . . absolutely terrible. I couldn't believe anybody was really like that. It wasn't 'til years later, when I saw Little Richard on the same bill as the Beatles, that I realized how good Paul's impersonation was.[6]

Various references to the Beatles' repertoire in the early 1960s suggest that Little Richard's "Long Tall Sally" and "Tutti Frutti" were favorites of the Beatles' audiences as early as 1961.[7] Richard's gospel-style shouting and falsetto screams are imitated in various Beatle performances, and an obvious salute is made as late as the 1969 *Abbey Road* album.

Furthermore, Richard is listed by both McCartney and Harrison as a "favorite singer" in a unique interview-poll published in a February 1963 issue of *New Musical Express,* one of Britain's most successful popular music magazines. Neither Presley nor rhythm and blues singer Chuck Berry are so honored in this poll.[8]

Chuck Berry

Although Berry is not listed as a favorite in the *New Musical Express,* the Beatles did record a number of his songs (some of which were never released) and frequently included them in their concert repertoire. While Berry's archetypical blues-influenced rock and roll songs were clearly favorites of the Beatles, and Harrison can often be heard imitating his guitar style, Berry's nasal, country-flavored vocal style was duplicated only by George (in "Roll Over Beethoven") with John adapting a more raucous style on Berry's songs.

Carl Perkins

The most country and western-influenced of any composer-performer recorded by the Beatles, Perkins represents the archetype of the rockabilly singer. Though often blues-based in their harmony, his songs (and performances) are generally less intense than rhythm and blues-influenced rock and roll, often substituting more lyrical melody lines for the accented and repeated blues notes found in the songs of such composers as Little Richard and Chuck Berry.

It is significant to note that the Perkins's songs chosen by the Beatles for performance, "Honey Don't," "Matchbox," and "Everybody's Trying to Be My Baby," are all humorous in tone and all assigned to the "non-singers" of the group, Ringo and George, perhaps with an intention of providing some relief from the Beatles' more serious efforts. It is also true, however, that both Harrison and Starr have, in the *New Musical Express* poll and elsewhere, expressed their admiration for country and western music to a far greater degree than have Lennon or McCartney.

The Everly Brothers and Buddy Holly

Virtually all commentators on the Beatles' music have been insistent on the Everly Brothers' influence on the early Beatles. Arnold Shaw, in *The*

Rock Revolution, states that the Everlys' style was very much in keeping
with the "Anglicized Kentucky Bluegrass" music which had been in-
fluencing young British musicians since the advent of the skiffle craze,
adding that the Beatles had once gone under the name of the "Foreverly
Brothers," demonstrating the closeness of that connection.[9]

Gillett refers to the Everlys' close country and western harmony style
and their "distinctive instrumental sound," often gained by a "rich
acoustical guitar accompaniment with a series of full chords linking
verbal phrases," as particularly noteworthy characteristics of their
style.[10] Both the vocal harmony style (usually alternating perfect fourths
with thirds and sixths in "authentic" Bluegrass style) and the rich
acoustical accompaniment, especially in the context of a driving, uptempo song, are clearly found in the Beatles' early music, although their
uses of both are somewhat personalized as will be seen. But the sustained, lyrical melodic style often shown by the Everlys is perhaps
equally important as an influence, a style which is often combined by
Buddy Holly and the Crickets with a call and response vocal exchange.
The recordings of both groups remained popular on the Liverpool charts
in the late 1950s and early 1960s, although Holly's were released
posthumously. Holly's "Words of Love" was recorded by the Beatles as
late as their sixth American album in tribute to one of their chief
mentors, ad reminiscences of both the Everlys' and Holly's style occur
even in the Beatles' mature style.

Uptown Rhythm and Blues

The term "uptown rhythm and blues"[11] is used here to refer to a mostly
black repertoire which is blues-influenced in its intensity and rhythmic
identity but possesses a greater harmonic variety and sophistication
than is usually associated with the blues tradition. Performers working
in this style include Chuck Jackson and Ben E. King (both mentioned by
McCartney and Lennon as among their favorite singers), the Drifters,
Smokey Robinson and the Miracles (whose "You've Really Got a Hold
on Me" was recorded by the Beatles in 1964), and the Shirelles. George
Harrison once declared that the Beatles sounded like "Male Shirelles"[12]
and their gospel-influenced call and response interaction can be heard
on many Beatle recordings including their "cover" of the Shirelles' hit
"Baby It's You." Songwriters Gerry Goffin and Carole King, also idols of
the early Beatles,[13] frequently composed in this "uptown" style for the
Drifters and Shirelles and their song "Chains" was included on the
Beatles' first album in 1963.

Other Influences

The *New Musical Express* poll provides a number of other possible influences: Harrison rates the Duane Eddy group as his favorite with guitarist Chet Atkins given as his favorite instrumentalist.[14] Neither of these two seem to have had a significant influence on Harrison, although both show aspects of the country and western guitar style that George draws heavily from in the early years, and Atkins's slicker, more commercial style is hinted at in Harrison's playing on "Till There Was You," included on the Beatles' first American album. A more significant instrumental influence is the guitar work of Carl Perkins. Many of his rhythmic mannerisms and articulation techniques, for example, partially muffled two or three note background riffs (i.e. short melodic fragments), usually on the off-beats, can be found in the Beatles' rockabilly recordings, especialy those composed by Perkins himself.

Some of the Beatles' choices listed in the poll are difficult to take seriously as possible influences on the Beatles' style although they may well constitute honest preferences. These dubious influences include, for Harrison, his listing of Eartha Kitt as his favorite singer and, for Lennon, his listing of Quincy Jones as a favorite band and Sonny Terry as a favorite instrumentalist. Although Lennon's latter choice might be seen as a token nod toward a more "authentic" black blues style, the former is more difficult to rationalize and may or may not be a sincere choice. Lennon's listing of Luther Dixon as his favorite composer seems legitimate enough since Dixon's composition "Boys" was included on the group's first British album. Similarly, McCartney's listing of Billy Cotton's "Trad" jazz band as his favorite must be considered questionable, although his reference to Goffin and King as favorite composers is certainly authentic enough.

Under the category of "tastes in music," Lennon's listing of "R and B" and "gospel" seems compatible with his listing of favorite singers and performers, but Paul's expressed preference for "modern jazz" (along with "R and R") seems strange at first glance, unless it is assumed that he is misapplying the title to refer to Billy Cotton's style. Actually, the Beatles were on record at that point as having expressed some enthusiasm for the Modern Jazz Quartet and Paul's listing may simply be another manifestation of that approval. George's preferences for country and western are understandable in light of his previous choices, and his mention of "Spanish guitar" music stems from an early interest in the guitar playing of Andres Segovia.

The list of potential Beatle influences could, of course, be far greater. The generalized account supplied here is not meant to be all-inclusive, even within an early-period context, but merely to provide an indication of the types and variety of styles which may have influenced the early Beatles. Other specific influences will become apparent from a survey of the Beatles' early recordings.

Early Recordings

The most complete and accurate Beatle discography is *All Together Now*, compiled by Harry Castleman and Walter J. Podrazik.[15] This work contains the salient information on all Beatle recordings released in America and England between 1961 and 1975, and the most significant early recordings from Germany and elsewhere. Particularly useful features of this discography include a seemingly accurate attribution for all Beatle compositions, a partial listing of Beatle songs written for others, and a listing of "bootleg" albums. These are generally illegal recordings of concerts (live, radio or television), studio out-takes (alternate versions never released), and audition tapes. The sound quality of these recordings is frequently very poor, but they do provide a glimpse into the early Beatle repertoire and their early performance style.

The Decca Audition

The audition tapes for Decca (recorded January 1, 1962) show the Beatles' eclectic tastes, or at least their desire to impress the Decca officials with their versitility. The repertoire ranges from such standards as "The Sheik of Araby" and "Red Sails in the Sunset" to the 1950s popular ballad "To Know Her Is to Love Her" (characterized by a bridge section with unusually varied harmonies), the Chuck Berry hit "Memphis," and some songs the Beatles were later to re-record and release: "Till There Was You," "Please Mr. Postman," and "Money." Three Paul McCartney originals are also included. "Like Dreamers Do" and "Hello Little Girl" are pleasant pop songs (later recorded by other British groups) with little to distinguish them from others in the period. However, Paul's "Love of the Loved" is a fascinating example of early harmonic adventurousness which clearly anticipates the sophisticated adult ballad style which the Beatles were to demonstrate so effectively in "Yesterday" and "Michelle."[16]

The Sheridan Session

The next Beatle recording to be discussed comes from a May, 1961, session in Hamburg, Germany, in which they accompanied singer-guitarist Tony Sheridan (an English singer particularly popular in Germany) on six songs, while recording by themselves one original instrumental ("Cry for a Shadow") and one vocal ("Ain't She Sweet") by Lennon.[17]

The entire session was released as an album in June, 1962, although a single release combining "My Bonnie" and "The Saints" had been issued and re-issued earlier. (The entire album was subsequently re-released in various versions after the Beatles had become famous.)

Although this version of "My Bonnie" is the one that first brought the Beatles to the attention of manager Brian Epstein, the vocal is, in fact, by Tony Sheridan with the Beatles backing him. The Beatles provide a typical, driving hard rock accompaniment combining an active boogie-woogie bass line (of remarkable virtuosity considering bassist Stu Sutcliffe's reputation as a weak player) and a Chuck Berry-influenced rhythm guitar figure alternating triads and added sixth chords. Harrison's lead guitar fills are a fascinating mixture of rockabilly fragments, blues riffs, and chordal Chuck Berry interjections. Harrison's solo is clearly Berry-influenced in its "bent" chords and repeated motives. The second chorus of the solo introduces a throbbing reiteration of the chord roots by the bass in a manner which evokes the "surfing" style of Dick Dale and Jan and Dean so popular in America in the early 1960s.

"Take Out Some Insurance on Me, Baby" and "Nobody's Child" are both blues-influenced ballads for which the Beatles provide rather cursory accompaniments. The former is provided with a lead guitar introduction more country and western than blues-like in essence, although Harrison's brief solo is properly idiomatic and fluid (despite an obvious wrong note), while "Nobody's Child" is provided only with a tongue-in-cheek rural blues lead guitar opening.

For "The Saints" ("Go Marching In"), the Beatles supply a rather primitive accompaniment enlivened only by a repeated lead guitar blues riff and the syncopated chords which emerge in the third chorus. Harrison's solo is again clearly Chuck Berry-influenced in its alternation of chordal interjections and linear blues motives. Also worthy of note is the "surfing" style reiteration of the bass in the middle chorus and a falsetto "ooh" by Sheridan a la Little Richard.

The Beatles' accompaniment to "Sweet Georgia Brown" is dominated by a rock piano in the style of Jerry Lee Lewis (probably played by

Paul) and a chanting vocal chorus. The piano is given the solo and the Beatles' backing is otherwise rather conventional.

The Beatle-accompanied recording of "Why?" (coauthored by Sheridan) is significant as a precursor of two early Beatle ballads. A Latin-rhythm commercial ballad which features a I–iii–ii–V chord progression, "Why?" seems to have influenced Lennon's "Ask Me Why" and "Do You Want to Know a Secret?" not only harmonically but also in its use of background vocals.[18]

The Beatles' recording of "Ain't She Sweet?," with vocal by John Lennon (released as a single in May, 1964), shows a typical driving Chuck Berry accompaniment and lead guitar solo along with Lennon's harsh rock and roll voice.

The Beatles' first recorded original composition, "Cry for a Shadow" (attributed to John and George), owes much to the clean articulations and controlled excitement of Cliff Richard's backup group, the Shadows, whose instrumentals the Beatles performed frequently in the early Hamburg days.[19] Its melodic material, presented by lead guitar with the standard string tremolo manipulation of tone, is typical both in its character and repetitiveness. The harmonic accompaniment, an alternation of I–vi moving to IV–V–I, is equally commonplace. The middle section, in the major submediant key and over soloistic tom-tom activity, is more improvisatory in nature and is accompanied by various vocal outbursts by the performers. The song proceeds in a typical manner (the melody drops an octave for variety at one point) and is thoroughly conventional in all but one aspect: a recurring introduction motive in which two guitars juxtapose a movement of thirds (G–B and A–C) against a reiterated dominant pedal G. This single gesture—more of a sonorous event than a melodic or harmonic statement—furnishes a distinctive touch that lends great individuality to the piece. It is the first of many such unique, identifying "sound-gestures" to appear in the Beatles' compositions. Some of these sound-gestures are simply compelling and easily identified refrains or "hooks," but frequently they are more fundamental events which owe their dramatic effect at least as much to sonority as to any particular characteristic of melody or harmony. More will be said about these sound-gestures in subsequent discussions.

BBC Radio Concert

The next recording worthy of attention is a bootleg release of a BBC radio concert in the summer of 1962, perhaps June 9.[20] None of the fourteen songs on this recording are Beatle originals, but a brief survey of them will yield more information about the group's early repertoire.

Only four songs can be considered authentic rhythm and blues-influenced rock and roll songs: "I Got a Woman" (recorded by Ray Charles, Elvis Presley and others), "A Shot of Rhythm and Blues" (recorded by Arthur Alexander), "I'm Gonna Sit Right Down and Cry" (recorded on Presley's first album in 1956), and "Slow Down" (recorded by Larry Williams).

The Beatles' version of "I Got a Woman" is closely modeled after Presley's, with Harrison's solo drawing heavily on the sort of chordal rockabilly fragments found also on Presley's recording, and with vocalist Lennon attempting to capture Elvis's vocal ornaments and breathless style.

"A Shot of Rhythm and Blues," based on a slightly rearranged blues progression, shows the Beatles alternating a unison vocal and a call and response interaction. As the background voices (harmonized in fifths) intone the refrain melody, Lennon delivers his repeated-note vocal interjections in a manner similar to that found later on "P.S. I Love You," the flip side of the Beatles' first British single.

The Beatles' version of "I'm Gonna Sit Right Down and Cry" is surprisingly dissimilar to Presley's original, performed in a style which is more rock and roll than rockabilly and not unlike their version of "I Got a Woman" in terms of syncopated rhythmic accompaniment. Distinctive features include the repeated use of a unison blues riff to provide continuity; a blues-based rather than rockabilly lead guitar solo; and the addition of an upper harmony voice to add sonority at climactic points, followed by a strategically placed unison squeal. These final gestures become particularly significant in original Beatle compositions recorded in the early years.

The fourth of these songs, Larry Williams's "Slow Down," is given an exciting performance similar to that eventually released commercially. The virtuoso arpeggio figure repeated by the bass is evidence that the more technically proficient McCartney has now taken over the bass guitar from Stu Sutcliffe.

A second general stylistic category relevant to this group of songs is that of the uptempo "pop-rock" song. The term "pop-rock" is used here to refer to songs that make use of the energy and rhythmic aggressivness of rhythm and blues-influenced rock and roll while failing to exploit in any consistent way the blues-based intensity (often gained from the use of blues-note dissonances) or the more intense performing postures associated with that style. These pop-rock songs also tend to stress a more sustained melodic flow than does rhythm and blues-influenced rock and roll.

In this case, the songs being discussed under the general category of pop-rock have a strong affinity with the rockabilly style as well (although this is certainly not always the case) and the Beatles' performance reflects this. For example, "Everyone Loves Someone" is performed in the Everlys' manner while "Crying, Waiting, Hoping" features the responsorial vocals of Buddy Holly and the Crickets (with George Harrison as lead vocalist). Perkins's "Glad All Over" is given a typical rockabilly treatment as is Freddie Fontaine's "Nothin' Shakin' But the Leaves on the Trees" (both lead vocals again by George).

"Lonesome Tears in My Eyes," recorded in 1956 by Johnny Burnette and The Rock 'N' Roll Trio, also combines a rockabilly slant with its pop-rock credentials. The Beatles, with lead vocal by John Lennon, evoke here a Latin-rhythm "Tex-Mex" style (actually a western "substyle" of rockabilly), complete with quarter note triplets in parallel thirds played by the lead guitar.

A third general category relevant to this collection of songs is that of the "popular ballad." These are generally taken at a slow or moderate tempo, emphasize lyricism to a greater degree, and are often more harmonically sophisticated than the uptempo pop-rock songs (or the rockabilly-influenced songs heard in this collection). Paul sings lead on two of these: "To Know Her Is to Love Her" and "Bound by Love" (the "Honeymoon Song"), and sings with John on "Please Don't Ever Change." The Beatles' treatment of this final Goffin-King song is clearly derivative of the Crickets' 1962 performance in its use of two-part harmony, and owes its identity as a popular ballad more to its occasional chromatic sophistication than to its arrangement. "Bound by Love" (from the 1959 film *Honeymoon*) is, like "Lonesome Tears in My Eyes," a Latin-rhythm piece with "Tex-Mex" rockabilly touches in the accompaniment. But there is a far greater emphasis on the lyrical flow here, and the effect is not unlike that found in the initial verse section of McCartney's "P.S. I Love You."

Two songs in this collection fail to fall comfortably into any of these three categories. "I Just Don't Understand," recorded in 1961 by actress-singer Ann-Margret and sung here by Lennon, shows the conjunct (i.e., stepwise) melodic flow and repetitive phrase structure of a traditional minor key folk melody, although the Beatles' superimposition of blues riffs lends a more intense aura. Perkins's "I'm Sure to Fall," with McCartney as lead vocalist, is an unadorned country and western ballad which might well have been the model for the Beatles' own "Love Me Do" in its phrasing and employment of vocal harmonies.

The Star Club

The final recording to be discussed here is a two-volume set made at the Star Club in Hamburg in late December, 1962, and released commercially only in 1977. This amateur recording, which includes Ringo on drums in place of Pete Best, was actually taped after the Beatles' first single release with Parlophone ("Love Me Do" / "P.S. I Love You"), and is discussed here as a final look at the Beatles' early repertoire.

The recorded performance at the Star Club includes only two Beatle originals: Lennon's "Ask Me Why" (the "B" side of the Beatles' second British single) and McCartney's "I Saw Her Standing There" (a rhythm and blues-influenced song found on the group's first album). These are not included on the American versions of the Star Club album which feature a slightly different selection than the original British release, as is often the case. The following discussion will be based on the combined repertoires of both.

Along with "I Saw Her Standing There" (which will be discussed in the next chapter), this collection offers several rhythm and blues-influenced or "hard rock" songs as they are termed in the 1960s: "Be-Bop-A-Lula," recorded in 1956 by Gene Vincent (with the lead vocal here sung by a German waiter); "Kansas City" combined with Little Richard's "Hey-Hey-Hey-Hey!"; "Your Feet's Too Big"; Chuck Berry's "Roll Over Beethoven," "Sweet Little Sixteen," and "Little Queenie"; Little Richard's "Long Tall Sally," "Hippy Hippy Shake," "Shimmy Shake," "Hully Gully," and "I'm Gonna Sit Right Down and Cry"; "Twist and Shout," a recent hit for the Isley Brothers; and two songs by Ray Charles: "Hallelujah! I Love Her So" and "Talkin' 'Bout You."

Most of the lead vocals here are taken by Paul (often in his "Little Richard voice") with John handling only "Talkin' 'Bout You," "Sweet Little Sixteen," and "I'm Gonna Sit Right Down and Cry," and George singing on "Roll Over Beethoven." Guest vocalists appear also on "Hallelujah! I Love Her So" and "Hully Gully."

The Beatles' versions of these songs are generally dynamic if conventional in detail. Many of them employ the same rhythmic alternation of triad and added sixth chord that characterizes the basic sonority of the accompaniment in previous recordings in this style. Harrison's solos continue to offer an interesting mixture of rockabilly and blues-influenced figures. His solos and fills in the Chuck Berry songs frequently derive closely from the original recordings, and his solos on "Long Tall Sally" and "Roll Over Beethoven" are similar to those appearing on the Beatles' later album versions. The recording of Tommy Roe's then popular hit "Sheila" seems a half-hearted vehicle for some solo drumming by Ringo and includes no bass guitar or lead guitar solo.

Two uptown rhythm and blues songs are included in this group: "Where Have You Been all My Life?" and "Mr. Moonlight," both with lead vocals by John. "Mr. Moonlight" is taken at a faster tempo than the Beatles' late 1964 recorded version but, except for a guitar solo in place of the later organ solo, this version is quite similar.

Three songs in this group can be best described as rockabilly. "Nothin' Shakin' But the Leaves on the Trees" is recorded here in a version that is somewhat more hard rock-oriented in its driving bass part and prominent drumming than their earlier BBC version, and features Paul as lead vocalist rather than George. Harrison is lead singer on two Carl Perkins's songs: "Everybody's Trying to Be My Baby" and "Matchbox." The Beatles' versions of both of these songs resemble those eventually released on 1964 albums, down to the dominance of rockabilly elements in Harrison's solos. (Ringo replaces George as lead vocalist on *Matchbox* in the later recording, however.) "Lend Me Your Comb," a 1957 hit for Carl Perkins, is given an Everly Brothers' treatment vocally and rockabilly elements dominate the accompaniment as well. Even the I–bIII–IV–V series of chords that link the second verse to the bridge suggests an Everly Brothers' mannerism; the Latin rhythm bridge evokes the "Tex-Mex" style encountered earlier.

Several types of ballads appear in this group. "To Know Her Is to Love Her" is a 1950s rock ballad with, as noted earlier, a harmonically rich bridge section. "A Taste of Honey" and "Till There Was You" are both Broadway show tunes and, as such, must be considered "adult" commercial ballads. Both are heard in versions closely resembling the Beatles' later recordings of them. Harrison's solo guitar work on the latter suggests the commercial jazz style of the versatile Chet Atkins.

A third "adult" ballad is "I Remember You," which had recently been a hit for the popular Frank Ifield whose British television show the Beatles had appeared on shortly before. The Beatles' rendition emulates the harmonica sound of Ifield's original, but the sharp, two-beat accompaniment suggests more the sound of Perkins's "I'm Sure to Fall" and the Beatles' "Love Me Do."

"Falling in Love Again," popularized by Marlene Dietrich and a likely favorite of the Beatles' German audience, is given a surprisingly straightforward rendering. Paul's vocal has a lyrical, almost sentimental quality, although the rawness of the accompanying sonority gives it the sound of a rock ballad. The guitar solo simply paraphrases the melody and the final major seventh chord (heard also on the Beatles' version of "Till There Was You") confirms the song's status as an adult ballad.

In contrast to the more or less reverent approach taken toward the last song, the adult standard, "Red Sails in the Sunset," (introduced by Paul as "the one you've come for") is given an uptempo rockabilly treatment, although Paul's vocal is appropriately lyrical and sustained. Surprisingly, Harrison's solo here is more hard rock-oriented than on many of the Chuck Berry songs discussed earlier.

Finally, the Latin rhythm standard "Besame Mucho" (played here "by request") is given an uptempo arrangement which is parody-like in some respects, especially the background vocals in their "cha-cha-boom" exclamations.

And so it is clear that the Beatles' performing repertoire remained eclectic even after their first British single was released. And, although an edited tape such as the one used as the basis of these Hamburg recordings can scarcely be considered definitive in such matters, the mixture seems more rhythm and blues or hard rock dominated than in the BBC tape recorded just a few months earlier. Still, rockabilly songs continue to play an important role as do ballads of various sorts and, increasingly, original compositions. (The original compositions naturally begin to dominate in concert performances as the Beatles' fame increases.) It is no exaggeration to suggest that the Beatles' musical range, at least in terms of performance, is already amazingly broad by late 1962.

But breadth does not guarantee genius, of course, and it remained for the Beatles to consolidate their musical experiences and to add their own unique ingredients before they could emerge as the masters of rock in the 1960s.

Early British and
American Recordings

Paul McCartney's "Love Me Do," the Beatles' first British single, was recorded in September, 1962, at the EMI studios in London under the supervision of George Martin. The session was a long one; seventeen "takes" of the "A" side were made before Martin called in a studio drummer to play the drum set, relegating Ringo to tambourine. (The version ultimately released as a single features Ringo's drumming while the album version has him on tambourine.) The song had been performed for Martin at the earlier audition and he chose it for the Beatles' first single in part because of Lennon's harmonica playing on it.[1]

The influences on this song are readily apparent. References have been made to Bruce Channel's hit single "Hey! Baby" as a model for John's harmonica introduction and fills[2] between vocal phrases, while Carl Perkins's country and western ballad, "I'm Sure to Fall," is similar to "Love Me Do" in some aspects of rhythm, melodic contour, harmonic scheme, and in the reliance on perfect intervals (e.g., fourths and fifths) in the vocal harmony. But significant differences do exist between "Love Me Do" and the Perkins's ballad, particularly in the vocal harmony. Whereas the country and western or rockabilly style frequently made use of perfect fourths in an attempt to gain the closest possible harmony (e.g., a melody note "C" harmonized by a "G" rather than the softer minor sixth "E" beneath), the Beatles' use of perfect fifths and fourths is the result of a specific preference for these sonorities. The readily available option of a third beneath the melody is consistently ignored. Furthermore, the voices do not proceed in similar motion as is so frequently the case in the country and western style, but are quite independent in their melodic direction.

This preference for perfect fifths and fourths, combined with an almost hypnotic repetition of one basic rhythmic motive, creates a nearly incantatory effect, reinforced by the simplicity and repetitiveness of the text. Thus, "Love Me Do" essentially owes its distinctive identity not to any extraordinary feature of melody or harmony (only the I, IV, and V chords are used), but to acute sensitivity to color and textural detail.

McCartney's "P.S. I Love You," the "B" side of the Beatles' single, was for some time, not given the attention or speculation that "Love Me Do" enjoyed almost from the beginning. Once the Beatles were solidly successful and it became evident that all their material had commercial potential, "P.S. I Love You" began to attract more attention from radio programmers and others. The song is a pleasant, if unremarkable, example of a popular love ballad in Latin rhythm.[3]

The sources for the song are again fairly obvious. The vocal introduction resembles Goffin-King's "Please Don't Ever Change" in its repeated note recitational melody over a chromatic chord progression. The opening measures of the verse are similar to the Latin "Tex-Mex" ballad "Bound by Love" in harmonic progression (i.e., I–ii–V–I), general melodic contour, and lyrical flow. The gospel-influenced call and response vocal style heard in the bridge is clearly modeled after the uptown rhythm and blues style and particularly resembles the bridge of "A Shot of Rhythm and Blues."

Despite these obvious derivations, "P.S. I Love You" does demonstrate some distinctive qualities. The verse section begins with a lilting ascending-descending phrase of two and one-half measures, the second of which is repeated a fifth lower for the second phrase while displaying an effective use of accented nonharmonic tones. But the most significant device occurs in the third, five-measure phrase as a surprising bVI triad is introduced and returns to the tonic chord via a bVII triad.

This is the first distinctive harmonic surprise to appear in a Beatles' composition and must be considered a bold gesture in this otherwise conventional context. The bridge, with its alternation of IV and I behind the call and response vocal pattern (with solo interjections by McCartney the second time), and the greater part of the verse remain commonplace and the overall result is a well-crafted, if eclectically influenced, love ballad with a single unique gesture.

The Beatles' second single, "Please Please Me," was recorded on November 26, 1962, and released as the "A" side of a single on January 12, 1963. Biographer Hunter Davies explains that Lennon wrote the song as a substitute for "How Do You Do It?," a song given to the Beatles by George Martin which was recorded but not released at their request.[4] "Please Please Me" proved to be a most successful choice, impressing manager and publishers alike, and rose to number one in England by February 16, 1963.

The song features Lennon's harmonica and a distinctive, descending verse melody against a reiteration of the tonic pitch highly reminiscent of the Everly Brothers' vocal style, in particular their recording of "Cathy's Clown." A series of eighth note guitar chords (I–bIII–IV–V) that links the initial four measure vocal phrase with its repetition is also characteristic of the Everlys, although the heavy percussion and bass sound achieved by the Beatles provides a sound quality not available to the duo.

The second, refrainlike section of the verse effectively contrasts with the harmonically static first section with its variety of diatonic chords (i.e., IV–ii–vi–IV in the first four measures) and response vocals. The bridge exhibits an unusually sinuous, chromatic melody revolving around the third of the IV and V chords.

Still, despite its undeniable popularity, "Please Please Me" contains no real surprises. It effectively uses striking vocal sonorities (especially the pedal-like reiteration of the tonic in the highest voice) and employs a good variety of melodic shapes, rhythmic figures, and diatonic chords. But, ultimately, the song presents no substantial stylistic advance.

The same might be said of the "B" side of the single, Lennon's "Ask Me Why." This song is similar in many respects to the Beatles' earlier "B" side, McCartney's "P.S. I Love You." It is a generally subdued, lyrical love song with Latin-tinged rhythmic accompaniment in which the second half of the verse (fulfilling a bridge function) changes briefly from the smooth commercial ballad style to a more intense, uptown rhythm and blues style.

The song is also comparable to the Tony Sheridan composition "Why?" (recorded earlier by the Beatles with Sheridan) in its prominent use of the mediant minor 7th chord passing to a supertonic minor 7th in the verse and the melodic rhythm of the verse.[5] Its use of three-part background vocals, which often take on a melodic function equal to the lead voice, is also shared by the Sheridan ballad. In fact, the many commercial ballad characteristics that dominate Lennon's song (e.g., the major and minor 7th chords in conjunct progression), suggest that his interest in that style may have been equal to McCartney's in this period.

The First British Album

On March 22, 1963, Parlophone and producer George Martin released the Beatles' first LP, *Please Please Me*. The album miraculously remained number one on the British *Melody Maker* charts for more than six months. It contained fourteen songs: both sides of the group's first two singles, six songs by other composers, and four new songs, one of which had been originally composed for and recorded by another British singer.

The six nonoriginal songs chosen by the Beatles demonstrate the varied influences to which they were still prone, even after their initial success. Probably the most surprising choices from a stylistic point of view are the two aggressively raucous rhythm and blues songs, Russell-Medley's "Twist and Shout" and Dixon-Farrell's "Boys." The first of these was the first completely ostinato-based song recorded by the Beatles. The second was their first released song based on a strict blues progression. Equally surprising is the vocal manner used in these performances. In both cases, the singer (Lennon in the first, Starr in the second) seems to make a conscious effort to emulate a frenzied "shout" style more associated with Little Richard than with the previous performers of the material (i.e., the Isley Brothers' 1962 recording of "Twist and Shout" and the Shirelles' 1960 recording of "Boys"). The style of these hard core rhythm and blues songs seems to have little in common with the Beatles' own compositions or releases at this point (only one original song on the album can be placed in the same category). It seems clear that the Beatles were anxious to declare their allegiance to the rhythm and blues roots which had helped them to establish their reputation as dynamic performers, a reputation documented by biographer Davies among others:

> The Beatles . . . played loud and wild and looked scruffy and disorganized, like some aboriginal throw-back. They had continued in the rock and roll style which had been the fashion when they left Liverpool for a series of bookings in Hamburg clubs but was now dying out, thanks to the Shadows. They'd become even more rock-and-rollish if anything, added extra pounding, volume . . . "

The uptown rhythm and blues style, more moderate both in tempo and in tone, is also well represented on the album. "Anna," composed by Arthur Alexander, "Baby It's You," a David-Bacharach-Williams collaboration recorded in 1961 by the Shirelles, and "Chains," composed by Goffin-King, all fall into this category. The first two demonstrate the typical alternation of I and vi chords—a device that characterizes many of the Beatles' attempts in this style.

Also included on the album is the triple meter ballad "A Taste of Honey." Earlier experiments by the Beatles with the adult commercial ballad style (e.g., the Lennon-McCartney "Love of the Loved" as well as their demonstration recordings of "Red Sails in the Sunset" and "Besame Mucho") make it clear that this choice was not unprecedented. In fact, George Martin's first positive reactions to the Beatles were in connection with Paul's singing of "Till There Was You" included on the Beatles' second British album.[7] It is likely that Paul's background and interest in such standards (derived at least in part from his bandleader father) was one of the main reasons for their inclusion on the early albums. The influence of their advisors (perhaps not sure of the potential market) and the desire to show off Paul's "pretty" voice in the best context also may have played a part in the decision.

The Beatles' arrangement of "A Taste of Honey" is, for the most part, conventional. It includes an out-of-tempo introduction in three-part harmony announcing the song by means of the refrain, and a subdued instrumental accompaniment featuring legato guitar arpeggios and brush strokes on the snare drum. Only some heavily accented guitar chords and vocalized "do do do do's" mark the arrangement as rock and roll, and even the switch to common meter (4/4) for the bridge is a convention of the song rather than a Beatles' innovation. The recording is important nevertheless for its demonstration of a self-consciously commercial vocal style on McCartney's part and for evidence that, even at this early stage, Ringo was capable of holding his own in the vocal harmony.

Of the Beatles' originals, four have already been discussed: "Love Me Do," "Please Please Me," "P.S. I Love You," and "Ask Me Why." Two others are medium tempo ballads: "Misery" and "Do You Want to Know a Secret?"

Lennon-McCartney's "Misery" qualifies as a ballad because of its moderate tempo and predominantly lyrical melodic line. Beginning with a rhythmically unaccompanied vocal introduction based on the third phrase of the verse, the verse melody demonstrates an unusually prominent use of descending major sixths in the first two (identical) phrases. The third phrase is basically an extended sequential repetition of the second, and features an especially poignant prepared major seventh appoggiatura at the cadence.

Harmonically, the verse exhibits a common progression (I–IV–I–IV–V–I), while the bridge section (and the final fadeout coda) alternate between I and vi (again reminiscent of the uptown rhythm and blues style) beneath a melody consisting of a descending diatonic scale.

This song was recorded by British singer Kenny Lynch and released the same day as the Beatles' first album with unspectacular results. While the song was included on the American Vee Jay album, it was not included on any Capitol album released in the United States. This suggests that the song was (rightfully) considered to be somewhat less interesting than most of the group's recordings in this period.

A more noteworthy song in many respects is Lennon's "Do You Want to Know a Secret?." The song was originally composed for Billy J. Kramer and the Dakotas and was released by that group on April 26, 1963, backed by another Lennon-McCartney composition, "I'll Be on My Way." The song was a number one hit in England for Kramer by June. The Beatles subsequently released their version as the "A" side of an American single in March, 1964, which rose to the second spot on the *Billboard* charts by May 9.

The "tempo rubato" vocal introduction (sung by George) evokes the melodramatic ballad style of the 1950s with its dramatic text. An equally dramatic musical setting is provided. The first line is delivered with a recitative-like repetition of notes and is harmonized by the minor form of the tonic and subdominant chords provided by a guitar tremolo. The second line is given even more extraordinary treatment. It begins over a bIII which proceeds to the Neapolitan chord (bII), and finally to V in preparation for the verse melody.

Despite this unique and undoubtedly tongue-in-cheek introduction, the melodic-harmonic characteristics of the verse strongly resemble those of both Sheridan's "Why?" and Lennon's "Ask Me Why." This is particularly evident in the song's prominent use of the mediant 7th chord. It appears immediately after the tonic chord in the first measure of the verse and is followed (as in the other songs) by the supertonic 7th chord (with the biii 7 inserted for chromatic movement here). This is in turn followed by a dominant 7th chord, and the entire two measure sequence is repeated (with variation) four times before moving to a subdominant, dominant, and finally submediant chord in the last phrase of the fourteen measure verse.

Although the descending-ascending contour of "Secret" is distinctive, its melodic rhythm is again similar to the two other ballads with the greatest amount of activity focused at the beginning and end of each phrase. The middle of the phrase contains longer note values or rests over which the harmonized background vocals contribute their countermelody. In all three of these songs, the melodic activity of the soloist and background voices in the verse is so closely intertwined as to make separation into melody and harmony (or background) virtually impossible at times.[8]

The bridge of "Secret" begins in the key of the subdominant and incorporates an interesting variation of a standard 1950s ballad progression, that is, I–vi–iii–ii –I–vi–iii–vi–V of original key. Still, the significance of "Secret" lies in its parallels with the other two ballads already noted and with the commercial ballad style in general, including aspects of "P.S. I Love You" and other ballads played by the Beatles in the early years. Clearly Lennon is modeling such compositions as "Do You Want to Know a Secret?" and "Ask My Why"—consciously or unconsciously—on pre-existing models, even while attempting, like McCartney, to add unique, personal touches of his own.

One original song on the album, Lennon's "There's a Place," must be placed in the pop-rock category, one which also includes "Please Please Me" and, less comfortably, "Love Me Do." Songs in this style, as suggested earlier, demonstrate some of the characteristics associated with rhythm and blues influenced rock: instrumental accompaniment techniques and special effects (e.g., string bending); an emphatic beat defined by percussion and guitars; and a generally restrained adaptation of rhythm and blues vocal techniques. But pop-rock songs also exhibit the influence of traditional popular song in their emphasis on sustained and singable melody (i.e., a "catchy" tune), a somewhat expanded harmonic vocabulary, and a more tightly controlled energy level, often combined with slicker, more commercial vocal and instrumental arrangements.

The popular song influence is immediately apparent in "There's a Place." The song begins with an instrumental introduction taken from a two-measure section of the verse and features Lennon's harmonica on a sustained major 7th chord. A two-measure phrase containing only three notes and sung mostly in thirds and sixths by Lennon and McCartney is repeated (with slight variation) four times in the first half of the verse over a conventional harmonic progression (I–IV–I–IV–V–vi–V) much in the manner of Lennon's "Misery." Unlike "Misery," but similar to Lennon's "Please Please Me," there is a second half to the verse. This makes use of the same basic melodic idea but is more harmonically diversified, incorporating a iii7 and the I7 heard in the introduction along with the other chords of the first section.

Again as in "Misery," the melodically contrasting bridge begins on the submediant. It proceeds with an unexpected major II, followed by a I and then an equally unexpected III.

But despite some unusual harmonic touches, "There's a Place" remains a rather ordinary pop-rock song (again not included in any American Capitol album) which shows obvious similarities to earlier Lennon compositions, for example, "Please Please Me" and "Misery."

McCartney's "I Saw Her Standing There" is the first recorded Beatles' composition patterned directly on the rhythm and blues style. The song was released as a single both by Duffy Pommer with the Graham Bond Quartet and the Beatles themselves as a "B" side in January, 1964. The Beatles' Version eventually rose to number fourteen on the *Billboard* charts.

Evidence of the rhythm and blues model can be seen in every aspect of the recording. Unlike their previous compositions with singable, catchy melodies of obvious and directional contour, "I Saw Her Standing There" displays a disjointed and syncopated melody that contains only a handful of notes (many of them "blues" notes). These are frequently displaced from the downbeat in direct contrast to the rhythmic squareness that characterizes most of their early works. The rhythmic accompaniment contributed by the rhythm guitar is equally syncopated (if slightly predictable), as opposed to the almost machine-like emphasis of all four beats in previous recordings. Only the percussion, assisted by rhythmic hand clapping, retains its metronomic quality. Of course, it is this metric insistence that gives life to the rhythmic deviations.

Despite the heavy arpeggio figures supplied by the bass guitar in typical rhythm and blues style, the recording shows an unusually sparse texture. Short syncopated fills from the lead guitar at phrase ends and pauses in the melodic line are the only sources of harmony. The second half of the verse exhibits a slightly fuller texture with its added vocal harmony and more active chording from the rhythm guitar. But the return of the beginning of the verse after the repeat shows even greater sparseness as the lead guitar reduces its contributions. The recording thus represents a striking departure from the sound ideal demonstrated in other Beatles' recordings or in the pop record market in general.

The vocal performance on "I Saw Her Standing There" is, in terms of the Beatles' previous works, equally exceptional. McCartney's vocal contains many subtle ornaments and changes in tone quality (e.g., the use of a "scratchy" quality in places and half-spoken, half-sung pickup notes). The manipulation of tone quality and use of embellishments are evident in other early Beatles' recordings, but none is as rich in vocal nuance.

The character of the melody itself, at least the first eight measures of the verse, can hardly be considered original to McCartney as a songwriter. Both melodically and harmonically, these eight measures could equally have been composed by Little Richard, Chuck Berry, Larry Williams, or many others working in the rhythm and blues tradition. The tendency to revolve around one pitch and the consistent use of flatted thirds and sevenths, both of which are manifested here, are characteristic of all of them.

The second part of the verse is exceptional in several ways. The use of parallel vocal harmony is in itself unusual within the mainstream rhythm and blues context. This type of texture is more readily found in the music of country and western-influenced groups such as the Everly Brothers. It is seldom used by the most famous rhythm and blues soloists who generally restrict vocal accompaniment to occasional responses or unison choruses.

The nature of the vocal harmony in this section is also worthy of note since the perfect intervals found in abundance here are seldom used at this quick tempo in any style (except perhaps for bluegrass). Also unusual in the rhythm and blues context is the use of the natural seventh scale degree in measure six after five occurrences of the flatted version in previous measures.

A far less subtle deviation from the rhythm and blues tradition occurs at measures eleven and twelve. Here, a falsetto "ooh" (harmonized a tenth below) coincides with a harmonic progression of IV–bVI. This type of minor third root progression is without precedent in the popular rhythm and blues idiom of the period, although similar progressions have been noted in certain Everly Brothers' introductions and some songs of Buddy Holly. The Beatles were undoubtedly aware of the impact of this brief musical effect on their listeners and acted accordingly. Three measures before its arrival, it is prepared with a change in bass guitar activity from eighth note arpeggios to repeated quarter notes. The result of this manipulation is a psychological ritard and a clear signal to the listener that something exceptional is about to happen. When the unexpected progression finally does arrive, its shock value is increased by the falsetto "ooh!." This intensity is maintained to the end of the verse by the boldness of the perfect intervals in the vocal harmony.

As in several previous Beatles' recordings, the instrumental texture undergoes a noticeable change in the bridge. The lead guitar assumes a prominent role for the first time by doubling the bass guitar arpeggios, breaking into a country and western-derived variant of that arpeggio, and finally contributing its most distinctive solo fill at measures seven and eight.

The most exceptional feature of the bridge, however, is its handling of tension. The subdominant harmony is insisted upon for the first six measures of the section and the eventual change to dominant is, presumably, accompanied by a release of tension. It would seem natural at this point to expect a direct return to the verse. Eight-measure subsections have been the norm in Beatles' compositions up to this point, and the dominant chord's arrival after such extensive preparation would seem to be the climax of the bridge. This is not the case, however, and the next two measures containing a return to the subdominant and a striking example of contrary voice-leading in the two vocal parts are heard as an unexpected extension of the phrase. This results in a new escalation of tension that propels the bridge back to the verse with more momentum than would have been possible after the expected eight-measure bridge.

Harrison's lead guitar solo is introduced by the kind of ecstatic screams first encountered in the Beatles' recording of "Twist and Shout." In that recording, the screams served to fill out phrase ends (and to pay homage to the original recording), and in this instance their function is in part similar. However, the screams also suggest—as does the introductory "count-down"—that what the listener is about to hear will be even more reckless than usual. This is true, at least to the extent that an authentically improvisatory solo is allowed to take place at all for the first time in a recorded Beatles' original and only the second time on any commercially released Beatles recording.

The solo exhibits a heavily reverbed sound over a relatively sparse texture of bass arpeggios and throbbing low rhythm guitar strings. Its linear continuity is more well developed than in the solo on "Boys," although the melodic line is still conceived in terms of two and four measure phrases and consists basically of a string of well-placed blues riffs, mostly in the low range with occasional higher chords for punctuation, and sliding grace notes in the country-western style. The second half of the solo features double stops (particularly perfect fourths) and string muffling and bending. The overall style can hardly be described as original (the solo in "Boys" is probably more remarkable for its use of silence), but the ideas emerge fluently and the solo shows a degree of continuity.

Single and Extended Play Releases

While "I Saw Her Standing There" represents a unique and successful exploitation of the rhythm and blues tradition, the Lennon-McCartney pop-rock song "From Me to You" is a less spectacular achievement. Released as the "A" side of a British single on April 12, the song rose to number one on the charts in just three weeks and remained there for six weeks. An American release of the song (the Beatles' first) issued on May 27 did not fare as well, reaching only number 116 on the *Billboard* charts (although the song did somewhat better when rereleased in early 1964).

Despite its almost immediate British success, there is little in "From Me to You" to distinguish it from other pop-rock songs of the time. While the melody features a nice balance of conjunct and disjunct motion (i.e., movement by skip), it is put together in a predictable manner with key phrases repeated either with slight variation or sequentially. Harmonically, the song is equally pedestrian; the verse section uses only the I, vi, IVb7, and V7 chords, while the only variety offered by the bridge is an augmented dominant seventh (V+7) and a falsetto "ooh."

The "B" side of the single, "Thank You Girl," was later rereleased as the "B" side of "Do You Want to Know a Secret?" in the United States and eventually reached number thirty-five on the *Billboard* charts. The song is only again typical of the pop-rock style in many respects, and demonstrates several characteristics seen previously in other Beatles' compositions. For example, the introduction, featuring a harmonica and wordless voices, is drawn from the latter part of the verse. The first half of the verse, based on an alternation of I–IV chords, employs one short pentatonic phrase that is repeated several times with slight variations and added vocal harmony.

The second half of the verse continues with the IV and V chords and a descending scale line that anticipates the bridge melody. The bridge, which once again begins on a vi and uses only the ii and V7 chords with it, features a descending scale line melody that is repeated (slightly varied) for the second phrase. The third phrase of this section is, for the first time in a Beatles' composition, identical to the third phrase of the verse.

Among the other noteworthy features is the varied use of instrumental texture and dynamics to reinforce formal divisions between phrases and sections. For example, the first two phrases of the bridge are accompanied by freely ringing lead guitar chords and reduced bass guitar and percussion activity, while the accompaniment for the last phrase returns to the throbbing eighth notes in guitar and percussion that characterize the recurring introduction section. Also of some significance is Ringo's modest drum solo, juxtaposed over the final repetition of the introduction which closes the song.

In terms of melodic-harmonic content, this song may well be the most simplistic since "Love Me Do." But, just as in the case of the Beatles' first single, the song is given great interest by the attention paid to textural variety and the exploitation of an almost hypnotic repetitiveness. At the same time, it must be stated that "Thank You Girl" demonstrates a more well developed use of melodic contrast than the earlier song, as well as more structural cohesiveness between sections.

The successful single "From Me to You" was followed a few months later by the issuing of an extended play release (45 rpm) by Polydor, the German company which had recorded the Beatles with Tony Sheridan. This release featured "My Bonnie" (with Lennon's vocal), "Why?" and "The Saints" (with Sheridan's vocals), and the Lennon-Harrison instrumental "Cry for a Shadow." The record did not sell particularly well, rising no higher than number thirty-eight on the British *Melody Maker* charts. An American single release by MGM Records in January, 1964, featuring "My Bonnie" and "The Saints" did somewhat better, rising to number twenty-six on the *Billboard* charts by March 24.

The Beatles' own British company, Parlophone, issued an extended play release featuring "Twist and Shout," "A Taste of Honey," "Do You Want to Know a Secret?," and "There's a Place" on July 12, 1963. Despite the fact that every song had appeared previously on the Beatles' first album, the record sold well, remaining on the *Melody Maker* charts for thirty-one weeks and holding the top ten for two.

A few days later; the group's American distributor, Vee Jay, released the album *Introducing the Beatles,* which strongly resembles the first British album *Please Please Me.* It contains twelve of fourteen of the songs included on the British release, omitting only "Ask Me Why" and "Please Please Me."[9] (American albums of this period normally have no more than six songs per side while the British versions frequently have eight. This difference accounts for many of the discrepancies in album content between Beatles' albums issued more or less simultaneously in both countries.) *Introducing the Beatles* made no real progress on the American charts until a huge publicity campaign was undertaken by Capitol Records in early 1964, at which point it was rereleased. It then began to sell very well and rose quickly to number two on the *Billboard* album charts (behind Capitol's first Beatles' album), remaining on the charts for forty-nine weeks.

On August 23, Parlophone released the Beatles' fourth single, "She Loves You," another Lennon-McCartney collaboration. The record rose to the number one spot on the *Melody Maker* charts after only two weeks and remained in the charts for thirty-one weeks. The single was released in America a few days later, this time by Swan Records. It sold poorly at first but enjoyed substantial success in early 1964 as "Beatlemania" hit the United States.

The vocal introduction (and refrain) of "She Loves You" is one of the most exciting to be found in any Beatles' composition. The high range and forcefulness of the unison melody, with its many dissonances against the harmony, give it an unusual intensity. The chord progression itself is an unusual one. The vi—V7/V–IV–I (with added sixth) pattern includes an unexpected minor third root relationship between the second and third chords, seen before only in the verse of "I Saw Her Standing There." The added sixth chord dissonance which concludes the section is an appropriately brilliant (if admittedly cliched) ending for one of the most striking and immediately singable refrains or "hooks" in the popular music of the period.

The verse itself is less spectacular. The melody shows a typical mixture of conjunct motion and small leaps with its most distinctive feature being an accented 4–3 appoggiatura. The vocal texture alternates between unison and harmony in thirds above the melody which occasionally creates minor seventh chords with the guitar accompaniment. The only other harmonic feature of any significance within this section is the unusual prominence of a minor subdominant chord with an added sixth. While this chord occurs in some Beatles' originals composed for others in this period, no Beatles' recording had made significant use of the chord, so the effect is relatively novel.

The refrain, introduced by another ecstatic falsetto "ooh," is identical to the introduction for the first four measures. The last four measures are notable mainly for the recurrence of the minor subdominant with added sixth and the augmented dominant seventh chord which follows it.

The instrumental accompaniment of guitars, bass guitar, and drums is somewhat fuller than usual and appears to be electronically "boosted" in comparison with some earlier Beatles' records. There is also an attempt to ensure continuous momentum by filling all vocal pauses with one of two pronounced guitar riffs, the first a typical rhythm and blues riff with flatted blues notes, and the second an arpeggio figure echoing the melodic movement of the refrain.

But, realistically, many of these harmonic and instrumental subtleties may have had far less to do with the song's great success than the simple appeal of the repeated "yeah yeah yeah" refrain. These "yeah yeah's" were to become almost synonymous with the group and its musical style. The term for Beatles-style rock and roll in many non-English speaking countries included the words "yeah yeah," and a vicar for the Church of England garnered a great deal of publicity by requesting that the Beatles tape a "yeah yeah" version of "Oh Come All Ye Faithful."[10] It is clear that, as a distinctive "sound gesture," the "yeah yeah yeah" refrain from "She Loves You" is unparalleled in the Beatles' early music.

The "B" side of "She Loves You" was another Lennon-McCartney effort, "I'll Get You." Since it exhibits no major innovations or surprises, this song can be dealt with quickly. Basically, "I'll Get You" is a medium tempo ballad with a Chuck Berry influenced eighth note chordal accompaniment similar to that found in "Misery." The song stresses conjunct motion against a commonplace harmonic progression that uses predominantly I, IV, V7, and vi chords in the verse, adding a couple of secondary dominant seventh chords in the bridge. Perhaps the most distinctive aspect of the song is its treatment of nonharmonic tones. The added sixth is prominent as in "She Loves You" and, in keeping with the Beatles' ballad style, there are a reasonable number of major and minor sevenths as well as a few ninths appearing in metrically prominent positions (as was also the case in "Misery"). The song is, otherwise, decidedly lackluster and was not included on any British album although it does appear on the Beatles' second American album for Capitol Records.

With the release of "She Loves You," the Beatles had been propelled into superstardom. Their triumphs included a Sunday Night Concert at the London Palladium, an exhilarating tour of Sweden, and a Royal Variety Performance at the Prince of Wales Theatre in London, where the Beatles charmed the rich and aristocratic of Britain.

It was in this atmosphere that Parlophone Records and George Martin released their second British album.

With The Beatles

With advance orders totaling 250,000 (surpassing the previous record of 200,000 for Presley's *Blue Hawaii*), *With the Beatles* immediately rose to number one on the *Melody Maker* charts, and remained there for twenty-two weeks. It eventually became the largest selling British album with over one million sold by 1968.

Six nonoriginal songs are included in the album. Five of these can be described as rhythm and blues-rock or uptown rhythm and blues, including Berry's "Roll Over Beethoven," later released as a single in Canada; "Please Mr. Postman," by Holland, Bateman and Gordy, the "B" side of the Canadian single; Drapkin's "Devil in Her Heart" (with both pop-rock and country-western overtones); Gordy and Bradford's "Money"; and Robinson's "You Really Got a Hold on Me," a 1962 hit for the Miracles. Most of these are given straightforward and rather derivative renditions. "Money" is supplied with a density of texture and a tension (due to a dissonant ostinato effect) not found on the original, but most are no more than tight and well-disciplined imitations with only minor variants.

The Beatles' version of Meredith Willson's "Till There Was You" is somewhat more remarkable. The song had, of course, been in the Beatles' repertoire almost from the beginning, and here it is given a smooth and polished performance in a commercial Latin-jazz idiom. Harrison's guitar playing had occasionally demonstrated commercial jazz mannerisms in earlier songs, but here those mannerisms define the arrangement completely. His acoustical guitar employs an unusually legato line, quarter note triplet countermelodies, rapid (usually muffled) off-beat chord arpeggios, and a harmonic vocabulary abounding with added sixth, major seventh, and ninth chords, all of which suggest commercial jazz style of such guitarists as Chet Atkins. McCartney's vocal shows little evidence of any jazzlike influences, however, and is as simple and unadorned as was his version of "A Taste of Honey." Once again, the selection manages to show off Paul's "pretty" voice while demonstrating the group's versatility—two virtues considered so important that "Till There Was You" was the first song played by the Beatles on their famous "Ed Sullivan Show" American debut several months later.

Of the eight Beatle originals included on *With the Beatles*, only Lennon-McCartney's "I Wanna Be Your Man" qualifies as rhythm and blues rock. The Beatles had originally composed the song for the Rolling

Stones, who had recorded it as their second single with some success. The rhythm and blues elements are restricted mainly to the verse. Here, a two measure blues-influenced melodic phrase emphasizing the 5th, b7th, and 9th of the tonic chord is repeated by vocalist Ringo a total of four times with varying endings. This occurs against a reiteration of the Ib7 chord with the 9th supplied by a repeated organ riff (played by Lennon). The instrumental texture is quite thick, juxtaposing a rather muddy tremolo rhythm guitar sound, an occasional chord or riff by the lead guitar, the Hammond organ riff, and a four note repeated bass ostinato and heavy, driving percussion.

The texture is lightened considerably in the refrain as a descending chromatic countermelody from the lead guitar breaks up the new harmonized melody over a series of secondary dominant chords (V7/V–V7–I–V7/ii–V7/V–V7–Ib7).

While the refrain clearly departs from the rhythm and blues idiom, Harrison's lead guitar solo launches back into it with a vengeance. Complete with accompanying screams and shrieks, it resembles the solo in the earlier original rhythm and blues rock song "I Saw Her Standing There" in its initial reliance on standard blues motives using flat thirds and sevenths, and its subsequent move to syncopated chords. The song's fadeout coda is a final indication of the frenzied rhythm and blues stance as lead guitar and organ both improvise blues riffs over a melee of shouts, whoops, and harmonized repetitions of the refrain line, "I Wanna Be Your Man."

Two compositions on the album, both by Lennon, are clearly derived from the uptown rhythm and blues style. The verse of "All I've Got to Do" employs a descending pentatonic melody that demonstrates vocal ornaments, melismas, and even pauses similar to those heard in such songs as "Baby It's You" and "Anna."

This quality is reinforced harmonically by the alternation of I and vi for the first six measures of the verse (see ex. 1).

(Ex. 1   "All I've Got to Do": verse, meas. 1–4)

The bridge, which exhibits a primarily ascending pentatonic melody in declamatory (speech) rhythm, begins on IV but also stresses the I and vi chords. The rhythmic accompaniment is also evocative of the uptown rhythm and blues style in its use of a distinctive syncopated rhythm (see ex. 2).

(Ex. 2　"All I've Got to Do": drum rhythm)

There are also some characteristically Beatle elements not associated with the uptown rhythm and blues style. The melody makes frequent use of prominent and expressive nonharmonic tones. Especially when the melody is doubled a third higher by the vocal harmony, dissonant fourths and elevenths are common. The inclusion of the minor subdominant can also be considered a Beatles' characteristic, although "Devil in Her Heart" features one in a comparable context.

"Not a Second Time" shares many characteristics with the previous song. The verse melody is again pentatonic (with the second phrase a variant of the first), and again an alternation between I and vi dominates harmonically. The bridge also employs the I and vi chords prominently, although ii7 and iii chords are included also. Once again, nonharmonic tones abound, especially ninths. The rhythmic accompaniment is syncopated in a characteristic way and a piano dominates the accompaniment sonority for the first time. A lower octave piano solo is also featured with a straightforward presentation of the melody, a characteristic shared by many uptown recordings.

Four of the five original pop-rock songs on the album are Lennon and/or McCartney compositions. Lennon's "It Won't Be Long" shares certain musical characteristics with the Beatles' more successful singles, for example, "Please Please Me" and "She Loves You." The most notable of these traits is a catchy and compelling introduction drawn from the refrain. In "It Won't Be Long," the introduction has sharply accented off-beats with interlocking cross-accents supplied by the background vocal responses over a vi–I alternation. A prominent lead guitar fill interjected at the end of the introduction guarantees the continuation of momentum into the verse (see ex. 3).

(Ex. 3　"It Won't Be Long": refrain, meas. 1–4)

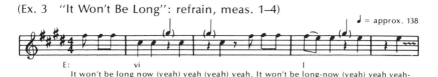

Melodically, the verse is similar to "Please Please Me" in general contour and phrase structure except for the effect of an elision or missing measure. In measure three, the measure-long lead guitar fill is played only once before the initial phrase repeats. The ear anticipates another measure of lead guitar to complete the usual four measure phrase and the effect is a startling one (see ex. 4).

(Ex. 4 "It Won't Be Long": verse, meas. 1–3)

The second, refrainlike half of the verse (which serves also as the introduction) also resembles its counterpart in "Please Please Me," exhibiting a comparable rhythmic momentum in the interplay between lead vocal and responses. Even the harmonic content here is similar in its alternation of vi and I chords, although the earlier song offered a greater variety of chords in this section.

The most striking harmonic effect occurs in the first half of the verse. The progression of the tonic chord to the flat submediant chord is unprecedented in the Beatles' compositions, although the same chord had occurred twice previously in a different context (in "P.S. I Love You" and "I Saw Her Standing There"). The effect of this flat submediant chord on the melody in "It Won't Be Long" is quite distinctive; three of the four pitches in the measure containing the chord are flatted. These alterations do not disturb the "singable" quality of the tune, but lend a certain degree of freshness and novelty.

Of course, the Beatles cannot be given complete credit as the innovators of this striking progression. The I–bVI progression, while certainly not widely used, had occurred in compositions predating the Beatles' by several years.[11] While it is reasonable to suggest that many of the earliest examples were unknown to Lennon, it is certain that both he and McCartney were well aware of two songs of rockabilly singers Carl Perkins and Buddy Holly, for example, Perkins's "Honey Don't" (later recorded by the Beatles), and Holly's "Peggy Sue." While Perkins's song exhibits a distinctly different melodic type, his placement of the chord—in the second and fourth measure of the verse, each time preceded by a tonic chord—is almost identical to Lennon's.

The bridge section is less dramatic, but succeeds in creating a relaxing contrast to the rhythmic agitation of the verse. The descending chromatic vocal countermelody (doubled a tenth below by bass guitar) and the unusual chord sequence generated by it (I–V+ –v–VIb7–IV–V7–V7/V–V7) are effects not encountered before in a Beatles' composition, although a similar chromatic descending line can be found in "A Taste of Honey." The device reflects the Beatles' tendency to keep background voices as active and melodically significant as possible.

With a penchant for unusual sound gestures such as the I–bVI chord progression, the distinctive lead guitar fill, and the alternating vocal "yeahs," "It Won't Be Long" can be considered comparable to the most successful pop-rock songs on the single releases. The popular and commercial nature of the song is confirmed by its ending, which features a gradually ritarded, smooth succession of chromatic chords, leading to a final three-voice major seventh chord on the tonic.

McCartney's "All My Loving" is similar in style to several singles from this period (especially "She Loves You") in its primarily smooth, conjunct melodic motion, the lack of overt rhythm and blues characteristics, and its enlarged harmonic vocabulary.

The verse melody consists basically of ascending and descending scale fragments, accompanied by a conventional harmonic progression until the last two measures of the second four measure phrase. Here, a supertonic chord precedes a subtonic (bVII) chord which in turn resolves to a dominant seventh in anticipation of the next phrase. The bVII–V progression (a minor third root relationship) was, in 1963, still something of a rarity, although within the space of two years, the same progression had become a cliché in several styles of popular music.

The bridge again features a descending chromatic vocal countermelody that generates an augmented chord in a manner reminiscent of the bridge of "It Won't Be Long." (This particular device is one which both Lennon and McCartney are to exploit with some persistence through 1968.)

Perhaps the most distinctive thing about the recording is its use of instruments. The lead guitar accompanies with a flow of eighth note triplets, an effect of unusual intensity at this rapid tempo, while McCartney indulges in a "walking," often stepwise bass pattern (heard for the first time in an original Beatles' composition). The lead guitar solo makes an equally unpredictable (and slightly incongruous) contribution with its country and western sound effects and melodic idioms. Country and western mannerisms had made occasional appearances in several other Beatles' songs, but seldom had the idiom been so consistently exploited.   "Little Child" and "Hold Me Tight" are both Lennon-McCartney collaborations. While both exhibit rhythm and blues characteristics in their instrumental accompaniments, the comparatively lyrical melodic flow (with many long note values), avoidance of blues flats or other rhythm and blues melodic idioms, and the harmonic variety mark both as pop-rock songs. This harmonic variety includes, in the case of "Little Child," a frequent usage of the minor subdominant and, in the case of "Hold Me Tight," an unusual juxtaposition of tonic and flat mediant chords (bIII).

Harrison's "Don't Bother Me," his only independent recorded composition to this point, can only be described as pop-rock. The song begins with an instrumental melody that later becomes a counter-melody in the bridge. The verse melody relies mainly on a single pentatonic motive which recurs in various guises, a procedure also found in some Lennon-McCartney songs. Original characteristics also occur: the song is the first original Beatles' composition to be in a modal-leaning minor key throughout (although some harmonic movement toward the relative major is evident). Harrison's harmonic sense is seen to be somewhat distinctive as well. The verse begins with the unusual progression of v–iv–III–i and later incorporates the unexpected major subdominant. The instrumental sound is also unique; a thick, tremolo-laden lead guitar dominates with its chords and fills over a multilayered percussion accompaniment featuring what the record liner notes refer to as "Arabian bongoes."

Harrison's "Don't Bother Me" may be neither the most unique nor the most successful of the Beatles' originals on the album, but it shows flashes of an independent musical personality while demonstrating the craftsmanlike approach so significant in his later work.

4

Success in the U.S.A.:
The Songs of 1964

The Beatles had to conquer America to become international superstars. This had never been an easy task for British artists, but manager Brian Epstein had arranged for Capitol Records (like Parlophone, a subsidiary of EMI) to record and to distribute the Beatles' songs prior to their visit. Capitol also contributed $50,000 to a lavish publicity campaign complete with posters, buttons, and saturation of the airwaves with pre-recorded radio interviews. By the time the group appeared on "The Ed Sullivan Show" on February 7, 1964, the American public had capitulated, even if the entire press had not. Along with the two appearances on "The Ed Sullivan Show," the group performed to record crowds at the Coliseum in Washington, D.C., and at Carnegie Hall.

One of the keys to the Beatles' American success in 1964 had actually made its first appearance in late 1963. The Lennon-McCartney collaboration "I Want to Hold Your Hand," recorded on October 19, had first been released by Parlophone on November 29 with "This Boy" as the "B" side. The song started out as number one on the *Melody Maker* charts and followed "She Loves You" as the best-selling single of the year in England.

"I Want to Hold Your Hand" is provided with a dramatic, ear-catching introduction drawn from the latter part of the bridge. The song begins with a forceful alternation of throbbing subdominant and dominant eighth note chords. The harmonic effect in this context is actually that of subtonic to tonic (bVII–I), a progression used sparingly in popular music of the period and therefore capable of a powerful impact.

The verse itself is somewhat less spectacular. The melody moves mostly by step in a narrow range, but uses its few leaps effectively and in

41

conjunction with harmonic surprises. The chord progression begins in a conventional manner with tonic and dominant seventh chords in the first two measures. In the second measure, a doubled chromatic bass line links the dominant chord to the submediant in the third measure. This is followed by a major mediant (III) which could be heard as a secondary dominant of the submediant (V/vi). But instead of returning to the expected submediant, the major mediant passes to the tonic chord and a repeat of the initial phrase. One major change is made on the repeat, however. The last note of the third measure leaps up to a falsetto octave, joined by a second voice at the interval of a fourth and a solo drum fill. This striking effect, along with the forceful alternation of the chords in the introduction and bridge, is one of the unique sound gestures in the Beatles' early music, and probably one of the chief contributors to the song's overwhelming popularity. The third phrase features a descending scale line (harmonized in places with thirds and fourths) over a IV–V–I–vi progression.

As in many previous Beatles' recordings, the bridge demonstrates a sharp reduction in texture and rhythmic momentum. The initial ii7–V–I–vi progression is reminiscent of the verse of "All My Loving" and the first two phrases of the melody are relatively lyrical with triadic leaps (often harmonized by thirds and fourths once again) using the seventh and ninth of the underlying chord. This lush lyricism is surrendered in the third phrase where harmonized voices in the upper range reinforce the dramatic chords of the introduction and the rhythmic momentum escalates to a new climax.

It is not difficult to understand the popularity of "I Want to Hold Your Hand." First of all, the song demonstrated a "sound" which, with its electronically boosted bass and guitars, was fresh to the ears of the American audience. Second, it combined a simple, singable melody with unusual rhythmic intensity and well-placed dramatic surprises. These qualities, combined with the massive publicity campaign, guaranteed that "I Want to Hold Your Hand" would launch the Beatles on an American success never before paralleled in the history of popular music.

The "B" side of this song in England was Lennon's "This Boy" (also known as "Ringo's Theme"), a slow ballad. "This Boy" was subsequently released (with "All My Loving") as a single in Canada, and on an American extended play release. Its popularity is attested to by its inclusion in the soundtrack of the Beatles' first feature film, *A Hard Day's Night*, in 1964.

The song is, nevertheless, reasonably conventional. It is the first Beatles' ballad built largely on a clichéd ballad progression of the 1950s: I–vi–ii–V7. This two measure progression is repeated four times in the verse beneath a three part vocal in which the lowest part is the "designated melody" (in all copyrighted arrangements), while the upper voice is equally or even more active melodically. Neither part demonstrates a distinctive contour, however; the lowest part revolves around the third scale degree and the highest revolves around the sixth scale degree. The upper part does contribute substantially to the harmonic interest of the song, though, creating major sevenths and added sixths against the accompanying chords. While this bit of harmonic sophistication tends to distinguish this ballad from the 1950s archetypes that use the same basic progression, the bridge section once again makes a strong reference back to that earlier style. While all of the original ballads have exhibited a noticeable change in texture or approach at the bridge, "This Boy" is the first to make use of a hyperemotional "confessional" style popular in the 1950s (and found in Ritchie Valens's 1958 hit "Donna" among others). The singer makes a dramatic appeal for the return of his girl friend as the harmony and melody engineer an appropriate increase in tension by the piling up of secondary dominants and their resolutions and a sequentially rising line. This melodic-harmonic intensity is reflected by Lennon's solo vocal; the first climax of the bridge is accompanied by sob-like appoggiaturas on each note, and the second is underlined by a sudden cutoff of the accompaniment which allows the soloist his last minute exhortations free from competition.

Despite the relatively sophisticated use of vocal harmony in the verse, Lennon's "This Boy" represents an archaic gesture, an attempt to reconstruct a 1950s ballad style no longer in general use by late 1963. In spite of the song's popularity, the clichés used here so self-consciously are seldom exploited again in a Beatles' ballad.

On January 13, 1964, while the Beatles were still concertizing in Paris, Capitol Records released "I Want to Hold Your Hand" coupled with "I Saw Her Standing There." by February 3, "I Want to Hold Your Hand" had catapulted to number one on the Billboard charts, a position it held for seven weeks, only to be deposed by "She Loves You," released earlier by Swan. On the same day, Capitol of Canada released an album, Twist and Shout, which was identical to the first British album except for the substitution of "From Me to You" and "She Loves You" for "Misery" and "I Saw Her Standing There." A week later, Capitol released *Meet The Beatles!*, an album that contained nine of the songs on the Beatles' second British album, *With the Beatles,* along with "I Want to Hold Your Hand," "I Saw Her Standing There," and "This Boy." The album rose to number one on the *Billboard* charts in just three weeks, remaining there for eleven weeks. (The reissued Vee Jay album, *Introducing the Beatles,* eventually rose to number two in the same period.) With success virtually guaranteed for any Beatles' recording released in January or February, various labels issued earlier recordings (e.g., the Tony Sheridan sessions) and new collections (e.g., Vee Jay's *Jolly What! The Beatles and Frank Ifield On Stage*). Some of the earlier singles such as "Please Please Me" did very well, and every release at least made the charts.

The Beatles' next new recording was released in mid-March by Parlophone in England and Capitol in the United States. This, their sixth single, featured Lennon-McCartney's "Can't Buy Me Love" and Lennon's "You Can't Do That." These songs are particularly significant among the Beatles' compositions as the first examples of a characteristic song type that combines obvious elements of the blues tradition with an unprecedented harmonic variety gained by a free use of minor chords.

"Can't Buy Me Love" breaks no new ground from a formal point of view. It begins with an exciting vocal introduction which is based on the refrain-like bridge section as in "She Loves You." But harmonically, the introduction is an unusual one in its fluctuation between the two minor chords iii and vi for the first four measures. The final three chords of the section clarify the key of the song but do little to prepare for the change of style that occurs in the verse. For, as the verse gets underway, it becomes evident that it is operating—both melodically and harmonically—within a traditional blues framework. In fact, this twelve measure section represents the purest example of the blues idiom yet encountered in an original Beatles' composition, surpassing the other rhythm and blues songs "I Wanna Be Your Man" and "I Saw Her Standing There" in terms of fidelity to that tradition. Not only does the melody make use of flat thirds and sevenths consistently, but it also makes use of the standard blues progression and the typical repetition of melodic phrases against a change in harmony (see ex. 5).

This verse section could conceivably have been composed by any of a number of people working within the blues or rhythm and blues style. Its appearance in "Can't Buy Me Love" is extraordinary because of the overall context in which it appears. Minor chords, such as those found

(Ex. 5   "Can't Buy Me Love": verse, meas. 1–4)

C: Ib7
Buy you a dia-mond   ring   my   friend   if   it   makes you feel al-right.

here in the introduction and bridge had, of course, been a part of the
rock and roll vocabulary from the beginning. They were most often
encountered within the context of repeating chord patterns within a
major key (such as the I–vi–ii–V7 cliché) or, occasionally, in a freer
mixture with major chords (as in some uptown rhythm and blues songs).
The accompanying melodies in the first type were almost exclusively
major in quality while in the second type they were of distinct minor key
implications only for short phrases within a dominantly major key
context.

But the situation that exists in "Can't Buy Me Love" is distinct from
both of these. Here, diatonic minor chords (including ii, iii, and vi) are
included in the refrain-like bridge of a song which is also characterized
by the chord progression and flatted thirds and sevenths of the blues
tradition. These two harmonic characteristics—the free use of minor
chords and the blues-like harmonic activity—had seldom been combined into one song previously. In "Can't Buy Me Love," however, there
exists what amounts to an alternation between the two harmonic styles
with the introduction and coda sections emphasizing a free use of minor
chords, the verse demonstrating a strict blues style, and the bridge
combining both within a few measures (see ex. 6).

(Ex. 6   "Can't Buy Me Love": refrain, meas. 1–4)

C: iii   vi   iii   vi
Can't buy me lo -   - ve,   lo - - ve,   can't buy me love. -

In this way the Beatles succeeded in extending and in lending harmonic variety to traditional blues material, while at the same time
preserving its melodic-harmonic and tensional qualities. And, in so
doing, they also managed to find a way of incorporating authentic blues
material into their basically popular style.

Lennon's "You Can't Do That" also operates within the formulas of
the blues tradition for its twelve measure verse (after a unique instrumental introduction that exploits a riff alternately using the natural and
flatted third almost as a microcosm of the song's contrasts). The har-

monic progression is identical to the conventional one used in the verse of the previous song, and the dissonant cross relations between the flatted thirds and sevenths of the blues tradition and the underlying major chords are even more evident. There are also some deviations from the blues idiom: melodic thirds are not consistently flatted; the melodic insistence of the fourth scale degree against the tonic chord is unusual for a blues melody (although the resultant clash does add considerably to the intensity of the song); and the phrase structure does not coincide with the harmonic structure in the traditional manner (see ex. 7).

(Ex. 7 "You Can't Do That": verse, meas. 1–4)

But the real surprise comes once again in the bridge. An entirely new atmosphere of natural sevenths and thirds is introduced along with a new emphasis on minor chords and secondary dominants (see ex. 8).

(Ex. 8 "You Can't Do That": bridge, meas. 1–4)

Like the previous example, "You Can't Do That" incorporates the blues progression and its traditional melodic idiom more or less strictly in the verse, while gaining variety and contrast by the use of a bridge whose melodic and harmonic content would seem to be incompatible with the blues style.

"Can't Buy Me Love" rose to number one in just two weeks and eventually earned the Beatles their second gold record (certified by the Record Industry of America). While "You Can't Do That" rose only to number forty-eight, the Beatles' domination of the charts was unprecedented in this period. In April, the Beatles held the top five spots on the *Billboard* listings including (in order): "Can't Buy Me Love," "Twist and Shout," "She Loves You," "I Want to Hold Your Hand," and "Please

Please Me." It was in this atmosphere that the Beatles' second American album, *The Beatles' Second Album,* was released on April 10 by Capitol.

The album contained five songs from the British album *With the Beatles* ("Roll Over Beethoven," "You Really Got a Hold on Me," "Devil in Her Heart," "Money," and "Please Mr. Postman") along with three original "B" sides ("Thank You Girl," "I'll Get You," and "You Can't Do That"), a cover of Little Richard's "Long Tall Sally" and an attractive if conventional pop-rock song by Lennon, "I Call Your Name," (originally composed for Billy J. Kramer with the Dakotas).

One June 19, a Parlophone extended play release was issued in England containing "Long Tall Sally" and "I Call Your Name" and two new covers: Larry Williams's hard rock song "Slow Down," and Carl Perkins's rockabilly song "Matchbox" with Ringo as vocalist.

A Hard Day's Night

The next new original releases were on the soundtrack album of the Beatles' first feature film, *A Hard Day's Night.* The American version, released by United Artists on June 26, contained seven new original compositions and "Can't Buy Me Love." (Instrumental versions of four songs taken from the soundtrack were also included.)

The film's title song, Lennon's "A Hard Day's Night," is one of the most distinctive pop-rock songs produced by the Beatles to that point. It begins with a complex polychord from the twelve string guitar and launches into a verse which combines a strangely static melody with elements of the blues tradition and novel harmonic effects characteristic only of the Beatles. The first two (virtually identical) four measure phrases make unusual use of the subdominant chord beneath the melodic fifth scale degree to create a distinctive dissonance common neither to the blues tradition nor to the pop-rock style in general. A subtonic chord (bVII) occurs in combination with a melodic flat seventh before returning to the tonic chord, although the melodic context here—a leap to the flat seventh as a consonance—is alien to the blues idiom (see ex. 9).

(Ex. 9 "A Hard Day's Night": verse, meas. 1–4)   ♩ = approx. 140

G: I   IV   I   bVII   I
It's been a Hard Day's Night   and I've been work-ing like a   dog - - .

These references to the blues tradition, both melodic and harmonic, disappear completely in the bridge as Lennon's lead vocal gives way to McCartney's. Melodically and harmonically, the first half of the bridge is very similar to the comparable section in "Can't Buy Me Love": a contrasting melodic idea that involves a short pickup phrase leading to a sustained pitch is introduced along with a harmonic progression which emphasizes the mediant and submediant chords. As in "Can't Buy Me Love," the second half of the bridge makes a harmonic transition back to the original key (see ex. 10).

(Ex. 10   "A Hard Day's Night": bridge, meas. 1–4)

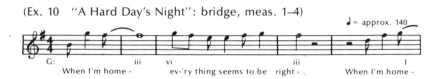

Other unique effects include an instrumental solo (played by George Martin on electric piano and Harrison on twelve-string guitar) that repeats a blues riff at breakneck speed, and a concluding chord arpeggio pattern that, like the opening polychord, juxtaposes the tonic and subtonic chords.

"A Hard Day's Night" was released as a single shortly after the album and quickly rose in the charts in both America and England. And, in many respects, the song is remarkable. It exhibits great melodic contrast; it makes a highly unusual use of blues characteristics; it combines these blueslike characteristics in the verse with a prominent use of minor chords in the bridge as in the rhythm and blues synthesis songs previously discussed; it exploits harmonic surprises; and it demonstrates some unique sound gestures such as the opening and closing polychordal configurations in the lead guitar.

Not all of the songs from the soundtrack are so extraordinary. Some are closely related in both style and effect to earlier Lennon-McCartney compositions. Complete with harmonica introduction and countermelodies, Lennon's "I Should Have Known Better" is comparable to Lennon-McCartney's "Thank You Girl" in many respects. Harmonically, the verse relies on an alternation of two chords (I and V7 in this case) and the result, as before, is motion without direction. Again, the melody is pentatonic for the first several measures, relies predominantly on three pitches, and emphasizes the sound of the added sixth sonority. Basically there is little in either harmony or melody that could not have been composed by a younger Beatle or any average pop composer.

Lennon's "I'll Cry Instead" provides another example of an alternating chord pattern (I–IV–I–IV), and makes use of only three basic chords (the third being a dominant seventh) in its sixteen measure verse. Melodically, this song is slightly more complex, however, exhibiting an interesting use of blues flats. The flatted seventh scale degree is accented against a subdominant chord creating an effective dissonance, and the flatted third alternates with the natural third depending upon the context. Also of note is the unusual textural effect produced as the full instrumental and vocal texture temporarily scales down to a voice and bass duet in which the bass guitar contributes an active walking bass pattern for the first time in the song. The bridge is quite conventional harmonically, beginning on the mediant and following a common progression back to tonic. Melodically, there is a bit more interest as the raised sevenths provide a contrast to the flatted sevenths of the verse as in "Can't Buy Me Love" and some other Beatles' songs of the period.

Like many of the songs on A Hard Day's Night, Lennon's "Tell Me Why" demonstrates many previously encountered characteristics, notably a dynamic vocal refrain harmonized with a mixture of fourths, thirds, and sixths over a I–vi–ii–V7 progression and a call and response pattern in the verse. There is little here of distinction, although the Beatles' energetic vocal sound provides some excitement.

Three of the songs on the American album may be considered ballads of various types. Lennon's "I'm Happy Just to Dance with You" exhibits a mixture of stylistic elements. Its tempo is faster than usual for a ballad, and it begins in a rhythmically aggressive fashion with an introduction drawn from the bridge. The rhythmic accompaniment for the verse, a pseudo-Latin pattern generated mostly by lead guitar, is also exceptionally active for a ballad. But Harrison's vocal delivery emphasizes the lyrical qualities of the melody, and the repeating chord progression (I–iii–ii–V7) and the occasional use of an augmented dominant seventh (V+7) are highly reminiscent of earlier ballads by Lennon, especially "Do You Want to Know a Secret?" The bridge (also serving as the introduction) evokes the uptown rhythm and blues style somewhat by its emphasis on the relative minor (vi) and its pentatonic melody.

Lennon's "If I Fell" is a more orthodox ballad in terms of tempo and instrumental accompaniment but has its unique qualities. The vocal introduction may be the the most significant of these. In a rare example of sensitive wordpainting, an extraordinary sequence of descending chromatic chords expresses what British musicologist Wilfrid Mellers describes as "the 'wonder' of falling in love"[1] (see ex. 11).

(Ex. 11   "If I Fell": Intro., meas. 1–4)   ♩ = approx. 112

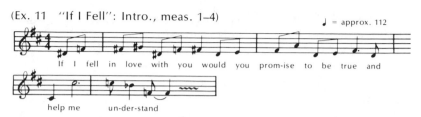

When the verse arrives and the key is stabilized, a slow moving, mostly stepwise melody and conjunct harmonic progression are introduced. The progression (I–ii–iii–biii°–ii7–V7) is once again similar to earlier ballads in its emphasis on the mediant chord followed by descending chromatic movement to a supertonic seventh chord. Meanwhile, the bridge exhibits an interesting ambiguity of key center between the original tonic and the subdominant, as well as more expressive wordpainting, this time involving a dominant ninth chord on the tonic and a minor subdominant to reinforce poignant passages (see ex. 12).

(Ex. 12   "If I Fell": bridge, meas. 1–4)   ♩ = approx. 112

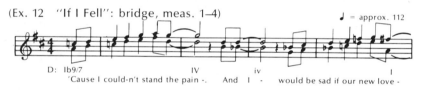

While this ballad shows strong resemblances to Lennon's (and McCartney's) earlier ballads, the work possesses a degree of sophistication, especially in regard to harmony and the expressive setting of lyrics, not found in the earlier songs.

The final song on the American album to be discussed is the Lennon-McCartney ballad "And I Love Her." One of the most frequently recorded of the Beatles' songs by other artists, its appeal is reasonably subtle.

Harmonically the song is fairly simple. It is the first original ballad to be predominantly in a minor key, and the verse alternates between i and iv for six measures before moving to the relative major by means of a bVI–V7/III–bIII progression. The bridge begins in the original tonic minor once again, moving to both bVII and v before once again heading toward the relative major. While the harmony is slightly unusual in its fluctuation between the minor tonic and its relative major, the song's most appealing attribute is undoubtedly its melody. The gentle dissonance produced by the appoggiatura ninths over the tonic minor chord retains its impact despite the liberal amount of repetition. The descending major triad found in the seventh measure is an unusually expansive melodic gesture for the Beatles. It contrasts effectively here with the repeated ascending lines of the earlier measures and also serves to reinforce the harmonic relief provided by the movement from tonic to submediant between measures six and seven (see ex. 13).

(Ex. 13 "And I Love Her": verse, meas. 5–8)

The melody of the bridge shares both the rhythmic characteristics of the verse and its motivic ideas; the descending triad noted above occurs prominently (in the minor form) in the bridge. The fact that the Beatles were well aware of the melodic riches of this song can be seen from the instrumental solo in which an acoustical guitar offers a delicate and generally unadorned rendering of the melody in a new key one half step above the old one. The idea of a key change to provide tonal variety was new for the Beatles at this point. It seems to acknowledge the fact that this song, despite its subtle and atmospheric use of nonharmonic tones, has an unusually limited harmonic pallette for this period.

The British (Parlophone) version of *A Hard Day's Night* was released two weeks after the American version. Like its American counterpart, it immediately rose to number one and remained high on the charts for several weeks. The British album contained all the original vocals found on the American release. The instrumental versions from the American soundtrack were replaced by "You Can't Do That," (the "B" side to an earlier single), and four new songs: Lennon's "Any Time at All," "When I Get Home," and "I'll Be Back," and McCartney's "Things We Said Today."

"Any Time at All" is another uptown rhythm and blues song. It begins with a rhythmically aggressive refrain employing short, biting, mostly pentatonic vocal phrases clearly separated by instrumental fills (mostly featuring acoustical guitar) over a harmonic progression which initially alternates between vi and I. The verse is both more lyrical and more harmonically varied, and incorporates a descending piano countermelody within its progression, once again notable for a minor subdominant chord: I–iii–vi–iv–I–V7–I.

"When I Get Home" also displays some elements of the uptown style, although these are mixed with traditional rhythm and blues and pop-rock characteristics. The dynamic vocal introduction, taken from the refrainlike second half of the verse, immediately presents the surprising "sound gesture" of the recording—a high-range four note pentatonic motive in parallel fourths which rises up to an sustains a high "A" (and the "E" below it) with unusual gruff-voiced intensity. When the first half of the verse arrives, it is relatively unspectacular in its rhythm and blueslike alternation between I, IVb7, and V7 and its short melismatic phrases recalling "Any Time at All" and other uptown rhythm and blues songs by Lennon.

After the excitement of the refrainlike section, the ten measure bridge offers no new surprises, relying for the first four measures on the I–vi progression again typical of the uptown style, the latter part of the bridge is of interest for its melodic-harmonic interaction; it features octave leaps to a dissonant ninth (against the subdominant chord). This is an excellent example of the Beatles' ability to incorporate unusual (for the style) dissonances without disturbing the melodic flow (see ex. 14).

(Ex. 14   "When I Get Home": bridge, meas. 5–6)

While the two previous songs are notable mostly for isolated details within a generally conventional structure, Lennon's "I'll Be Back" is one of his most significant achievements in this period, both from a melodic and harmonic point of view. The song defies effective categorization as either pop-rock or medium tempo ballad. It demonstrates the strong harmonic progression and rhythmic accompaniment often associated with pop-rock, yet it shuns the spectacular ear-catching effects of that style. Furthermore, it exhibits a melodic line that can only be described as lyrical, and its mellow, acoustical guitar dominated sonority contradicts the sharply assertive sound ideal identified with the pop-rock style.

Carl Belz, commenting in his book *The Story of Rock* on a slightly later Lennon-McCartney composition, refers to a "Popular folk style"[2] which may be the most appropriate term for "I'll Be Back" and other similar songs composed beginning in 1964 by the Beatles and others. The word "popular" is important in the stylistic label because the popular, commercially recorded folk songs of the period generally exhibited a more sophisticated approach to harmony than that found in the revived, "authentic" folk songs, some of which had become part of the skiffle repertoire. The popular folk style generally embraced both the quieter, less intense, and often introspective tone of many traditional folk ballads (frequently with balladlike or narrative lyrics) and the straightforward, unemotional melodic styles of these works. Of course, virtually all of the Beatles' music may be considered folklike in some respects, for example, range, phrase groupings, and patterns of conjunct and disjunct motion. But songs such as "I'll Be Back" are considered "popular folk songs" not merely because of these general attributes but also because they demonstrate a certain restraint in approach and a lack of intensity not characteristic of the Beatles' earlier work.

"I'll Be Back" begins with an acoustical guitar strum on the tonic major chord. The mode changes to the parallel minor after just two measures and one of Lennon's most attractive melodies is introduced. The melody, harmonized in thirds, is basically a simple one; it begins with a poignant ascending minor sixth leap to the upper voice (a rare gesture in a Beatles' melody) and proceeds to revolve around the third of the scale (see ex. 15).

(Ex. 15   "I'll Be Back": verse, meas. 1–4)   ♩ = approx. 126

A min.:   i   III   bVII   VI   V7   IV V   I
You know, -   if you   break my heart I'll go -   But I'll   be back a-gain - .

But the melody derives most of its distinctive quality from the harmony beneath it (as is so often the case in the best of the Beatles' melodies). The initial movement to the relative major chord (bIII) is not by itself exceptional, but it becomes so as the progression continues with a subtonic chord (bVII) and a submediant chord (bVI). The submediant drops a half step to the dominant and the six measure phrase cadences in the tonic major. This progression emphasizing the major mediant and submediant chords along with the unexpected subtonic gives an almost modal feeling to the piece, a feeling intensified by the fluctuation between the major and minor tonic. This modal flavor (also hinted at in earlier compositions) has been compared variously with similar tendencies exhibited in some Renaissance music and English folk music among others.[3] But, while the similarities are real, they are somewhat beside the point. The significance of these modal experiments lies not in their kinship with past styles, but in their demonstration of the Beatles' desire to enlarge substantially the harmonic vocabulary typically available to rock music in 1964.

The six measure phrase just described is immediately repeated before passing on to the first of two bridge sections. There is little to suggest any popular folk style here. Melodically, the bridge is typical of Lennon's pop-rock style; three similar pentatonic phrases are presented, the first two separated by a substantial vocal pause. The harmonic scheme is also a conventional one; the initial movement is to the relative minor (vi) and the progression also touches on ii, IV, and V7 before returning to the tonic minor after a cadential pattern similar to that of the verse.

After the verse is repeated, the second bridge is introduced. Like the first, it exhibits few "folklike" qualities and is typical of bridge sections in many of Lennon's songs in its melodic use of a sustained note followed by a group of similar phrases with shorter note values. Harmonically, this bridge is slightly more distinctive. It features a descending chromatic countermelody and an unexpected resolution of a dominant chord (up a minor third rather than up a fourth) before returning to a cadential pattern similar to those encountered earlier and a final repeat of the verse.

The inclusion of two separate bridge sections in "I'll Be Back" is formally unique and most likely dictated by text considerations. But the song's most remarkable qualities are concentrated in the verse: the elegant simplicity of its melody; its rich, modally-tinged harmonic variety; and the poignant lyrical delivery that lends a new seriousness and pathos to an otherwise standard lament.

"I'll Be Back" is paralleled in many respects by McCartney's "Things We Said Today." It begins with a vigorous acoustical guitar strum which asserts a minor key, and the verse melody revolves around a single pitch, the tonic in this case. But significant differences abound as well. The revolving melody makes use of the tonic, flat third, flat seventh, and fifth scale degrees in a manner similar to the earlier rhythm and blues influenced songs "I Wanna Be Your Man" and "A Hard Day's Night" while exhibiting even less sense of melodic direction. And, unlike "I'll Be Back," there is no real harmonic change beneath the melody; the tonic minor chord merely alternates with the dominant minor for the first eight measures (see ex. 16).

(Ex. 16 "Things We Said Today": verse, meas. 1–4) $\quad$ = approx. 140

A min.: i   v7   i   v7   i   v7   i   v7
     You say   you will love -   me, -   if   I   have to go. -

This almost hypnotic repetition ends in the ninth measure. Here, lead guitar arpeggios usher in vocal harmony in thirds and typically pop-sounding harmony including chromatic motion, dominant ninth chords, and a progression of triads along the circle of fifths beginning with the relative major chord. This four measure phrase gives way to the return of the initial verse phrase and the entire sixteen-measure section repeats, ending this time on the tonic major.

While the verse may evoke a traditional folk style in its simplicity and repetitiveness, the bridge section has little to do with either the traditional or popular folk style. The instrumentation takes on a rocklike boldness with the addition of a piano, and the harmony alternates between I–IVb7 and V7/V–V7. The only surprising event is the use of a flat supertonic (b11) to bridge the gap back to the original tonic.

"Things We Said Today" and "I'll Be Back" both demonstrate a primarily acoustical accompaniment and, in part, the serious tone often associated with the popular folk style. But both songs are eclectic and show distinctive pop-rock elements as well. "Things We Said Today" is probably more notable for its repetitive use of blues motives in a hypnotic, nonblues context; "I'll Be Back" for its modally enriched lyricism. Both songs are key examples of the Beatles' increasing maturity and musical sophistication.

A number of singles taken from *A Hard Day's Night* were released in both England and America in June. The title song was paired with "Things We Said Today" on a Parlophone release and with "I Should Have Known Better" on a Capitol release. Both rose quickly to number one. Capitol released two more singles on July 20: "I'll Cry Instead" backed with "I'm Happy Just to Dance with You" and "And I Love Her" backed with "If I Fell." All songs did reasonably well on the charts with "And I Love Her" rising to number twelve on the *Billboard* charts.

Something New

The same day, Capitol released their third Beatles' album, *Something New*. Its title notwithstanding, there was very little new music on the album. Five of the songs had been released in the United Artist's *A Hard Day's Night* album, while three others, "Things We Said Today," "Any Time at All," and "When I Get Home," had appeared on the Parlophone version of the same album. Two covers, Larry Williams's "Slow Down" and Carl Perkins's "Matchbox," had also been released earlier in England on a Parlophone extended play and were to be released on a single in America a month later. The album also included "Komm, Gib

Mir Deine Hand," a German version of "I Want to Hold Your Hand," which had been released in Germany previously. (A German version of "She Loves You" had been released in both Germany and America.)

In the next few months, a series of rereleases of earlier Beatles' hits were issued by the Oldies label, for example, "Love Me Do" / "P.S. I Love You" and "Please Please Me" / "From Me to You," as well as new collections, for example, *The Beatles Versus the Four Seasons* from Vee Jay; *Ain't She Sweet* from Atco; and *The Beatles' Story* from Capitol which featured narration, interviews, a medley of their hits, and one cut recorded live at a Hollywood Bowl concert.

The next new release was issued in late November by Parlophone and Capitol and contained Lennon's "I Feel Fine" and McCartney's "She's a Woman." "I Feel Fine" rose quickly to number one on the American and British charts while "She's a Woman" lagged slightly behind.

Both "I Feel Fine" and "She's a Woman" are heavily rhythm and blues influenced pop-rock songs with a number of unique features. "I Feel Fine" starts off with a sustained guitar pitch distorted by amplifier feedback that crescendos into the ostinato riff which dominates the song. The lead guitar riff combines rhythm and blues elements with a distinctive 4–3 appoggiatura which has little to do with that tradition (see ex. 17).

(Ex. 17 "I Feel Fine": intro, meas. 1–3)

G: V7   IVb7
    Lead Guitar

The verse melody similarly combines blues characteristics with the same appoggiatura for the first four measures and in the last four measures moves down in typical blues progression fashion (V7–IVb7–I). The bridge provides a dramatic contrast to this blueslike activity. As in the earlier rhythm and blues syntheses such as "Can't Buy Me Love," the flatted sevenths are replaced by natural ones and the harmonic progression (I–iii–IV–V) is far more typical of the pop-rock style than of the blues. The long note values (in three-part harmony) also contrast with the almost constant syncopation of the verse.

McCartney's "She's a Woman" comes as somewhat of a surprise. His earlier solo compositions tended to demonstrate a sophisticated, rather commercial harmonic sense combined with a subtle melodic style. Neither characterization seems particularly appropriate for "She's a Woman" at first glance. The song begins with heavy off-beat "chops" by the electric lead guitar with the bass downbeats contributed shortly thereafter; it is immediately clear (at least by the fourth measure) that this song will be an excellent example of pounding, hardcore rhythm and blues. The verse melody, presented in McCartney's husky "Little Richard" voice, uses an archetypical blues figure for its first two four measure phrases (the ascending minor sixth being slightly unusual but not contrary to the style). The twenty-four measure harmonic pattern is basically that of an extended twelve measure blues progression with the IVb7 interjected twice in the first eight measures (see ex. 18).

(Ex. 18   "She's a Woman": verse, meas. 1–2)

C: Ib7   IVb7
     My love don't give me pre-sents.

But beginning with measure nine, the melody takes on a distinctive quality that relates it to "I Feel Fine." It begins to exploit consistently a 4–3 dissonance over the IVb7, and continues this exploitation (after a return to the initial motive in measures thirteen through sixteen) through the descending V7–IVb7 pattern in measures seventeen through nineteen. After the first verse, filling riffs are provided by piano which use standard blues motives but which also hint at the same 4–3 dissonance that characterizes part of the melody.

As in "I Feel Fine," the bridge emphasizes the mediant chord, first passing to an unexpected dominant seventh chord on VI, and then to IVb7–V7 as in the previous song.

Harrison's lead guitar solo shows the influence of rockabilly figures (as had his brief solo in "I Feel Fine"), and the song fades on the accented off-beat chop that began it beneath McCartney's excited exclamations.

Both songs are significant for their demonstration of the Beatles' continuing efforts to draw uniquely on the rhythm and blues tradition while simultaneously expanding it by the juxtaposition of unexpected contrasts and by the incorporation of unusual subtleties of melodic detail.

Beatles For Sale

On December 4, Parlophone released *Beatles For Sale,* an album marked by an unusual number of covers of previous hits. Chuck Berry's "Rock and Roll Music" was included as well as a medley of Leiber-Stoller's "Kansas City" and Little Richard's "Hey-Hey-Hey-Hey!" Roy Lee Johnson's uptown rhythm and blues song "Mr. Moonlight" was provided with a particularly unimaginative rendition, and rockabilly singer Buddy Holly was represented by "Words of Love." Carl Perkins contributed two more to the Beatles' cause—"Everybody's Trying to Be My Baby" (sung by George) and "Honey Don't" (sung by Ringo).

Of the Beatles' eight original songs, two are rockabilly influenced pop-rock songs by Lennon: "I Don't Want to Spoil the Party" and "I'm a Loser." "I Don't Want to Spoil the Party" resembles Lennon's earlier "I'll Cry Instead" in its melodic repetition of the fifth scale degree and its reliance on the tonic chord for the first eight measures of the verse. The next four measure phrase offers more harmonic variety with its vi–V7/vi–ii7–V7 progression, and the final phrase returns to the initial melodic idea with the introduction of an unexpected subtonic chord. The bridge combines a typical Lennon balance of long note values and short, syncopated melodic ideas with another progression (I–vi7–V7/V–IV–V) that is generally conventional but shows subtle deviations in its resolution of a secondary dominant. Stylistic characteristics associated with rockabilly include the consistent country and western riffs contributed by the lead guitar, the country and western inspired solo, the two-beat bass pattern, and the constant vocal harmony, generally in thirds and sixths.

"I'm a Loser" also demonstrates a reliance on rockabilly-influenced instrumental techniques. After an introduction drawn from the bridge section, the verse melody again hovers around the third and fifth scale degrees. But this time the prolonged tonic chord is replaced by a repeated four chord pattern comparable to one which appears twice in the bridge of "I Don't Want to Spoil the Party," that is, I–V–bVII–I. The verse is also notable for an almost comical leap of a fifth into the lowest part of Lennon's range, a gesture clearly derived from country and western music. The two-beat rockabilly bass pattern of the verse changes to a four-beat walking pattern in the harmonically conventional bridge, and again longer note values alternate with shorter syncopated ones melodically.

Three Lennon-McCartney collaborations on the album may be considered mainstream pop-rock: "Every Little Thing," "What You're Doing," and "Eight Days a Week." Of the three, "Eight Days a Week" is the most significant, both for its clear demonstration of harmonic techniques and because it later rose to number one as a single release on the American charts.

The song begins with an instrumental introduction that defines the key chord progression of the verse, that is, I–V7/V–IV–I. This progression is distinguished by a harmonic characteristic increasingly typical of the Beatles' music—the unexpected resolution of a dominant-type chord up a minor third. While the context here is not identical, for example, to the second bridge in "I'll Be Back," the verse in "I'm a Loser," or the bridge in "I Don't Want to Spoil the Party," the principles are similar. A dominant or secondary dominant is introduced (with or without a seventh), but instead of resolving up a fourth (standard procedure in classical and popular traditions), it resolves up a minor third to another major chord. In the two songs just discussed, this unusual resolution only interrupts the expected resolution which follows immediately thereafter. In the verse of "Eight Days a Week," the expected resolution never occurs and is replaced by a return to the tonic chord.

The melodic phrase that dominates the verse in "Eight Days a Week" is also somewhat unusual in its minimal usage of nonharmonic tones. The melody simply moves up and down the chord, occasionally by step but more frequently by leap. Lacking any single distinctive feature, it relies completely on the novelty of the underlying harmonies for interest (see ex. 19).

(Ex. 19   "Eight Days a Week." Verse, meas. 1–4)

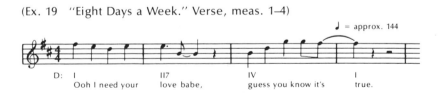

The eight measure bridge is notable mostly for its use of perfect fourths in the vocal harmony, perhaps the most extensive since "Love Me Do." But the song lacks any single dramatic ear-catching sound gesture and, therefore, it is somewhat surprising that it was so successful as a single release.

McCartney's "I'll Follow the Sun" is, at least in some respects, a more remarkable song. It is an archetypical example of the popular folk style discussed earlier in its subdued acoustical accompaniment (with some contributions from a mellow electric lead guitar) and narrative-style lyrics. It is also one of McCartney's most impressively original songs both melodically and harmonically.

After a brief introduction, the song begins with a tonally ambiguous first phrase (see ex. 20).

(Ex. 20   "I'll Follow the Sun." Verse, meas. 1–4)   ♩ = approx. 138

C: V   IVb7   I   II7

One day -   you'll look   to see I've gone.   But to-(morrow)

The first ascending leap of a fourth generates all of the melodic activity here, but in an unpredictable way because of the unusual progression in which dominant seventh chords are denied their expected resolutions more often than not. The latter half of the verse is more conventional, working its way back to the tonic by means of a I–iii–V7/V–V7–I progression. The bridge is also relatively standard for a McCartney song in its use of a chromatically descending vocal countermelody and a minor subdominant chord in a progression of ii7–iv–I. But despite its predictable moments, "I'll Follow the Sun" represents one of the finest examples of the harmonically enlivened popular folk style developed by the Beatles in mid- and late 1964.

Two songs on the album, Lennon's "No Reply" and McCartney's "Baby's in Black," are examples of the uptown rhythm and blues style. "No Reply" is in the mold of Lennon's earlier songs "Any Time at All" and "All I've Got to Do." The opening chord progression of IV–V7–I (with added sixth) in the relatively subdued first half of the verse gives way to greater harmonic variety in the more dramatic refrainlike second half, which begins on the relative minor and features a particularly effective use of a major seventh chord on the subdominant. McCartney's "Baby's in Black," the first of his songs to draw so heavily on the uptown idiom, is in the black vocal group style of "Mr. Moonlight" and "You've Really Got a Hold on Me." The verse is unusually simple, melodically and harmonically, but the brief, two measure bridge interlude is somewhat bolder with its vi–V7/V–IV–V progression recalling "Eight Days a Week" among others.

Eleven days after the release of *Beatles For Sale,* Capitol Records released the album *Beatles '65* which miraculously stayed on the *Billboard* charts for seventy-one weeks. This collection included the singles "I Feel Fine" and "She's a Woman" along with "I'll Be Back" from the British *A Hard Day's Night* album, and eight songs from *Beatles For Sale*: the covers of "Rock and Roll Music," "Mr. Moonlight," "Honey Don't," and "Everybody's Trying to Be My Baby," and the original pop-rock songs "I'm a Loser" and "I'll Follow the Sun." Seemingly, producers George Martin and Dave Dexter (coproducer for the American release) were interested in demonstrating the Beatles' versatility to American as well as British audiences.

Beatles' Compositions for Others

While space does not permit any extended discussion, mention must be made of the many Beatles' compositions written for and performed by others in 1963 and 1964. In some cases, these songs had already been recorded by the Beatles (e.g., "I Saw Her Standing There") or were later to be recorded by them (e.g., "I Call Your Name"). But, in most cases, these compositions (primarily written by McCartney) were recorded only by the singers or groups to whom they were given. Some of these recordings did quite well on the charts: Billy J. Kramer's recordings of Lennon's "Bad to Me" and McCartney's "I'll Keep You Satisfied" rose high on both the American and British charts. Many of those songs are pleasant examples of pop-rock and mid-1960s balladry but are, on the whole, less distinguished than most of the songs recorded by the Beatles.

Some exceptions to this generalization do exist, however. Two McCartney ballads for British singing duo Peter and Gordon, "A World Without Love" and "I Don't Want to See You Again," demonstrate an especially effective use of borrowed chords (i.e., chords "borrowed" from the parallel minor key). Both of these songs had great success on the charts, but the two most extraordinary songs composed for others—"Love of the Loved" and "It's for You" composed for Cilla Black—were less successful commercially. Nevertheless, they are outstanding examples of the Beatles' early skill in adapting the harmonically sophisticated adult commercial ballad style to their own ends.

The verse of McCartney's "Love of the Loved" is unique among his songs with its progression of I–iii–v–iv–bVI–V7–I. The Lennon-

McCartney collaboration "It's for You" is equally remarkable for a melody similar to "I'll Follow the Sun" in its construction and harmonic progression of i–III–IV–iv–III7–bVI–bV–ii–i. Both songs are particularly significant as precursors of the Beatles' more famous essays in the adult commercial ballad style, "Yesterday" and "Michelle."[4]

Style Characteristics in the Early Period

Form

The most common form for Beatles' songs in this period is the standard popular music pattern of verse-verse-bridge-verse. Refrain or refrainlike sections, notable for their greater intensity and sense of climax, frequently substitute for the bridge or occur in the second half of the verse. These refrain sections, in part or whole, often serve as well for the introduction (e.g., "She Loves You" and "When I Get Home"). This basic pattern is often extended by the repeat of the bridge and verse sections, with an instrumental solo (often based on the verse) occurring before or between these added sections.

The most common lengths of the verse and the bridge are eight, twelve (the standard blues progression length), and sixteen measures with others occurring occasionally. Within these sections, phrase repetition is typical. The most common phrase (or phrase group) patterns are as follows: a a b (e.g., the verse of "Can't Buy Me Love"); a a' (a variation of "a") b a (e.g., the verse of "I Don't Want to Spoil the Party" and "Eight Days a Week"); a a b c (e.g., the verse of "I Feel Fine"); and a a b b' (e.g., the verse of "I Want to Hold Your Hand" and "She Loves You"). Occasionally, a short phrase is repeated, often with variation, even more frequently (as in the verse of "Love Me Do" and "Thank You Girl") and sometimes a phrase is repeated a step higher (i.e., sequentially) as in the bridge of "From Me to You."

Melodic Characteristics

The Beatles' melodies generally resemble those of other popular and rock songs in this period in their reliance on predominantly conjunct motion with occasional leaps of a third or a fourth. In many of the Beatles' melodies, these leaps are most distinctive when they coincide with a move to the relative minor chord, some unexpected harmonic change, or some unusual instrumental activity as in the verse of "I Want to Hold Your Hand" and "From Me to You." "I'll Follow the Sun" provides a rare example of a melody that is based primarily on ascending leaps, while "Misery" shows an unusual number of descending leaps of a sixth.

More specific melodic types (sometimes overlapping) that occur are:

1. Repeating or revolving melodies that emphasize one or two pitches (e.g., the verse of "I Don't Want to Spoil the Party"). Frequently these melodies are heard over chord progressions that are equally insistent and repetitive, the result of which is a purposefully static quality that contrasts graphically with later activity (e.g., "A Hard Day's Night" and "Things We Said Today").
2. Scalar melodies with strong directional contour (e.g., the verse of "Please Please Me" and the bridge of "Thank You Girl"). These are relatively rare and generally descending in type, although the verse melody of "All My Loving" is predominantly ascending.
3. Blues-influenced melodies. These naturally occur in the early rhythm and blues influenced songs (e.g., "I Wanna Be Your Man" and "I Saw Her Standing There") and in the rhythm and blues synthesis songs of 1964 (e.g., "Can't Buy Me Love"), but can also be heard in a more subtle context (e.g., "Things We Said Today").
4. Pentatonic melodies. These dominate most frequently in compositions by Lennon (e.g., "Thank You Girl"), especially his uptown rhythm and blues songs (e.g., "All I've Got to Do").

The use of nonharmonic tones is one of the Beatles' most distinctive characteristics in this period (and throughout their career generally). For example, the dissonant fourth scale degree against the tonic chord (usually resolving to the third scale degree) is a crucial melodic aspect as early as "She Loves You" and plays an even more significant role in later songs such as "I Feel Fine" and "She's a Woman." Nonharmonic sixths, sevenths, and ninths are also frequently important in determining the character or originality of a Beatles' melody as in the verse of "And I Love Her."

Harmonic Characteristics

The most individual and distinctive stylistic elements in these early songs occur in the use of harmony. The Beatles' harmonic vocabulary can be described in terms of three categories of chords:

Category I

This includes the chords most frequently encountered in the Beatles' music and that of their contemporaries, for example, I, IV, V and, in descending order of frequency: vi, ii, iii, V7/V, and V7/ii.

Category II

This includes chords that are encountered less frequently than those in category I, but which remain relatively common, for example, augmented and diminished chords, major and minor seventh chords, and the minor subdominant (iv) and dominant (v) chords.

Category III

This includes chromatic chords that are, by and large, unique to the Beatles' music and seldom, if ever, found in the pop music of their contemporaries, for example, bIII, bVI, III, VI, and bVII. The first four of these are chromatic mediants, that is, chromatic chords that lie a major or minor third away from the tonic (or the preceding chord). The III and VI chords can be considered chromatic mediants only when they operate outside of any secondary dominant context and are heard as an unexpected interruption of a conventional progression.

While the use of chords in this category constitutes the most obvious novelty of the Beatles' harmony, the unusual contexts established for chords from categories I and II are often equally effective, especially in the songs of mid- and late 1964. For example, the verse progressions for "I'll Follow the Sun" and "Eight Days a Week" are striking because of the unexpected relationships (often of the chromatic mediant type) between chords which are, on the whole, rather common. The rhythm and blues synthesis songs (e.g., "Can't Buy Me Love") are remarkable not because mediant and submediant chords dominate the bridge, but because these chords provide such a dramatic contrast with the rhythm and blues style of the verse.

Instrumental and Vocal Arrangements—Sound Gestures

For the most part, the Beatles' instrumental and vocal arrangements are typical of the popular music and rock of this period. While Lennon's use of harmonica may have been original at the time of conception, the gesture was a commonplace one by the time that "Love Me Do" and the other early singles were released.[5] Similarly, while the electronic boosting of guitar and bass was relatively novel in the early singles, recording concepts and techniques were changing quickly and other groups (e.g., the Rolling Stones) were soon exploiting this fuller, more penetrating sound.

Even in this early period, the Beatles were capable of impressive versatility in their overall sound, ranging skillfully from mellow commercial jazz to acoustical folk, country and western, bright pop-rock, and dynamic rhythm and blues. Harrison's solos and many of his filling riffs often borrowed heavily from the country and western idiom regardless of the style of a given song, but rhythm guitar, bass guitar, and occasional keyboard instruments adapted themselves appropriately. Ringo's drumming, notorious for its nonvirtuosity, was nevertheless skillful in many respects; his variety of stylistic effects matched those of Lennon and McCartney and his occasional solos and fills are both economical and effective.

The Beatles' vocal arrangements are equally varied, including unison or double-tracked vocals; continuous or occasional vocal harmony (often used to expand the texture at climactic points); a constant "wall of sound," that is, vocal accompaniment in sustained chords to provide density of texture; vocal countermelodies; and call and response interaction of various types. All of these techniques are reasonably widespread in this period, but some of them, for example, the prominent use of countermelodies and call and response interaction, are particularly associated with the Beatles as is the use of perfect fourths and fifths in the vocal harmony.

Related to the Beatles' ability to exploit a wide range of vocal and instrumental effects is their talent for devising distinctive, ear-catching sound gestures with which a given song is immediately identified. These sound gestures range from the "yeah-yeah-yeah" refrain of "She Loves You" to the blueslike ostinato riff which begins "I Feel Fine" and may well be the most important attribute of many of their songs in terms of audience appeal.

Lyrics

It would be misleading to suggest that the Beatles' lyrics were substantially more "meaningful" than those devised by their contemporaries in this period. While some of the songs of mid-and late 1964 show a new elegance of phrasing (e.g., "I'll Be Back," "Things We Said Today," and "I'll Follow the Sun"), others are as pedestrian as ever (e.g., "She's a Woman" and "I Feel Fine"). There is little evidence of the originality and wit for which Lennon was praised on the publication of his two books, *In His Own Write* in 1964, and *A Spaniard in the Works* in 1965. In fact, Lennon's attitude toward lyrics seems to have been somewhat casual:

> To express myself . . . I could write *Spaniard in the Works* or *In His Own Write*, the personal stories which were expressive of my personal emo-

tions. I'd have a separate songwriting John Lennon who wrote songs for the sort of meat market, and I didn't consider them—the lyrics or anything—to have any depth at all. They were just a joke.[6]

The Achievement of the Early Period

The Beatles' lyrics may not have substantially surpassed those of their contemporaries in 1963 and 1964, but their many musical attributes were far superior. While the various musical influences on the Beatles remained clear throughout 1963 and 1964, the group still succeeded in expressing a marked individuality through their music. This individuality was achieved only with a self-conscious and purposeful effort. Lennon has stated that "we'd take things out for being banal, cliches, even chords we wouldn't use because we though they were cliches."[7]

Armed with this determination to be unique, the Beatles began their assault on 1965.

5

Help! and Rubber Soul: The Songs of 1965

While the Beatles' first project of the new year, the recording of songs for their next film, *Help!*, had already begun in February, and various collections of earlier material had been issued in the first three months, the first new single did not appear until April 9 in England and April 19 in America.

The "A" side was Lennon's "A Ticket to Ride," later included as part of the *Help!* soundtrack. "Ticket to Ride" rose immediately to the top of the British charts and, while its rise in America was less dramatic, it eventually was awarded a gold record there for sales of over a million.

As one might imagine, there is no huge leap in quality or sophistication from the songs of 1964, although "Ticket to Ride" does demonstrate some unique qualities. Like "I Feel Fine" before it, the song is dominated by a lead guitar ostinato figure, in this case played on Harrison's twelve-string guitar. But this ostinato is not blues influenced; it is based on an arpeggiation of the tonic triad with a prominent leap of a fifth, and has an accented dissonance on the second scale degree.

While the verse melody initially resembles the earlier "She Loves You" in contour and use of the fourth scale degree, the total effect is quite different. Where "She Loves You" changed harmony virtually every measure, "Ticket to Ride" stays with the tonic chord for six measures before a change is heard. The triadic ostinato is repeated (at a majestically moderate tempo) through all of this while the rhythm guitar and bass add to the stark, austere effect by their emphasis of the root and fifth of the tonic chord. Finally the harmony changes (as we are told that the girl is "going away") and a ii–V progression brings the eight measure section to a close (see ex. 21).

(Ex. 21   "Ticket to Ride." Verse, meas. 1–4)

Again, the second half of the verse serves the function of a refrain, beginning predictably on the relative minor chord with a pentatonic melodic figure, which contrasts nicely with the distinctive half-steps of the first part. The harmony changes to IV, back to vi, and then, surprisingly, to a subtonic chord. The result is unusually dissonant (none of the three melody notes in this measure are consonant with the chord) and unusually poignant. When the verse opened with the words "I think I'm gonna be sad," the music gave us cause to doubt it. Now, the fact that "She's got a ticket to ride" suddenly becomes the cause of pain, almost despair; the dissonance suggests that the impassive strength exhibited in the first half of the verse has a vulnerable side to it.

The bridge is less expressive, reminiscent of the bridge of "Please Please Me" in its melodic type and exclusive reliance on the IVb7 and V7 chords. And yet, overall, the song combines power and poignance more effectively than any Beatle composition to that point.

Lennon's ballad, "Yes It Is," the "B" side of "Ticket to Ride," is another mixture of old and new. It makes use of the sort of triplet rhythm accompaniment seen last in "This Boy" and the underlying chord progression of the verse begins in a conventional enough manner, that is, I–IV–ii–V7. But the melody and vocal harmony lines immediately bring about unusual complications: the subdominant chord is made a ninth chord and the supertonic chord is made an eleventh chord, complete with sharp major second dissonances which never really resolve. The repeat of the melodically simple first phrase sees the substitution of a subtonic chord for the supertonic chord; the resultant dissonance is less sharp (the effect of an added sixth chord is produced), but the subsequent resolution to the dominant chord (a minor third root relationship) makes a striking effect, similar to that heard as early as "All My Loving" but more dramatic here because of the slow ballad tempo. The remainder of the verse is more comonplace with its I–vi–IV–bVII–vi–I progression, although even here the last three chords make an unusual effect.

The bridge is almost completely conventional and recalls the bridge in "This Boy" in its clichéd progression of ii–V7–I–vi and its wall of sound vocal harmony. Even the melodramatic vocal exclamations of the soloist heard in "This Boy" make a return appearance here.

Still, despite its similarities to the earlier ballad, "Yes It Is" represents no "archaic gesture." And it is interesting to note how Lennon and the Beatles insist, in 1965, on embellishing simple structures (especially in the verse) which they once would have presented in their original stereotyped form.

The months of June and July were unusually busy ones, even given the frequently frantic schedule of the Beatles. On June 12, the Beatles were awarded the prestigious M.B.E. (Member of the Order of the British Empire), an honor which they accepted in their typically glib fashion, much to the chagrin of some older M.B.E. holders. From June 20 to July 4, the Beatles made another European tour with concerts in France, Italy, and Spain. On June 24, Lennon's second book, A Spaniard in the Works, was published, again to generally favorable reviews. And, ten days earlier, a new Capitol album, Beatles VI, had been released and, as usual, rose quickly to the top of the American charts. Most of its eleven songs had been released earlier, either on Beatles for Sale or as singles, for example, "Eight Days a Week" and "Yes It Is." Two were covers of Larry Williams's 1958–59 hits, "Dizzy Miss Lizzy" and "Bad Boy," and two were new compositions by McCartney ("Tell Me What You See") and Harrison ("You Like Me Too Much"). Both make an unusual use of electric piano in an idiom that combines elements of country and western music and barrelhouse piano style. McCartney's song also makes an effective use of claves, scratch gourd, and tambourine in lieu of the full drum set for much of the song, and employs an internal pedal gained by the reiteration of the fifth scale degree (reminiscent of "A Hard Day's Night") as a special effect. Melodically, both songs are simple and repetitive, with McCartney's exhibiting a distinctive octave leap and a greater sophistication in its use of nonharmonic tones. Harmonically, their basic vocabularies are conventional, even rather limited for 1965 songs, although Harrison's shows an unusually rich concentration of major and minor seventh chords and dominant ninth chords within that context. On the whole, both are attractive, if undistinguished pop-rock songs.

On July 23, six days before the release of their second film, the title song, Lennon's "Help!," was released, rising quickly to number one in both America and England. While far from profound, the lyrics from "Help!" show an insight into human relationships that is more penetrating than usual:

When I was younger, so much younger than today,
I never needed anybody's help in any way.
But now these days are gone, I'm not so self-assured.
And now I find I've changed my mind, I've opened up the doors.

In the previous chapter, Lennon was quoted to the effect that he did not always take his lyric-writing seriously, despite his widely touted literary successes. But, in 1964, a gradual change began to occur in both him and McCartney. Part of this was, in all probability, a result of the natural processes of maturation and the knowledge gained from extensive trial and error. But there seems to be little doubt that the influence of folk singer Bob Dylan is also in evidence here. Despite his relative lack of success in the popular charts, Dylan's impact on the popular music world was enormous. The Beatles had become fascinated by Dylan in 1964; they had all attended his 1964 London concert and had met with him afterward. Dylan's reputation at that point rested largely on his ability to write lyrics that were considered to be both poetic and "meaningful" in a socially-relevant sense. This had not been a particular preoccupation of any of the Beatles, of course, and Dylan's influence did not make itself apparent overnight. Some writers have detected Dylan-like turns of phrase as early as "I'm a Loser" and "I Don't Want to Spoil the Party,"[1] but his influence commences as a reasonably consistent force only in the songs of 1965 when many of the Beatles' songs begin to demonstrate the sort of thoughtfulness and striving for unique imagery that is associated with Dylan. And, in the same period, even Dylan's musical influence is felt from time to time as will be shown later in this chapter.

Musically, "Help!" is typical Beatles pop-rock. It begins with an ear-catching introduction which is drawn from the refrain. The verse melody is very repetitive and recitativelike, revolving mostly around the third scale degree. The background voices provide a melody that is unusually well developed and easily matches the primary melody in interest. The harmonic foundation of the verse, that is, I–iii–vi–IV–bVII–I, demonstrates good harmonic variety, but little unique other than the bVII–I cadence. The refrain shows surprisingly little contrast, relying on the fourth scale degree as extensively as the verse relied on the third scale degree. The repetitive motive repeats twice against changing chords with interesting effect; the initial motive, hovering tentatively and dissonantly over a submediant chord, makes a colorful metaphor for the singer's insecurity. Each time it is repeated, it becomes more secure in its harmonization (first against a subdominant chord, and finally as the root of the dominant seventh chord) as the singer gains in confidence for his final pleas. This sort of expressive word painting had occurred earlier in Beatle compositions as before of course, but it becomes an increasingly significant part of their most successful accomplishments from this point on.

The "B" side, McCartney's "I'm Down," could hardly provide a greater contrast to "Help!." It is a frenzied, rhythm and blues rock song which has been compared to Little Richard's "Long Tall Sally,"[2] whose place it assumed as the final number on all live Beatle concerts in 1965. And the song is certainly similar to Little Richard's (and several other rhythm and blues hits) in many respects: the refrain makes use of a standard twelve-measure blues progression while the verse reshuffles the same chords and the opening line of the verse is chanted fiercely on a single pitch (typical of the style in general). The melodic phrasing and long gaps between phrases also recall "Long Tall Sally" as does the spirit, if not the detail, of the accompaniment. There are some differences, however. Whereas Richard's song stressed the flatted third against the tonic triad, McCartney's uses the ninth of the chord. Also, "I'm Down" exhibits a well-developed call and response vocal relationship not heard in "Long Tall Sally." Otherwise, there are surprisingly few touches of originality—no unusual emphasis on the fourth scale degree or stylistically contrasting refrain as in "She's a Woman." "I'm Down" demonstrates that, despite his increasing sophistication and empathy for the adult commercial ballad style, McCartney's affection for raucous and somewhat primitive rhythm and blues had not dimmed since 1962.

The film *Help!* received its premier July 29 at the London Pavilion. Directed by Richard Lester (also director of *A Hard Day's Night*), the film has been described as "a surreal parody of the expensive gimmicky thrillers that were so popular at the time, such as *Goldfinger* and *Thunderball*."[3]

While *A Hard Day's Night* had received almost unanimous acclaim, the critics were more divided about *Help!*. Still, its box office success was substantial and the soundtrack album remained on the American charts for an impressive forty-four weeks and on the British charts for twenty-eight.

As usual, the British Parlophone release (on August 6) and the American Capitol release (on August 13) differed considerably. A total of seven songs (including "Help!" and "Ticket to Ride") had been newly composed for the film; they were surrounded by instrumental music from the soundtrack on the American release, while the British release included instead a group of seven songs, some of which had been released earlier as singles or on albums.

Four of the five new songs were pop-rock songs, including McCartney's "Another Girl" and "The Night Before"; Lennon's "You're Going to Lose that Girl"; and Harrison's "I Need You." The remaining song is a rather unique ballad by Lennon, "You've Got to Hide Your Love Away."

McCartney's two pop-rock songs show similar compositional approaches and a typically Beatle-like combination of rhythm and blues intensity with harmonic variety and novelty. The verse of "Another Girl" exploits the flatted notes of the blues tradition along with a I–bVII–I–IV chord pattern, while the bridge provides a great contrast with its temporary modulation to the flat sixth scale degree (bVI). While mediant, and especially chromatic mediant relationships between individual chords had increasingly become a Beatle trademark (in both Lennon and McCartney compositions), actual modulation (however brief) to remote keys remained unusual; bridge or refrain sections had most frequently begun on the submediant or subdominant without any real sense of modulation. Here, the modulatory effect is startling, perhaps even more so when a return to the original key is made via another chromatic mediant relationship.

Other points of interest include the chromatically descending line of the vocal introduction and brief refrain, and the fluidity of Harrison's new guitar fills, heard throughout the album.

"The Night Before" is most notable for its use of a repeated I–bVII–IV–V ostinato. While never before used by the Beatles, the progression was used extensively in 1964 and 1965 by groups as widely disparate as the Kinks and Paul Revere and the Raiders. The second half of the verse offers some variety with its initial vi–iv alternation, but the original ostinato progression returns for the final four measures of the section. The bridge offers more substantial contrast; the blueslike intensity of the verse is replaced by a sinuous chromatic melody (cf. the vocal introduction of "Another Girl"), and a sequential chord progression which concludes with vi7–V7/V–V in preparation for the return of the verse.

Like McCartney's two songs, Lennon's "You're Going to Lose that Girl" makes little pretense of literary quality, social relevance or connection with the film plot. It does, however, show off the composer's original harmonic sense effectively and, in the process, exhibits some similarities to "Another Girl." The song begins innocuously enough with a call and response vocal introduction (drawn from the verse) over a I–vi–ii7–V7 progression. But when the verse begins, a chromatic IIIb7 chord replaces the vi and the progression becomes a fresh and appealing one, especially when enlivened by the poignant appoggiaturas of the vocal responses. But the most unusual effect comes in the bridge. As in "Another Girl," a three-part harmonized vocal is assumed (although call and response vocal interaction continues) and a temporary modulation to the flat mediant is made via the reharmonization of a note common to both keys as in McCartney's song (see ex. 22).

(Ex. 22 "Another Girl." Verse, meas. 20 and bridge, meas. 1–3)

While "Another Girl" alternated I and V7 in its brief stay in the new key, Lennon's song alternates I and IV. And where "Another Girl" returned to the original tonic by means of a major third root progression between the bridge tonic and the original dominant (i.e., bIII–V), "You're Going to Lose that Girl" returns with an even more surprising diminished fifth progression between the bridge subdominant and a secondary dominant in the original key which is never resolved (i.e. bVI–V7/V). This degree of stylistic consistency between Lennon and McCartney songs is seldom so obvious, but it does demonstrate that significant cross-fertilization still occurs at this point, in compositional matters as well as in details of arrangement and performance.

In its tempo and intensity level, Harrison's "I Need You" lies between a typical pop-rock song and a medium tempo ballad. In terms of its melodic-harmonic content, the song is probably the simplest on the album. Only conventional diatonic chords (and one secondary dominant) occur in generally predictable patterns. Melodically, the song is scarcely more distinctive except for a poignant use of the dissonant second scale degree against the tonic chord and a 4–3 dissonant appoggiatura in the steel guitar-sound melodic fills. While "I Need You" is certainly a pleasant, well made song, it is further demonstration that, at least at this point, Harrison is less adventurous in his compositional choices than Lennon or McCartney.

Lennon's "You've Got to Hide Your Love Away" is, at least in terms of tempo, a slow ballad with each beat subdivided into triplets (normally notated in 12/8 meter). The effect, however, is quite different from such songs as "Yes It Is" and "This Boy." For the song is the first to make use of a completely acoustical instrumental accompaniment (including twelve-string and six-string guitars, tambourine and maracas, and two flutes in octaves for a brief instrumental solo in the final measures) and this, along with the persistence of its chord pattern and Lennon's droll vocal delivery, clearly evoke a "traditional" folk style and particularly the style of Bob Dylan. This influence is seen even more clearly in the song's lyrics. As in "Help!," the text offers a serious, in this case cynical, look at love comparable to many of Dylan's ballads. While this sort of bitterness and even world weariness has been implied in earlier Beatle songs, here it becomes overt—the primary focus of the song:

How could she say to me, "Love will find a way?"
Gather 'round all you clowns, let me hear you say,
Hey! You've got to hide your love away.

Melodically, the verse stays within the relatively small range of a fourth and divides into repeated two-measure phrases—characteristics which both Dylan and the Beatles demonstrate in several songs. The refrain makes use of a half-sung, half-shouted octave leap on "Hey," a common gesture in Dylan's style. Harmonically, the verse demonstrates a very active harmonic rhythm with a chord change on almost every beat, a characteristic more frequently found in Dylan's songs than the Beatles' (although not really common in either). But the progression itself is more typical of the Beatles. The first four chords of the verse pattern (I–V–bVII–I–IV–bVII–IV) duplicate the verse pattern in Lennon's earlier "I'm a Loser," and is, in general, more varied than most of Dylan's. Still, the source of the song remains clear, even if Lennon has outdistanced his model somewhat in terms of harmonic interest.

Along with the seven songs of the soundtrack, the British version of the *Help!* album contains the version of "Dizzy Miss Lizzy" released earlier on *Beatles VI* as well as two original compositions from that album, Harrison's "You Like Me Too Much" and McCartney's "Tell Me What You See." Also included are a new cover of country and western singer Buck Owens's hit, "Act Naturally" (with Ringo as lead vocalist), two original compositions by Lennon and McCartney which will be discussed in connection with the *Rubber Soul* album, and McCartney's "Yesterday," released as a single in America a month later and perhaps the best known of any Lennon and/or McCartney composition.

"Yesterday" is a distinctive recording for a number of reasons. Since it employs an accompanying string quartet, along with throbbing acoustical guitar chords, it is the first Beatle recording which could not be repeated in the same form for a typical live concert performance. "You've Got to Hide Your Love Away" had, of course, used solo flutes, but these could hardly be considered as fundamental to the essence of the song and were easily replaced. The Beatles had substituted and left out instruments in live performance before, and they were to attempt it even with "Yesterday" when the song began to achieve great popularity. But the results had little to do with the original recording and were not particularly convincing as a representation of the song. This, then, represents the first important step toward "studio rock"—music which, because of its complexity or technical requirements, cannot be performed effectively out of the studio.

There had been earlier "neoclassical" arrangements for rock songs, notably the 1964 Rolling Stones' hit, "As Tears Go By," which had used harpsichord and a string ensemble employing "classical" motives and mannerisms. But McCartney's use of a string quartet (presumably arranged by producer George Martin) differs from the Rolling Stones' in two important ways: first, the recording "presence" of the quartet in McCartney's song is greater so that its contribution seems both more immediate and intimate; second, while the style of the quartet is really more "Romantic" than "Classical" in historical terms, it is generally restrained and avoids both the busyness and the commercial sounding lushness often associated with "orchestrated" arrangements for pop singers. At the same time, it contributes some subtle touches to the song, especially in its use of a sustained, inverted pedal effect in the first violin which reinforces some particularly effective dissonances.

Still, these differences are not dramatic ones and it seems clear that the use of the string quartet in itself could not have accounted for the song's massive popularity. The reasons for this must be sought in the melodic-harmonic qualities of the song itself, as well as in McCartney's typically naive and charming presentation.

And, to be sure, the song does demonstrate some distinctive qualities. The verse melody exhibits a nice balance of conjunct and disjunct motion and an expressive use of nonharmonic tones which lend real poignance to key phrases of the lyrics (e.g., a dissonant ninth illustrates the singer's troubles "far away" with a dissonant fourth scale degree for his troubles "here to stay"), while an expressive use of dissonance occurs also in the bridge (see ex. 23).

(Ex. 23 "Yesterday." Verse, meas. 1–4)

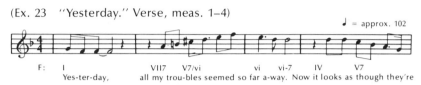

Harmonically, the verse exhibits only one measure of the tonic chord before an elaborate "tonicization" (or brief modulation) is made to the submediant by means of a vii7–V7/vi progression (actually ii7–V7 in the key of the submediant), a typical adult commercial ballad characteristic. This single, isolated measure of tonic throws off the symmetry of the phrase, and the addition of the next three two-measure phrases results in a somewhat unusual seven measure phrase.

The first measure of the bridge repeats the vii7–V7/vi progression of the verse against the melodic third scale degree, the result being a half-note anticipation dissonance, again typical of the commercial ballad style.

But "Yesterday" is not exclusively an adult commercial ballad; it shows characteristics associated with the rock ballad and pop-rock styles as well. The prominent use of the vi–V–IV progression in the bridge (suggested also in measures three and four of the verse) is typical of rock ballads in general, while the unexpected chromatic mediant relationship found between measures seven and eight is especially typical of earlier Beatle pop-rock songs (i.e., vi–II7–IV–I).

"Yesterday," therefore, is a synthesis of the adult commercial ballad style, the rock ballad and the pop-rock style. Still, it is certainly not the first of these; such songs as "Yes It Is" and "And I Love Her" show a relatively sophisticated use of elements associated with the commercial ballad style in combination with traditional rock characteristics, and the still earlier ballads "Love of the Loved" and "It's for You" offer even a more striking synthesis of styles.[4]

While "Yesterday" may well be the most famous and successful example of its kind, the differences between it and a number of earlier songs are a matter of degree rather than type of genre.

The single of "Yesterday" (backed by "Act Naturally") was released only in America and quickly climbed to number one, remaining on the charts for eleven weeks. After a series of reissues of earlier singles and a new single containing "Boys" and the medley of "Kansas City" and "Hey-Hey-Hey-Hey!" from earlier albums, the Beatles released a new single in early December in both Great Britain and America featuring McCartney's "We Can Work It Out" as the "A" side and Lennon's "Day Tripper" as the "B" side.

"We Can Work It Out," a medium tempo pop-rock song which rose to number one in both England and America, is given its characteristic sound by the use of a harmonium played by George Martin, and a unique interrelationship between melody and harmony. The initial phrase of the verse is, in terms of melody alone, quite simple in its repeated focus on the first (tonic) and second scale degrees. And the basic harmonic structure seems equally simple in its insistence on the tonic chord. But the simplicity is deceiving, for as the melody (harmonized in sixths) moves from the first to the second scale degree, the third of the tonic chord (in both harmonium and guitar) moves up to the dissonant fourth scale degree to parallel it a sixth below. The effect is an almost bitonal juxtaposition of the tonic and subtonic chords. This vertical juxtaposition is expressed horizontally in the third measure as the phrase concludes with a clear reference to the subtonic. After this initial phrase is repeated, the eight measure verse ends with a IV–I–IV–V pattern in which the final dominant also briefly exhibits a suspension of the dissonant fourth above the root (see ex. 24).

(Ex. 24 "We Can Work It Out." Verse, meas. 1–3)

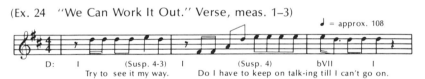

D: I   (Sus.p. 4-3)   I   (Sus.p. 4)   bVII   I
       Try to see it my way.   Do I have to keep on talk-ing till I can't go on.

The bridge introduces two unusual and contrasting elements. The section begins in the key of the submediant (vi) and the harmonium provides a sustained internal pedal on the sixth scale degree, a pedal which is consonant for the first three measures but becomes dissonant in the fourth against the dominant of the submediant. This suspended dissonance of a fourth is resolved to a third in the conventional manner (recalling the last measure of the verse) but, at this point, a remarkable rhythmic gesture is introduced: quarter note triplets which occur first in the melody itself and subsequently in the instrumental accompaniment, the effect of which is akin to a brief switch to triple meter (see ex. 25).

(Ex. 25   "We Can Work It Out." Bridge, meas. 3–6)

D: vi7   IV+6   V susp. 4/vi   vi - 7   IV maj. 7 vi
        and there's no time -   -   for fus-sing and fight-ing my friend.

Fifteen years after its release, it is easy to underestimate the novelty and uniqueness of the relatively subtle effects demonstrated in "We Can Work It Out"; they lack both the excitement of the earlier ear-catching sound gestures and the shock value of the daring chord juxtapositions of more recent songs. Nevertheless, it is important to note that the Beatles themselves felt compelled, by 1965, to introduce such unique elements into their music whether or not they would contribute greatly to the commercial palatability of their songs.

Lennon's "Day Tripper" is a hard-driving, uptempo pop-rock song dominated by a blues-influenced ostinato riff similar to that used in "I Feel Fine." And, just as the verse of "I Feel Fine" emphasized the nonharmonic fourth scale degree against the tonic chord, so too does the verse of "Day Tripper." The melody begins with a descending motive that begins on the dissonant fourth scale degree against the tonic chord, and the effect, especially when the melody is harmonized a third below, is a striking one, suggesting an eleventh chord on the tonic. As in a typical twelve-measure blues pattern, the initial melodic idea (which includes a flat seventh) is repeated while the progression moves to IV and back to I. But where the dominant seventh chord would normally occur, a V7/V is introduced along with a refrain section in three-part vocal harmony. The secondary dominant never receives its expected resolution but passes instead (after four measures) to IV (another unexpected chromatic mediant relation) to begin a highly unusual progression: V7/V–IV–V7/vi– (or V/ii)–V–I.

The combination of an ear-catching ostinato figure, a distinctive chord progression, the idiosyncratic use of the dissonant fourth scale degree, and some elements from the rhythm and blues style makes "Day Tripper" a typical example of the Beatles' mature pop-rock style, a style which was soon to be abandoned as the Beatles began to undertake the most dramatic stylistic change of their brief recording career.

Rubber Soul

In early December, the Beatles released *Rubber Soul*, an album which represents a major departure from the Beatles' accustomed practices in a number of ways. While George Martin is still listed as the album's producer, there is little doubt that the Beatles themselves exercised more control over the various parameters of recording and final selection of material than had previously been the case.[5] As usual, the American and British versions of the album differ substantially; two of the songs on the American release had been released earlier on the British *Help!* album, and the British *Rubber Soul* contains four songs not included on the American version. Such differences had not been of great consequence in the past since there is little evidence of any particular focus or theme for any of the preceding albums, British or American. While the mixture of various genres is not identical from album to album, there is no specific sense of identity to be violated by any version of any album. But all this changes with *Rubber Soul*. And, since it is the American version that could be expected to be the most widely disseminated (the Beatles' record sales had been far greater in America than in England since early 1964), it is reasonable to assume that any unique sense of identity or character possessed by the album would be most completely developed in the American version.

Wilfrid Mellers has stated that the title, "Rubber Soul," "hints at greater flexibilities of irony and compassion."[6] While it may be this literary idea as much as any single musical idea that most completely binds together all of the songs on both versions of the album, the use of the word "soul" clearly has no specifically musical implications insofar as any reference to the popular black rhythm and blues style of the period is intended. In terms of the influence of black music, probably no Beatle album has as little "soul" as this one.

While the album title appears to have little musical significance, the album cover may provide a hint as to the Beatles' musical intent. The four Beatles are pictured in decidedly "rustic" attire—a far cry from the conservative "mod" fashions displayed on earlier covers. This folklike western image is reflected in the music to some extent by the limited use of the electric guitar and, more significantly, by the general lack of broad, ear-catching pop-rock musical gestures.

Although McCartney's "I've Just Seen a Face" does not appear on the British album (having been included on the British version of *Help!*), it begins the American version of *Rubber Soul* and may be considered typical of the album in style and approach. The recording makes use exclusively of acoustical guitars—one twelve-string and two six-string folk guitars. After a half-speed introduction featuring the guitars in parallel thirds, the tempo quickens to an undanceable speed and McCartney's tight, country-flavored vocal enters with a melody distinguished only by its typical Beatle-style use of accented nonharmonic tones over the stereotyped I–vi–IV–V chord progression. The country-western aura is confirmed by the added vocal harmony in the chorus. Lennon adds his equally flat-toned voice in a duet of thirds and fifths over an even more basic harmonic progression. Since the instrumental accompaniment is equally devoid of any specific rock and roll gesture (the twelve-string solo approximates bluegrass style in rhythmic regularity, and the dull percussion off-beats fail to contribute much energy), the overall result is the Beatles' first authentically country and western (as opposed to country-rock or rockabilly) song—a genre not normally considered palatable to the popular market of 1965 by the recording industry.

"I've Just Seen a Face" is followed on the album by a song even further removed from the rock tradition—Lennon's "Norwegian Wood." This song, a traditional narrative ballad, uses a predominantly acoustical accompaniment and, in the verse, a generally simple, sequentially descending mixolydian melody in triple meter (exhibiting unusual activity only at the end of the first phrase) over a repeated tonic chord (see ex. 26).

(Ex. 26   "Norwegian Wood." Verse, meas. 1–4)

The harmonic stagnation of the verse is relieved somewhat in the bridge (with which McCartney apparently assisted)[7] which mixes the major and minor modes with interesting harmonic effect. But, in general, the effect is quiet and subdued, resembling neither the earlier Beatle ballads nor their pop-rock songs. The song does demonstrate a somewhat problematical use of the Northern Indian sitar, an instrument which attracted Harrison's attention when employed for certain scenes in the Beatles' second film. The use of the sitar here fails even to suggest the instrument's subtle potential or idiomatic use, but instead serves as a sort of "exotic guitar."[8] But the role of the sitar notwithstanding, "Norwegian Wood" remains a distinctive and unusual song with lyrics which represent one of the clearest examples of the sequential unfolding of a "tale" yet found in the Beatles' output.

Similar in this respect and in their generally folklike posture are Lennon's "Girl" and the Lennon-McCartney collaboration "In My Life," both on side two of the American album. The instrumental accompaniment of "Girl" is again predominantly acoustical, and the verse melody is typical of the narrative style with its many repeated notes and primarily conjunct motion, although the Beatles' characteristic use of nonharmonic tones affords the line an expressive interest not found in most folk songs. Harmonically, the song is relatively simple; the verse initially relies on the i, iv, and V chords in a minor key with some movement toward the relative major and, in the four-measure refrainlike section of the verse, the clichéd I–vi–ii–V7 progression. The bridge, with a temporary modulation to the subdominant, suggests the melodramatic recitative style of early rock before returning to the original key with the refrain section and the introduction of a folklike guitar countermelody.

Lennon and McCartney's "In My Life" evokes the passivity of a restrained folk ballad, eschewing both the blues-derived qualities of the typical pop-rock song and the harmonic suavity associated with the slicker commercial ballads. However, the song is not completely without guile. Although its basic harmonic structure is not extraordinary (the occasional use of a borrowed minor subdominant is its most distinctive feature), the use of nonharmonic tones is extremely sophisticated and lends a real poignance to the lyrics (see ex. 27).

(Ex. 27 "In My Life." Verse, meas. 1–4)

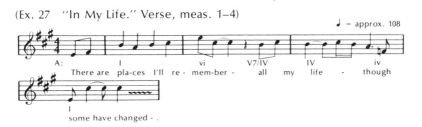

Overall, the song's restrained use of percussion and moderate tempo combines with a then unique section of pseudo-Baroque counterpoint (played by George Martin on piano) and introspective lyrics to evade precise categorization in the conventional pop genres of the day. But, again, the majority of its stylistic indicators suggest the popular folk ballad, and its credentials in this area are attested to by popular folksinger Judy Collins's subsequent recording of the song.

Like several other songs on *Rubber Soul,* McCartney's "I'm Looking Through You" demonstrates a split personality in its combination and alternation of elements from the pop-rock and folk or country and western styles. The acoustical guitar introduction sets the tone with the mixture of folk and country and western characteristics which continues throughout most of the song. The harmonic structure displays a nice variety of chords, but remains diatonic and lacking in surprises while the melody is unusually expansive in its reliance on leaps of a third. The instrumental accompaniment is solid, but strongly suggests the rock idiom only in the final measures of the verse, in which flatted thirds are introduced in the melody and McCartney's vocal quality takes on a biting edge. The more restrained posture recurs in the bridge, which features fragmented, country-style guitar interjections. While this stylistic juxtaposition is somewhat less subtle than in previous songs, "I'm Looking Through You" demonstrates many of the same folklike characteristics of those songs and shares with them a general disregard for the danceable characteristics commonly associated with the current pop-rock style.

Perhaps the most distinctive example of this disregard for the social dance conventions of rock music on *Rubber Soul* is the ballad "Michelle." "Michelle," attributed mainly to McCartney with Lennon given credit for assistance with the bridge, is, like "Yesterday," an "adult" popular song, an indication of which can be seen in the relatively large number of cover versions recorded in the first few months after its release by performers who appealed primarily to an adult audience.

Musical characteristics that suggest the adult commercial ballad (and especially the popular French chanson) include a melodic-harmonic relationship more sophisticated than usual in its incorporation of minor sevenths and added sixths; descending chromatic harmonies in two different contexts; the use of augmented sixth chord relationships (resolving down by half-step to the dominant chord); its frequent modal touches; and the occasional use of French phrases incorporated effortlessly into the lyrics. But "Michelle" is more readily defined as "adult" popular music by its tempo, general mood of restraint, and consistency in the exploitation of adult ballad characteristics. Recorded at too fast a tempo for the traditional rock ballad (an almost undanceable speed in that style), it lacks the energy and aggressiveness of the faster pop-rock types. Even the earlier hybrid songs such as "I'm Happy Just to Dance with You" contained several direct references to the rock idiom (especially in the role played by guitars and percussion) which are lacking in "Michelle."

"Popular" melodic-harmonic elements have, of course, always played an important role in the Beatles' style, but here these elements are presented in their original context, undiluted by elements from the blues-derived rock tradition. Chromatic passages take on widely divergent meanings when played by a quietly mellow electric guitar and accompanied by soft, pattering percussion as in "Michelle" and by the energetic, biting guitar and percussion combination found in so many other Beatle songs. By eliminating almost all aspects of rock instrumentation and energy, and by focusing on the commercial, popular elements of their musical vocabulary, the Beatles have here succeeded in producing another successful "adult" song—one which may also have achieved popularity among the young but whose relationship to the social dance tradition of their generation is minimal.

While the songs discussed up to this point all, for varying reasons, fall outside the social dance tradition (unlike virtually all previous Beatle compositions), some songs on *Rubber Soul* modify typical rock dance styles rather than depart from them. In this category is Lennon's "It's Only Love," one of the two songs to appear on the British *Help!* album. "It's Only Love" mixes the rock ballad style and uptempo or moderate tempo rock in a manner similar to that found in some earlier Beatle songs, but is differentiated from them in its complexity and approach to musical detail.

The basic melodic-harmonic materials of the song reflect its stylistic mixture. The introduction begins with a conventional (especially for Lennon) alternation of tonic and submediant harmonies. The verse melody is unusually square from a rhythmic point of view, and its harmony incorporates, in the first eight measures, a I–iii progression and an augmented dominant chord reminiscent of several earlier ballads, along with a use of the subtonic chord characteristic of more recent pop-rock songs. The remainder of the verse and the bridge are without distinction except for a repeated bVIII–I relationship in the latter.

But the most outstanding manifestation of the song's complexity and attention to detail is the multiplicity of sounds and tone colors in the instrumental accompaniment. Six different guitar effects occur, ranging from a vigorous acoustical strum to a tremolo on the electric lead guitar.

The various individual and combined effects are made possible by the most extensive multiple tracking to be found on any early Beatle album; this degree of detail in instrumentation in itself indicates an artistic intent the self-consciousness of which has few precedents in the Beatles' earlier compositions ("Yesterday" being a possible exception).

However significant a departure from or modification of the rock tradition may be suggested by these seven songs, *Rubber Soul* does not represent a complete break with the past, as shown by the five remaining songs.

McCartney's "You Won't See Me" is in many respects a typical pop-rock song for this period. The instrumental accompaniment is syncopated and rhythmically aggressive in the standard manner. The verse relies on a repeated chord progression identical to that used in "Eight Days a Week," along with a pattern generated by a descending countermelody comparable to one heard in the earlier "Hold Me Tight" among others. And yet the song does demonstrate some subtleties which differentiate it from earlier works and the most significant of these is the shared melodic interest. The vocal melody (which lacks the intensity of delivery heard in most earlier pop-rock songs) is characterized by long gaps between phrases and these gaps are filled by reasonably well developed melodic activity contributed by the bass guitar—which clearly transcends its function as a harmonic anchor here—and the accompanying piano. So while the song remains a conventional pop-rock song in most respects, it also represents a subtle extension of that tradition.

Lennon's "Wait" also exhibits elements typical of the Beatles' mature pop-rock style but, again, modifies them in some unusual ways. In this case the most interesting deviation from the Beatles' earlier pop-rock style is the song's handling of momentum. While the refrain section of the verse and the bridge display a traditional pop-rock continuity, the main section of the verse is characterized melodically by rhythmic stops and starts which disrupt the metric regularity associated with that style.

Harrison's "Think for Yourself" is even more prototypically pop-rock in style, although it also shows the originality of Harrison's harmonic sense more clearly than any other song since "Don't Bother Me" with its initial verse progression of ii–V–bIII–IV–I. The song makes use of the standard, uptempo pop-rock instrumental accompaniment with the addition of a "fuzz tone" (i.e., electronically distorted) bass guitar, an innovation popularized by the Rolling Stones earlier that year. This is paired with a verse melody of a type which is to become increasingly characteristic of Harrison with its drooping, often three-part vocal line replete with nonharmonic tones. In the bridge, the melody line closely resembles the accompanying instrumental riff found in the Beatles' earlier recording of "Money," not only in contour but in its pedal-like repetition against changing chords (i.e., IVb7–I–bVI).

Like Harrison's composition, Lennon and McCartney's "The Word" stands firmly in the pop-rock tradition while exhibiting a few interesting eccentricities. The verse is very blueslike for the first several measures in its juxtaposition of the minor tonic triad in the three-part vocal and the major tonic triad in the accompaniment. Such dissonant cross-relations constitute the essence of the blues tradition and have, of course, been heard in other Beatle songs, but never has the cross-relation itself been focused on so completely and dramatically. The initial melodic idea is repeated, in blueslike fashion, against a subdominant chord and again against the tonic. This is followed by a series of syncopated chords (similar to those in "Wait") which move from supertonic back to tonic via the circle of fifths. But more remarkable effects are to be found in the bridge; the three-note lead guitar riff against the vocal melody is closely related to the bridge vocal melody in "Think for Yourself" and, like it, is repeated in pedal-like fashion against changing chords (i.e., I–IV–bIII–IV). Also pedal-like in effect are the harmonium perfect fifths (played by George Martin) which appear in an instrumental bridge section before and after the vocal coda.

"Run for Your Life" is a Lennon composition of which little need be said. Based on the durable rock cliché of I–vi alternation, the song contains only two different phrases—a four-measure phrase associated with the verse and a two-measure phrase associated with the chorus. The country and western-inspired lead guitar solo is typical of many such Beatle pop-rock tunes, and only a consistent use of nonharmonic tones lends a hint of distinction to the song.

The basically traditional nature of the last three songs notwithstanding, the American version of *Rubber Soul* clearly represents a new departure in the Beatles' music insofar as it demands a redefinition of much of its material in a context unrelated to the social dance function previously considered germane to rock music. Whereas earlier Beatle experimentation had generally been concerned with innovations of harmony, melody, and—to a lesser degree—instrumentation, in *Rubber Soul* the Beatles moved to deny the very social and functional origins of rock and demanded that their music be experienced exclusively as an aural product. This is not to suggest that the Beatles' music on *Rubber*

Soul cannot be or has not been danced to, but rather to assert that much of the music is no longer primarily concerned with expediting the dance.

Furthermore, most of the songs contained on the album are unified in their demonstration of a new approach to rock—an approach that focuses on musical detail rather than on the massive, ear-catching sound gestures associated with earlier songs. This disregard for the traditional requirements of simple, massive effects and dance potential was manifest in some earlier Beatle compositions, but no previous album was so consistent in its denial of commercial conventions. This disregard may, paradoxically, have been made feasible only by the absolute guarantee of commercial success for any Beatle venture in 1965, and the relatively generous amount of studio recording time justified thereby.

A second specifically musical attribute shared by several songs on *Rubber Soul* involves those compositions that may be classified as country, folk, or a combination of the two in terms of the influences they display. Both country and folk elements were, of course, contained in earlier Beatle songs, but only as modifiers of the pop-rock tradition, not as a main component or main stylistic feature.

The Beatles' intention was not, in any case, to produce folk or country music, but rather to consolidate both with pop-rock to produce a genuine hybrid form as opposed to the merely folk or country-flavored songs they had produced earlier. Neither the disregard for the conventions of commercial rock nor the new preoccupation with musical detail necessarily presupposes a turn toward these styles; rather, the country and folk styles are used simply as a source for melodic-harmonic material and sound ideas that had not been drained of their potential for originality by overexposure on the popular market. Country and folk music styles had been familiar to the Beatles for many years, and it is understandable that their early attempts to break from the stiff requirements of the commercial rock market should draw heavily on them in some cases. And, of course, the influence of Bob Dylan, manifested clearly in the *Help!* album, cannot be overlooked as a contributing factor to the Beatles' experimentation in this area.

Still, the Beatles' experiments with folk and country music had little effect on the well-established folk-rock style of the 1960s, which was still primarily concerned with dance suitability. The folk-rock groups, as exemplified by the American group, the Byrds, opted for a more substantial and aggressive rock accompaniment featuring a solid, eminently danceable beat. Compared to the music of the Byrds and their many imitators, the Beatles' understated style on *Rubber Soul* was almost tantamount to a return to "purity."

Furthermore, the Beatles did not seem particularly anxious to pursue the folk and country-influenced genre they had created. In *Rubber Soul*, they managed to achieve great popular success while violating many tenets of the "Top Forty" tradition. (None of the songs on the album were released as singles, although several received airplay on AM radio, notably "Michelle.") They showed an unprecedented lack of concern for the restrictions of the period and made of their music something that seemed fit more for listening than for dancing. While the Beatles were soon to re-embrace some aspects associated with the rock dance tradition, their ability to transcend the limitations of that tradition becomes more and more evident in 1966.

'Revolver' and the Songs of 1966

The year 1966 was, for the Beatles, one of great activity and great change. George Harrison married, leaving Paul as the group's only bachelor. Lennon began a short-lived film career with a role in *How I Won the War.* McCartney wrote the soundtrack for the film *The Family Way* and, it is reported, began a preliminary study of western classical composers from "Bach to Stockhausen."[1]

This was also the last year in which the Beatles presented live concerts. A two-part tour beginning in June and concluding in late August brought them (for the last time) to Germany, Japan, the Philippines and, later, to the United States. The repertoire for this tour consisted of songs from 1963 and 1964 (e.g., "I Wanna Be Your Man," "Baby's in Black," "I Feel Fine," and Chuck Berry's "Rock and Roll Music"), from 1965 (e.g., "Day Tripper," "Yesterday," "I'm Down," and two pop-rock songs from the British version of *Rubber Soul*: "Nowhere Man" and "If I Needed Someone"), and the second single of 1966, "Paperback Writer." The more subtle and esoteric songs on *Rubber Soul* were not attempted, and many of the songs on the soon to be released *Revolver* album would have been nearly impossible to re-create on stage because of their studio-engineered complexity.

The year also saw a certain amount of controversy in connection with the Beatles. The group was accused of snubbing the wife of the Filipino president while on tour, while back in the United States discontent was being expressed over the cover art of the Beatles' first album of 1966, *"Yesterday" . . . and Today,* a cover (later withdrawn) on which the Beatles posed amidst "slabs of raw, red meat and decapitated baby dolls."[2]

But a greater controversy arose when a teen magazine, *Datebook*, reprinted certain remarks made earlier by Lennon in which he suggested that the Beatles were more popular than Jesus Christ and that "Christianity will go. It will vanish and shrink."[3] The reaction to this was particularly harsh in the southern United States where bonfires of Beatle records became a fairly common event in the summer of 1966 and several local radio stations removed the Beatles' records from their play lists. While this outrage spread somewhat into the midwest, Lennon eventually offered a retraction of sorts and the controversy gradually subsided with little or no permanent effect on record sales and no real dampening of enthusiasm among most hardcore Beatle fans.

This period was also one in which the Beatles became increasingly involved in "consciousness-expanding" hard drugs. While the group's members had used "pep pills" as early as their Hamburg days and had encountered marijuana in 1964 (with the encouragement of Bob Dylan among others), their first experience with L.S.D. was in 1965 when, it is reported, a dentist friend slipped it into their coffee.[4] While each of the Beatles eventually experimented with the drug, Harrison, and particularly Lennon were the most profoundly affected. Lennon's drug experiences became more frequent through 1966 and he began to study *The Psychedelic Experience*, a book coauthored by Richard Alpert and drug advocate and cult leader, Timothy Leary, based on *The Tibetan Book of the Dead*. It is probable that this involvement and Lennon's desire to appear "experienced" had some influence on the lyrics he (and the other Beatles) wrote in 1966 (especially beginning with the *Revolver* album) and perhaps on his desire to achieve unique, "hallucinatory" instrumental and electronic studio effects as well.

But drug-induced experience was not the only factor that influenced the Beatles toward such experimentation. McCartney's fleeting experience with such avant-garde composers as Berio and Stockhausen not only whetted his appetite for "advanced" electronic techniques, but provided him with some preliminary notions of how to achieve them. Furthermore, producer George Martin almost certainly had a significant role in the realization of some of the Beatles' "special effects." While Martin's classical background (which included free-lance work as an oboist) is unlikely to have brought him into much contact with the serious avant-garde, his experiences with the production of sound effects in connection with the comedy records of Peter Sellers and others was put to good use by the Beatles.

Finally, 1966 was marked by an increasing enthusiasm for classical

Indian music on Harrison's part. In August, after the American tour was completed and *Revolver* had been released, Harrison went on vacation to India in order to study sitar with the well known Ravi Shankar whom he had first met in June. While there, he encountered Ravi's "guru" or spiritual leader, and both George and his wife became interested in Indian religion—an interest that was to become stronger and, later (in 1967), was to affect the other Beatles.

While the year brought with it a variety of new experiences and, as will be demonstrated, a significant expansion of the Beatles' musical resources, its beginning was not a particularly auspicious one for the group. The first American release (February 21) was a single featuring Lennon's "Nowhere Man" backed by "What Goes On?," a collaboration attributed to Lennon and McCartney and, for the first time, Richard Starkey (Ringo). "Nowhere Man" rose only to number three on the *Billboard* charts, with "What Goes On?" climbing no higher than eighty-one. The single was not released in England since both songs had appeared previously on the British *Rubber Soul* album. And, in fact, each demonstrates a kinship of sorts with the songs on that album—"Nowhere Man" in its generally restrained pop-rock approach and pensive lyrics, and "What Goes On?" in its clear references to the country and western style.

"Nowhere Man" is unusually lacking in intensity for an uptempo pop-rock single. Its characteristic sound is demonstrated in the opening measures as unaccompanied three-part vocal harmony intones the simple verse melody which is to dominate the song.

While the song is reasonably appealing in its directness and simplicity, it is more remarkable for its lyrics. As in several of the songs on *Rubber Soul,* the lyrics are thoughtful and socially relevant, although a certain "preachiness" of tone is more evident here than in those songs on the American *Rubber Soul:*

"He's a real Nowhere Man / Sitting in his nowhere land.
Making all his nowhere plans for nobody.
Doesn't have a point of view / knows not where he's going to.
Isn't he a bit like you and me?"

"What Goes On?," on the other hand, exhibits little concern for "significance" in its lyrics, relying on the tried and true formula of a wronged lover's lament. Musically, it is hardly more distinctive. The song is clearly in the mold of Buck Owens's "Act Naturally" (the "B" side of the "Yesterday" single), also sung by Ringo, with its fragmented, half-muffled guitar interjections, ringing idiomatic guitar solo, and simple, flat-voiced vocal harmony providing its country and western credentials.

The Beatles' next single release, following "Nowhere Man" by three months, combined McCartney's "Paperback Writer" with Lennon's "Rain." This single met with more success than the previous one, rising to number one in both England and America and earning a gold record in the United States. Still, "Paperback Writer," the more popular of the two sides, is scarcely more distinctive than "Nowhere Man." Like the earlier song, its lyrics show a concern with social criticism in its depiction of a struggling young author:

(Second verse)

"It's a thousand pages, give or take a few;
I'll be writing more in a week or two.
I can make it longer if you like the style.
I can change it 'round and I want to be
a paperback writer—paperback writer."

Like "Nowhere Man," the song opens with an a cappella vocal introduction with overlapping entrances reminiscent of the complex "choral" style of the Beach Boys among others. This is followed by an uptempo lead guitar riff which recurs intermittently throughout the song. The riff, which combines characteristics of those in both "I Feel Fine" and "Day Tripper," introduces a verse melody of unusual simplicity and repetitiveness in its frequent alternation between the fifth scale degree and the flat seventh against a dominant seventh chord on the tonic. The a cappella vocal introduction returns twice, along with the lead guitar ostinato, and a simple countermelody is eventually added to the verse. But the effects still remain relatively conventional and the song as a whole seems far less imaginative than many of its immediate precursors.

Lennon's "Rain" is, generally speaking, a more remarkable work despite its lack of popularity (the song managed to climb only to number twenty-three on the *Billboard* charts). Like "Paperback Writer," it demonstrates at least a hint of social commentary in its lyrics:

"If the rains come, they run and hide their heads.
They might as well be dead.
If the rains come."

The moderate tempo song begins with a four-measure instrumental introduction which establishes an unusually rich and active texture gained by the juxtaposition of a slightly distorted lead guitar riff with extraordinarily active bass and drum parts. The verse itself is again fairly simple, especially in harmonic terms. It relies for the most part on a I–IV–V–I progression for the first five measures with an alternation of IV–I accounting for the final four measures of the section. Melodically, the verse is distinguished by an ascending major sixth leap at the beginning of each phrase and a threefold recurrence of a descending perfect fifth at the end of the section. This perfect fifth becomes an important harmonic component in the refrain which once again focuses on comparatively elaborate vocal harmony. The underlying harmony is again based on an alternation of tonic and subdominant, but here the initial tonic is represented only by the root and fifth of the chord against a bass pattern of quarter note triplets which also employ the root and fifth of the chord. Above this is heard sustained vocal harmony in fourths (again on the root and fifth of the chord) which incorporates scooped articulations and rapid ornamental melismas that hint at the Indian classical vocal style. A particularly striking effect is achieved in the third measure of the refrain where a polychord effect results from the juxtaposition of the subdominant chord in the guitar with the continuing outline of the tonic chord in the bass guitar, a conflict reinforced by clashing vocal harmonies. An added vocal countermelody in the third verse also provides some polychordal conflict, but the most extraordinary (if somewhat superficial) gesture of the song comes in the final verse where Lennon's lead vocal is presented in a version derived from an experimental tape-reversed effect—a stroke which Lennon apparently came upon quite by accident.

"It was the first time I discovered it. On the end of "Rain" you hear me singing it backwards. We'd done the main thing at EMI and the habit was then to take the songs home and see what you thought a little extra gimmick or what the guitar piece should be. So I got home about five in the morning, stoned out of me head, I staggered up to me tape recorder, and I was in a trance in the earphones, what *is* it—what *is* it? It's too *much*, you know and I really wanted the whole song backwards almost and that was it. So we tagged it on the end. I just happened to have the tape the wrong way round, it just came out backwards, it just blew me mind. The voice sounds like an old Indian."[5]

This strange effect is clearly "prepsychedelic," a gesture of the type that was to become increasingly frequent in the Beatles' music and is often associated with fantastic, drug-induced experiences but which, as seen here, may derive from any of a number of sources.

On June 20, Capitol Records released "*Yesterday*" . . . *and Today*, a miscellaneous collection of songs including the American singles "Yesterday," "Act Naturally," "Day Tripper," and "We Can Work It Out"; four songs from the British version of *Rubber Soul*: "Nowhere Man" and "What Goes On?" (released earlier as singles), "Drive My Car," a Lennon-McCartney collaboration, Harrison's "If I Needed Someone," and three Lennon compositions later included in the British version of *Revolver* released the next month: "And Your Bird Can Sing," "Doctor Robert," and "I'm Only Sleeping."

Although straightforward, energetic, and danceable pop-rock in its general posture, use of repeated guitar ostinato and underlying harmonic structure, Lennon and McCartney's "Drive My Car" nevertheless bears a resemblance to some of the songs on the American *Rubber Soul* (and, to a lesser extent, the single "We Can Work It Out") in its ironic lyrics and especially in its use of a dissonant pedal effect (involving the reiteration of the nonharmonic interval of a fourth in the vocal harmony above both tonic and subdominant chords) and the prominent use of the flat third (and augmented fifth) asserted vocally against the accompanying dominant seventh chord in a manner recalling the abrasiveness of "The Word."

Harrison's "If I Needed Someone," also on the British *Rubber Soul*, is, in its restrained pop-rock style, generally comparable to Lennon's "Nowhere Man." Similarities between the two include the prominence of the three-part homophonic vocal texture and even a certain likeness in the ascending-descending contour of the narrow, conjunct melodies. Harrison's song also includes a layered, lead guitar-bass guitar ostinato comparable to that found in "I Feel Fine" in its stress on the nonharmonic fourth scale degree. This ostinato, based on the tonic chord, continues throughout the entire verse while the guitar chords assert four measures of tonic, two of subtonic (bVII), and two final measures of tonic. The effect of this ostinato is again related to the pedal-induced effects seen in other *Rubber Soul* songs, although here the polychordal effect is more pronounced. The harmonic texture is further enriched by a number of nonharmonic tones in the top line melody and accompanying harmony parts. The bridge is more conventional, basically following a ii–V–I pattern in the key of the supertonic with a melody similar in style to that found in the verse.

Two of the three Lennon compositions later included on the British *Revolver* are relatively conventional examples of the Beatles' mature pop-rock style, although both demonstrate unique touches and a fairly well-developed satirical sense. "And Your Bird Can Sing" is a sarcastic love lament introduced by an infectious uptempo lead guitar riff in thirds which serves also as a solo and a coda. The melodic-harmonic materials of the verse are relatively simple: the tonic chord is asserted for four measures before the progression continues with a ii–IV–I pattern notable only for its minor third root relationship. The melody is equally simple, relying frequently on repeated notes along with a triadic figure with which the background vocals assist. The bridge exhibits a new lead guitar riff outlining a chromatically descending chord progression not unlike those found in Beatle songs as early as "It Won't Be Long" and "All My Loving." "Doctor Robert" is generally assumed to be a salute to the friendly dentist who introduced the Beatles to L.S.D., containing as it does such lines as "Take a drink from his special cup, Doctor Robert," and "You're a new and better man, he helps you to understand." Another uptempo song, it makes use of a syncopated ostinato (featuring a slightly distorted lead guitar) which emphasizes the nonharmonic fourth scale degree once more. The verse melody is again fairly simple, alternating two elements: a three note descending scale line ending on tonic, and a blues motive containing a flat seventh scale degree.

Once again the harmony remains on tonic for several measures before changing, this time to VIb7 (and briefly V) which later turns out to be a secondary dominant asserting a new key on the supertonic, also the key of the bridge. The bridge presents a passage of ornamented pseudopolyphony again recalling "Paperback Writer" and several Lennon compositions of the period.

The lyrics of "I'm Only Sleeping" also contain hallucinatory implications but the music here illustrates them far more graphically by its incorporation of well coordinated, double-tracked tape-reversed electric guitar passages. This special effect (a similar one having been used in "Rain") is used for a countermelody, a fairly extended solo, and a brief coda. Each time, the fluid, rapid ornaments and the hint of a pedal effect combine to suggest the Indian classical style. Neither the melodic nor the harmonic aspects of the song are particularly striking, although the initial verse progression (i.e., i–iv–bIII–bVI–bIII–V–i) is more harmonically active than in many Lennon songs of the period, as is the eight measure refrainlike section. The hallucinatory tape effects remain the song's most significant attribute, however, and link it more closely to the experimental mood of the American *Revolver* than either of the other two Lennon compositions.

Revolver

Released in early August by both Parlophone and Capitol Records, *Revolver* has been heralded by most critics as a major achievement. Mellers has described the album as a great advance that is no longer relatable "to the conventions of commercialized popular music." It is, he states, "both verbally and musically an extraordinary breakthrough . . . the songs complement one another without exactly forming a sequence."[6]

While the content of the British and American albums differs—the British version containing also the last three songs discussed in connection with the American *"Yesterday"* . . . *and Today* album—the sequence of those songs shared by both remains the same. Both begin with Harrison's *"Taxman,"* a blues-influenced hard rock song that goes further than any previous Beatles' record toward the distorted, hard-edged sound often associated with the emerging psychedelic style. The song begins with a brief prelude in which isolated tape effects, guitar fragments, and the sound of coughing are juxtaposed with two different voices (at different tempos) counting off the song's tempo—a glimpse into the staged, worldly confusion of the recording studio. The very first Beatles' album, *Please Please Me* (April, 1963), had also begun with such a countdown to introduce "I Saw Her Standing There" and the contrast between the two introductions may be seen as a symbolic gesture underlining the loss of innocence—both musical and social—which had occurred between the two albums. The song is launched with a heavy bass ostinato figure based on the first, fifth, and flat seventh scale degrees and reinforced rhythmically by sharp bass drum strokes and equally sharp (and distorted) lead guitar chords on the Ib7 chord. Throughout the song, the texture is extraordinarily sparse and hard-edged—an effect due in part to the infrequent use of the full drum set and the ringing cymbals which had been such an important part of the group's earlier sound.

Harrison's melodic and harmonic materials are also relatively sparse and tightly controlled. The twelve-measure verse dwells on the Ib7 for eight measures before moving to a brief refrainlike section with a bVIIb7 chord. The refrain also employs the IV chord for a single measure before returning to Ib7 in the final measure. The nine-measure bridge features a more frequent alternation between Ib7 and bVIIb7 (with a single bIII occurring in the song's coda). The verse melody is dominated by two motives that recur, slightly varied, in the bridge: a typical blues motive based on the fifth, flat seventh and octave in the first measure; and a descending triadic figure beginning on the ninth of the chord and ending on the fifth, found in the second measure (see ex. 28).

(Ex. 28   "Taxman." Verse, meas. 1– 2)   ♩ = approx. 144

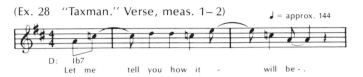

D: Ib7
Let me   tell you how it   -   will be - .

   This melodic phrase occurs twice in the verse, each time answered by sharp guitar chords of a Ib7 with the flat third added—the same cross-relation dissonance (both major and minor third occurring in the same chord) that was displayed so prominently in "The Word" among others. While these motives are not exactly novel, the unrelenting intensity that they produce, especially when combined with the abrasive lead guitar sound, is unusual for a Beatles' composition. A clearly contrasting bridge section had alleviated the intensity of "The Word" and, while the texture does exhibit some variety in the nature and activity of the percussion accompaniment, the activity of the bass ostinato (as well as its occasional doubling by the lead guitar) and the use of background vocals, no real contrast is provided in "Taxman." The song is tension-filled from beginning to end.
   The lead guitar solo and brief coda further reinforces this intensity and marks the first significant break from the often country and western or rockabilly-tinged pop-rock style of the earlier albums. The distorted solo is characterized by rapid hand tremolos; an extensive use of both extremes of the instrument's range, including several octave shifts between ranges; unusually flexible rhythm, often oblivious to the bar line; and, most significantly, a melody line obviously influenced by the sitar technique in its use of rapid ornaments and turns using both semitones and quarter tones (achieved by string bending) and a modally conceived melody line virtually free of blues clichés.
   Although most of these techniques also occur in the solos of some of the other progressive lead guitarists of the period (e.g., Eric Clapton, then of the Yardbirds; Mike Bloomfield of the Paul Butterfield Blues Band; and Roger McGuinn of the Byrds), this solo nevertheless represents a major departure from the Beatles' accustomed solo style.[7]
   In Harrison's lyrics, cynicism and social consciousness are blended in

a manner similar to many recent Beatle compositions as he takes aim at the ample tax bite of the British government:
(Second verse)

Should five percent appear too small,
Be thankful I don't take it all.
'Cause I'm the Taxman.

The sarcasm of "Taxman" is superseded by irony and pathos as it is followed by McCartney's "Eleanor Rigby," one of the most famous Beatle compositions of the period. Innumerable critics have lauded this song for the haunting imagery of its lyrics. George Melly has suggested that here the Beatles have

rebuilt the Liverpool of their own anonymous childhoods . . . the big soot-black sandstone Catholic churches with the trams traveling past, the redbrick terrace houses with lace curtains and holy-stoned steps, the parchment-faced old spinsters who kept a canary, did a bit of dressmaking, or had been 'in service'—all the lonely people.[8]

The instrumental accompaniment is provided exclusively by a string octet, arranged by McCartney and Martin, making this song the first on which the Beatles themselves make no such contribution. As in "Yesterday" (which also employed an acoustical guitar), the strings evoke a "classical" effect, but in the earlier song their warmth and "Romantic" lyricism added poignance and even sentimentality. Here, the somewhat more austere arrangement of the string quartet "distances" or neutralizes the emotional quality of the lyrics by enclosing them in an "archaic" and therefore objective framework.

The melodic-harmonic qualities of the song are somewhat less remarkable. The song begins with an eight-measure refrain (which recurs once in the middle of the song) consisting of one repeated four-measure phrase. This phrase alternates submediant and tonic chords with a melody combining stepwise and triadic motion and a prominent use of the familiar added sixth sonority (see ex. 29).

(Ex. 29 "Eleanor Rigby." Refrain, meas. 1–3)

The verse, which employs a repeated period of five measures, again relies on the tonic and submediant chords with mostly triadic melodic movement and an expressive use of nonharmonic tones which give a unique character to the primarily descending melody. The first two phrases of the period feature the raised sixth scale degree (i.e., C sharp) which suggests the dorian mode, while the final phrase uses the natural sixth scale degree (i.e. C natural) to gain a more affective half-step movement (see ex. 30).

(Ex. 30 "Eleanor Rigby." Verse, meas. 1– 5)

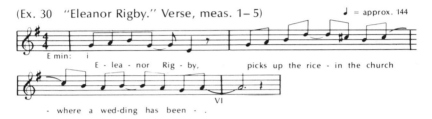

This is followed by an eight-measure section (again a repeated four-measure period) which may be considered a second, more subdued refrain. While the basic chord progression once again consists primarily of i (tonic) and VI, a greater poignance is achieved by the prominent use of the nonharmonic fourth scale degree and the chromatic counter-melody played by the strings—a countermelody comparable (if not identical) to those heard in McCartney's "Michelle" and Lennon's "And Your Bird Can Sing" among many others (see ex. 31).

(Ex. 31 "Eleanor Rigby." Bridge, meas. 1– 4)

While the large leaps in the vocal melody also contribute to the distinctive quality of this section, the use of rhythmic syncopation here is similar to that found in the other two sections, as is the basic harmonic scheme. In fact, it may be suggested that, despite the compelling text and several subtle melodic touches, the song as a whole offers less richness of detail and more thinly disguised repetition than most other Beatle compositions.

"Eleanor Rigby" is followed on the British version of Revolver by Lennon's "I'm Only Sleeping" and, on the American version, by Harrison's "Love You To," the Beatles' first serious attempt at incorporating aspects of classical Indian music into their own. "Love You To" begins with a traditional descending glissando on the "chikari" or sympathetic strings of a sitar against an equally traditional tamboura drone consisting of the tonic and fifth of the scale. While only the tabla player is listed on the record jacket, it seems clear that Harrison is also employing a specialist on both sitar and tamboura since, in the rubato "alapa" section which follows, the characteristically subtle exploration of the nuances of the raga shows both a technique and a stylistic sensitivity which would have been unavailable to Harrison at this point.

This is followed by a "gat" section with a steady pulse maintained by the tabla and an acoustical guitar strumming on open fifths to support the tamboura drone. Here, the verse begins with a vocal melody that exhibits two identical phrases emphasizing the sixth and fifth scale degrees, and a third phrase that winds its way up to the tonic and descends with an ornamental melisma which suggests the classical Indian vocal style to some extent (see ex. 32).

(Ex. 32 "Love You To." Verse, meas. 1–4)

C: (Drone)

Each day just goes so fast - , I turn a-round it's past - .

This is followed by a two-measure connecting phrase from the sitar, a phrase which is subsequently used both as a link between phrases and as a countermelody. This phrase leads into a brief vocal refrain, consisting of a single measure, beginning on the flat seventh scale degree and descending to the fifth. This measure is repeated after a measure of the sitar's solo phrase which also concludes the section (see ex. 33).

(Ex. 33 "Love You To." Refrain, meas. 1–2)

C: (Drone)

Love me while you can.

Along with this refrain section is introduced a new element—a sustained, electronically-produced pitch on the flat seventh scale degree which recurs periodically and implies the subtonic chord (bVII), the only hint of harmonic change in the drone-dominated piece.

Harrison's "Love You To" was not received with great enthusiasm by

either the general public or the critics. While the former found it austere
and difficult, the latter found it superficial—an unsuccessful attempt at
imitating a sophisticated style beyond Harrison's experience and com-
prehension.[9] But it is unfair to suggest (as some critics do) that Harrison
was attempting to reproduce the complete essence of the classical
Indian tradition, since it is clearly a synthesis of that style with the
Beatles' pop-rock style that he is seeking here.[10] While lacking detailed
knowledge of the subtleties of that classical tradition, Harrison would
certainly be aware that his melody lacked the subtle inflections of the
"authentic" Indian style just as he would have known that the music of
his master, Ravi Shankar, did not normally feature the strumming of an
acoustical guitar. If, in this case, Harrison's song is unsuccessful, it is not
because it incorporates only the superficial characteristics of Indian
music (e.g., the drone) but because it fails on its own terms, that is, it fails
to provide sufficient melodic or rhythmic interest to compensate for the
lack of harmonic variety. It is, of course, in just this area that classical
Indian music excels, and those passages in which the sitar is allowed to
range freely (especially in one solo section) are very convincing and
effective. Harrison does not allow enough space for the soloist to pursue
his natural course of events but, once again, the song is an attempt at a
synthesis in which neither tradition is allowed to dominate the piece.

Harrison's rather daring experiment is followed on both albums by
what is probably the most conventional song of the album—McCartney's "Here, There and Everywhere." Whereas Harrison's "Love You
To" blended a certain amount of mysticism with its love lyrics,
McCartney's lyrics are unabashedly and naively celebratory, a posture
which had become increasingly rare since the *Rubber Soul* album.

Musically, the song also represents an updating of an earlier tradition.
The rubato introduction recalls Lennon's "If I Fell" in its chromatic
twists (see ex. 34).

(Ex. 34   "Here, There and Everywhere." Intro, meas. 1–3)

The verse is based harmonically on a series of conjunct chords also
similar to those heard in "If I Fell" as well as other early ballads (see ex.
35).

(Ex. 35   "Here, There and Everywhere." Verse, meas. 1– 5)   ♩ = approx. 90

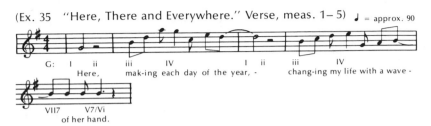

(Ex. 35 melody notation)

G: I   ii   iii   IV   I   ii   iii   IV
     Here,   mak-ing each day of the year, -   chang-ing my life with a wave -

VII7   V7/Vi
of her hand.

There are, however, some subtle differences that mark the song as a more recent attempt. The first four measures of verse melody feature more expansive leaps (which recall the introduction) than are typical of early ballads, and the second four measures of the section first suggest a modulation to the relative minor with a ii7–V7–i progression in that key before settling back into the original key with a melodic contour echoing the first phrase.

The brief four-measure bridge is generally straightforward in its III–i–iv–V7–i progression in the key of the parallel minor, but the effect made by the return to the major mode is as elegant as it is simple (see ex. 36).

(Ex. 36   "Here, There and Everywhere." Bridge, meas. 1– 4)

♩ = approx. 90

G: bIII   i   iv   V7
   I want her   ev-'ry-where   and if she's be-side me I know I need

   i   iv   V
   ne-ver care.   But to love her is to need her -

So, despite the resemblances to some earlier ballads, this is clearly a mature, well-made song with a melody notable for its expansive leaps (often to dissonant notes) and a unique tonal relationship between the verse and the bridge.

From McCartney's sophisticated commercial ballad, *Revolver* moves next to the sublime with "Yellow Submarine," a Lennon-McCartney collaboration described as a "children's song"[11] which comes closer to a fairy tale in its guileless poetry than any Beatle song to that point:

In the town where I was born, lived a man who sailed to sea.
And he told us of his life in the land of submarines.
So we sailed up to the sun, till we found the sea of green.
And we lived beneath the waves in our yellow submarine.

The naive charm of the lyrics is well matched by the musical setting. A sixteen-measure verse, sung by Ringo, alternates two short phrases for its entire length which are harmonized simply but effectively by a nice variety of diatonic chords. The refrain is even simpler with its alternation of tonic and dominant chords beneath a melody replete with repeated notes (while exhibiting some contrapuntal independence in the vocal harmonies).

But the song is most remarkable for its studio effects which range from the insertion of a two-measure brass band solo to various "sea sounds" (a specialty of producer George Martin) such as the breaking of waves (produced in a washtub), whistles, bells, and captain's commands barked in Lennon's most cockney accent.

Of course, this sort of humorous "novelty" song was hardly a new invention in 1966, but the melody as well as the gimmicks proved surprisingly durable and the song, coupled with "Eleanor Rigby" as the only single from the album, remained high on both the British and American charts for several weeks.

While drug implications have been denied for "Yellow Submarine," Lennon has attributed the lyrics for "She Said She Said" to an acid trip encounter with Peter Fonda.[12]

She said—I know what it's like to be dead.
I know what it is to be sad.
And she's making me feel like I've never been born.

Musically, "She Said She Said" demonstrates the same distorted "psychedelic" sound heard in "Taxman." After an introductory lead guitar figure anticipating the vocal melody, the verse begins with a repeated harmonic pattern of I–bVII–IV which recalls McCartney's earlier "The Night Before" and several non-Beatles' songs from the period. The initial melodic phrase consists of two motives: a leap of a fifth, and an ascending-descending line harmonized in thirds except for a final perfect fourth (see ex. 37).

(Ex. 37 "She Said She Said." Verse, meas. 1– 3)   ♩ = approx. 108

Bb: I   bVII   IV   I   bVII
      She said -   I know what it's   like to be dead - .

A distinctive sound is achieved here (as in so many other Beatle songs) by a judicious use of nonharmonic tones, notably the sustained melodic fifth scale degree against the changing chords and the accented nonharmonic sixths, sevenths, and ninths. The last four measures of the ten-measure verse employ a single phrase—a basically descending motive which concludes with an ascending leap of a fourth recalling the opening phrase of the verse (see ex. 38).

(Ex. 38 "She Said She Said." Verse, meas. 7– 8)   ♩ = approx. 108

The refrain melody resembles the verse in its combination of leaps and stepwise motion (although descending rather than ascending scale lines are the rule here) and also shows a similar use of nonharmonic tones. It is also notable for a shift to triple meter in the third measure, an effect that squeezes together the declamatory phrases in a manner which is both natural and artistic. This effect is magnified when, in the fourth and fifth measures, it is followed by a pair of spacious and widely separated phrases (introduced by a surprising minor dominant chord) at the words: "When I was a boy / Everything was right" (see ex. 39).

(Ex. 39 "She Said She Said." Bridge, meas. 1– 5)   ♩ = approx. 108

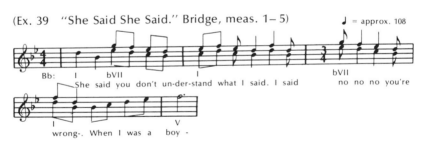

The contrast with the rhythmically cramped dialogue of the earlier measures graphically depicts both the idyllic recollections of boyhood (usually more imagined than real) and the tension of much adult conversation.

Other points of interest include the frequent sharing of melodic interest between voice and guitar, and Ringo's active drum accompaniment featuring the economical, layered fills which increasingly become a hallmark of his style in this period. Still, the song's greatest achievement lies in the masterstroke of word painting described above which lends real pathos to an otherwise undistinguished text.

The great variety of genres encountered on side one of *Revolver* continues on side two with McCartney's "Good Day Sunshine," a "period" piece which self-consciously evokes an old-time "barrelhouse" style in its use of piano (played by George Martin) and harmonic structure.

The song begins with repeated piano chords on the dominant, breaking into a striking vocal introduction which exhibits deft, across-the-bar syncopation based on an alternation of V/V and V/ii chords before a return to V7. The most explicit "barrelhouse" gestures are in the verse; the piano-dominated accompaniment exhibits idiomatically chromatic lines and a boogie-woogie bass pattern. The chord progression of I–V/ii–V/IV–V–I is also a typical barrelhouse mannerism and recalls Lennon's 1965 "I Call Your Name" as well as a more recent hit, "Day Dream," by the Loving Spoonful, a song which also shares the nature-celebration theme of "Good Day Sunshine" (see ex. 40).

(Ex. 40 "Good Day Sunshine." Verse, meas. 1– 4)   ♩ = approx. 120

This colorful, if uncomplicated, verse section alternates throughout with the syncopated refrain that also serves, in modified form, as a brief, fadeout coda. While the song's most distinctive characteristic may be its old fashioned "period" flavor, its subtle syncopations demonstrate that the Beatles' innovations begin in 1966 to extend to rhythm as well as melody, harmony, and instrumentation.

"Good Day Sunshine" is followed on the British album by Lennon's "And Your Bird Can Sing," a song also displaying some barrelhouse mannerisms in its instrumental accompaniment. On the American album, it is followed by McCartney's "For No One," one of the most elegant songs ever composed by the Beatles. Again, it features an unusual instrumental sound, this time supplied by a harpsichord played by McCartney. The verse melody that begins the song is characterized by an expansive motive based on repeated notes outlining an ascending tonic arpeggio with expressive nonharmonic tones occurring in the fifth and sixth measures. Harmonically, this is supported by a progression generated by a descending diatonic bass line in the manner of Lennon's 1964 "Help!" (see ex. 41).

(Ex. 41   "For No One." Verse, meas. 1– 4)

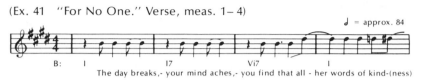

B: I   I7   Vi7   I
The day breaks,- your mind aches,- you find that all - her words of kind-(ness)

The descending bass line and accompanying diatonic progression is broken in the sixth measure with an unexpected subtonic (bVII) triad, a chord which has frequently occurred in similar contexts in other Beatle songs. The bridge melody (in the key of the supertonic) presents a strong contrast to the verse with its active, conjunct contour which changes directions frequently and contains virtually no repeated notes. A particularly attractive gesture is found in measures three and four where bass and piano begin an octave doubling of the vocal melody but continue to ascend as the vocal melody descends, resulting in an artfully simple counterpoint which is followed by a 4–3 dissonance resolution on the original dominant chord.

As in most Beatle compositions of the period, the momentum is increased by additions to the instrumental texture. The return of the verse features piano and bass along with the original harpsichord sonority, and this is followed by a lyrically ornate French horn solo. The bridge returns as before, but the next verse combines the vocal melody with fragments of the horn solo. The final bridge section remains unchanged until the addition of horn octaves to its final 4–3 suspension on the dominant. The song ends here, leaving not only the dominant chord unresolved, but the rather bitter narrative of the love lament as well.

McCartney's elegant if basically conventional ballad is followed by Harrison's "I Want to Tell You." This song is similar in effect to neither "Taxman" nor "Love You To" but, rather, to the personal pop-rock style heard previously in such mature songs as "If I Needed Someone" and "Think for Yourself." The "fadein" introduction features an arpeggiated lead guitar riff comparable to that found in the former in its use of an implied 4–3 suspension, while the declamatory verse melody is similar to that found in the verse of the latter as is the alternation between solo and harmonized phrases. The eleven-measure verse melody further resembles its counterpart in "Think for Yourself" in its phrase construction; in both cases the second phrase provides an extension of an idea introduced in the first. The harmonic progression of the verse is thoroughly conventional, except for the addition of a figure incorporating a dissonant flatted ninth over the dominant chord in the seventh measure, an effect made even more grating by the tritone interval between the upper voices in the piano accompaniment.

While the bridge melody is generally undistinguished (restricted mostly to the first, second, and third scale degrees), the harmonic progression is typical of Harrison's non-Eastern style in its free mixture of major, minor, and, in this case, diminished chords as well as in its lack of strong tonal direction. The brief coda contains the only obvious Indian mannerisms of the song as the middle part of a three-part vocal engages in an unusually ornate melisma including some rapid turns. Still, Harrison's trademarks are clear; this is a song in which neither conventional excitement nor sensuality are sought, and in which some of the most attractive and accessible characteristics of the Beatles' earlier pop-rock style are avoided in order to achieve a distinctive if somewhat ascetic effect.

Speaking of the next song on the album, McCartney's "Got to Get You into My Life," Lennon refers to the Beatles as doing their "Tamla Motown bit."[13] The reference is to two recording labels then prominent in the recording of two updated forms of the uptown rhythm and blues tradition—"motown," a relatively commercial style, and "soul," a more intense, improvisatory style which owed less to contemporary popular music, especially in harmonic terms. While neither of the terms "soul" and "motown" were (or are) used with much precision, certain characteristics can be associated with both of them and McCartney's song demonstrates some of each. The brass-sax riffs that begin the piece and dominate the texture evoke the soul band sound, although they are in places more lyrical and less rhythmically active than would be typical of the uptempo arrangements for famous soul singers of the period such as James Brown and Wilson Pickett. Meanwhile, the repeated, evenly accented quarter note bass line (reinforced by the percussion) and the use of a descending chromatic sequence at one point are characteristics associated more with the motown style of groups such as the Supremes.

Musically, the song exhibits characteristics associated with several past Beatle songs. The repeated-note, triad-based verse melody resembles the verse melody of "For No One" for the first few measures (although a dramatic ascending leap of a seventh to a dissonant note is characteristic only of the current song) and the harmonic alternation between tonic and subtonic chords over a tonic pedal for the first eight measures recalls Harrison's "If I Needed Someone" (see ex. 42).

(Ex. 42   "Got to Get You into My Life." Verse, meas. 1– 4)

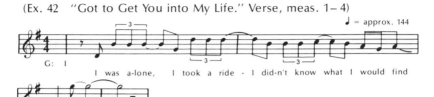

The second eight measures of the verse begin by exploiting a descending chromatic line in the harmony which is almost identical to that heard in a comparable section of "Eleanor Rigby" as well as in some motown songs of the period such as "Stop in the Name of Love," recorded in 1965 by the Supremes (see ex. 43).

(Ex. 43   "Got to Get You into My Life." Verse, meas. 9– 12)

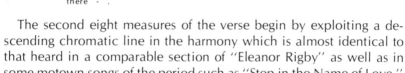
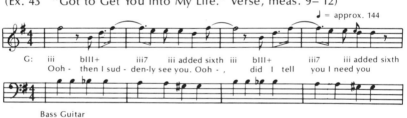

In the brief, six-measure refrain, McCartney's voice takes on a harsher quality more apropos of the soul style, and a blueslike intensity is achieved for the first time as he shouts flat thirds against the major tonic chord. The brass-sax riff also takes on a new edge here and demonstrates the use of blues flats for the first time.

But aside from the novelty of the soul-motown instrumental style accompaniment, the song exhibits little that is new or particularly striking in either the music or the love song lyrics. However, the final composition on *Revolver,* Lennon's "Tomorrow Never Knows," falls into a completely different category.

Even more than "She Said She Said," "Tomorrow Never Knows" represents a quintessential "hallucinatory" song with lyrics derived from Leary's *Psychedelic Experience:*

Turn off your mind, relax, and float down-stream.
It is not dying, it is not dying.
Lay down all thoughts, surrender to the void.
It is shining, it is shining.

But while "She Said She Said" was given a rather conventional musical setting, "Tomorrow Never Knows" is accompanied by the most elaborate and well developed use of electronic sounds and concrete music effects (i.e., the manipulation of prerecorded sound material) heard to that point in any Beatle song or any other song in the rock idiom.

The song begins with a tonic drone asserted by an Indian tamboura and reinforced by throbbing eighth notes on bass guitar and an unusually simple and repetitive drum pattern. The first unusual effects encountered are synthesized "bird cries," which, as Wilfrid Mellers suggests, may derive from jazzman Charles Mingus[14] or any of a number of avant-garde "serious" composers. The basic melodic material is surprisingly simple. As in "For No One," the eight measure melody is basically a terraced unfolding of a tonic chord with a repeated move to the tonic pitch by way of a flat seventh (see ex. 44).

(Ex. 44 "Tomorrow Never Knows." Verse, meas. 1– 4)

C: (sitar)
Turn   off your mind, re - lax   and float   down   -   stream.

As in Harrison's "Love You To," this use of the flat seventh scale degree is accompanied by the intrusion of a taped collection of pitches suggesting a subtonic chord. Shortly thereafter, a passage of tape-reversed string sound combined with other tape-reversed concrete effects builds to a brief but frantic polyphonic string solo. This merges into a tape-reversed lead guitar solo with an exaggerated fluidity which suggests the classical Indian style. As the song progresses, Lennon's vocal is given a "distanced" echo quality as the electronically and tape-generated texture builds in density to a final coda in which tape-manipulated piano and other instrumental sounds are added to the final collage.

While the techniques exploited here would hardly have been considered sophisticated by serious composers of electronic music, their application to an Indian-influenced instrumental texture in a rock album were considered miraculous and groundbreaking. And so, on the basis of these and other such revolutionary qualities, it is not surprising that the overall impact of *Revolver* was extensive. Still, the significance of the more conventional songs can best be determined by a comparison with the stylistic norms and accomplishments of the entire Beatle repertoire in the years 1965–1966.

Style Characteristics: 1965–1966

Form

As in earlier Beatle songs, the most commonly occurring pattern is verse-verse-bridge (or refrain)—verse with repeats and instrumental solos extending the form by at least one additional bridge and verse section depending on the song's tempo. As before, the verse sections occasionally have two distinct subsections, the second sometimes filling the role of a refrain. This particular pattern occurs almost exclusively in McCartney's songs (e.g., "Eleanor Rigby").

Eight measure sections remain the rule although, as before, there are a number of "irregular" or asymmetrical section lengths, perhaps the most famous of which is the seven measure verse of "Yesterday." The songs of *Revolver* are similar in this respect to earlier albums; most have eight measure sections, while two have ten and one ("I Want to Tell You") has an eleven measure verse.

Varied repetition of a phrase or phrase pair (occasionally reharmonized) remains typical (e.g., "Yellow Submarine" and "Norwegian Wood") with any third phrase generally providing contrast (e.g., "We Can Work It Out") and with an occasional return to the first idea for the fourth phrase (e.g., "You Won't See Me"), a form more common in earlier songs. There is a greater tendency in this period toward songs that are "through-composed" (i.e., contain no obvious or direct repetition) in a given section but which demonstrate motivic links between phrases (e.g., "For No One," "Here, There and Everywhere," and "She Said She Said").

Melody

The characteristic use of the prominent nonharmonic fourth scale degree seen in the earlier songs continues in this period (e.g., "Ticket to Ride" and "Day Tripper"), while the use of nonharmonic tones in general becomes both more extensive and sophisticated in songs of various styles by Lennon, McCartney, and Harrison (e.g., "Eleanor Rigby," "Here, There and Everywhere," "In My Life," and "She Said She Said").

Certain melodic types fall into disuse during this period, including those associated with the rhythm and blues synthesis style so significant in 1964 and the uptown rhythm and blues style. While blues-influenced melodies do not disappear completely, there are relatively few which exhibit an obvious and consistent use of blues motives (e.g., "The Word" and "Taxman"). The only distinctively new melody type to become at all prominent in this period is the terraced, triadic melody with repeated notes, a type which is encountered three times on the *Revolver* album (i.e., "For No One," "Got to Get You into My Life," and "Tomorrow Never Knows").

Harmony

Certain distinctive characteristics heard in earlier songs continue to be developed in this period, especially in the early stages. The unexpected chromatic mediant relationships introduced in 1963 are exploited to an unprecedented degree in such early 1965 songs as "You're Gonna Lose That Girl" and "Another Girl" but play a comparatively minor role thereafter. However, the use of the subtonic chord (bVII) as a distinctive component of many chord progressions becomes increasingly common in later 1965 and 1966, especially in songs composed by Lennon and Harrison (e.g., "Taxman" and "She Said She Said").

Chromatic chord sequences generated by descending chromatic countermelodies which occur as early as the 1964 "All My Loving" occur frequently in this period, especially in songs composed by McCartney (e.g., "Michelle," "Eleanor Rigby," and "Got to Get You into My Life").

Meanwhile, characteristic diatonic progressions are by no means eschewed in 1965–1966. The *Rubber Soul* album is particularly notable for its use of conventional diatonic progressions, and even some of the songs of *Revolver* contain progressions that hearken back to the early Beatles' style (e.g., "Here, There and Everywhere"). Finally, dissonance-producing pedal effects and static ostinatos become relatively common in 1965 (e.g., "We Can Work It Out," "Think for Yourself," and "If I Needed Someone") and the use of the drone pedal becomes a prominent feature in some of the Indian-influenced songs (e.g., "Love You To" and "Tomorrow Never Knows").

Rhythm

While the Beatles' experimentation with rhythmic effects in 1965–1966 is by no means as extensive as their experimentation with other musical parameters, there are some examples of increased interest in this area, notably in metric shifts and extensive syncopations across bar lines (e.g., "She Said She Said" and "Good Day Sunshine").

Instrumental and Vocal Arrangements—Sound Gestures

There is little question that the Beatles' uses of distinctive and/or innovative instrumental arrangements are among their most remarkable achievements in this period. Their distinctive instrumental arrangements range from the relatively subtle folk and country and western techniques displayed in *Rubber Soul,* to the use of conventional instruments not normally heard in the rock idiom (e.g., the flute in "Hide Your Love Away," the string ensemble in "Yesterday" and "Eleanor Rigby," and the French horn solo in "For No One") to the Indian-influenced and psychedelic techniques (e.g., the sitar in "Norwegian Wood" and "Love You To" and the lead guitar sound and style in "Taxman") to the sophisticated collages of electronic sounds and concrete music effects (e.g., "Rain" and "Tomorrow Never Knows"). And, of course, the increased possibilities of studio enhancement (e.g., overdubbing and mixing) that became available to the Beatles in this period unquestionably have an effect on the subtlety and complexity of even the most conventionally arranged songs (e.g., "It's Only Love").

Vocal arrangements continue to make extensive use of responsorial techniques in this period, but a somewhat more realized use of choral effects and even a pseudopolyphony emerges in this period (e.g., "Paperback Writer" and "Dr. Robert").

There are, in 1965–1966, fewer examples of the sort of broad, ear-catching vocal gestures that so frequently marked the introductions and refrains of the earlier singles. To a certain extent, these distinctive gestures are replaced by the use of instrumental ostinatos similar in type to the one that characterizes the 1964 "I Feel Fine" and which recur frequently in the single releases of 1965 by both Lennon and McCartney (e.g., "Day Tripper" and "Paperback Writer").

Lyrics

The sort of conventional love song lyrics (both celebration and lament) that characterized virtually all of the Beatles' early songs are considerably less in evidence in this period. Due in part to the influence of Bob

Dylan and in part to the Beatles' increasing awareness of their own significance as musical leaders and trend setters, many of the lyrics in 1965–1966 show a new seriousness of tone and even a certain degree of cynicism. Conventional love songs do not disappear completely (as shown by "Here, There and Everywhere" on the *Revolver* album), but a new emphasis on social criticism, along with a tendency toward the revelation of drug-inspired, hallucinatory experiences become the dominating factors in the Beatles' lyrics.

7

Sergeant Pepper
and the Singles of 1967

With *Revolver*, *"Yesterday"* . . . *and Today*, and *A Collection of Beatles Oldies* high on the charts, the four Beatles took a four-month respite from their recording activities. Lennon went to Germany and Spain to make *How I Won the War*, a United Artists film directed by Richard Lester in which he made his solo acting debut as musketeer Gripweed. Meanwhile, Ringo vacationed in Spain while George travelled to India to begin a more intense study of classical Indian music.

In November, Paul composed the soundtrack music for *The Family Way*, a Warner Brothers film directed by John and Ray Boulting. While this "solo" recording falls outside of the scope of this study, it should be remarked that the music shows the same lyrical poignance and often novel harmonic sense that McCartney displays in so many of his mature songs, while also demonstrating his fondness for commercial clichés. And, while the score is generally unobtrusive as a soundtrack, it is also very repetitive and cannot be considered a particularly important contribution to his output.

A far more significant contribution to the Beatles' music is the single record released in the middle of February, 1967, which combines McCartney's "Penny Lane" with Lennon's "Strawberry Fields Forever." The single soon reached number one on the British *Melody Maker* charts. In America, "Penny Lane" eventually rose to the number one spot while "Strawberry Fields Forever" rose no higher than number eight.

This eighth place position was, however, quite an achievement considering the nature of "Strawberry Fields Forever," a song that Mellers has referred to as the "strangest Beatle song thus far"[1] and which is certainly the most unconventional single released by the Beatles to that point.

Lennon's lyrics involve a dreamlike (and at least partially drug-inspired) reconstruction of a childhood memory—"Strawberry Fields" being a Salvation Army school whose annual picnic he attended more than once with his Aunt Mimi.

The most significant aspect of the song is its incorporation of avant-garde effects within the idiom of a western popular song. The two previous Beatles' songs that had made extensive and serious use of electronic or tape-manipulated effects, Harrison's "Love You To" and Lennon's "Tomorrow Never Knows," had both been heavily Indian-influenced and the contexts in which the new effects appeared were, therefore, in themselves alien to the western popular music tradition. Such is not the case with "Strawberry Fields Forever"; while some of the melodic, harmonic, and rhythmic elements may be ambiguous or unusual, they clearly remain within the boundaries of the prevailing popular music style.

A synthesized flute trio, with material taken from the verse accompaniment, serves as an introduction to the song. The melody of the refrain-like first section begins with a motive reminiscent of Lennon's "Run for Your Life" in its use of the accented nonharmonic fourth scale degree against the tonic chord as Lennon sings: "Let me take you down / 'cause I'm going to. . . ." The tonality is blurred slightly at the words "Strawberry Fields" in the third measure, however, as the melody comes to rest on the flatted seventh scale degree over an ambiguous chord defined by the lead guitar as a minor dominant seventh (v 7) (see ex. 45).

(Ex. 45 "Strawberry Fields Forever." Refrain, meas. 1–4)

As Lennon intones the words "nothing is real," the tonality is further clouded by a variant of the previous triplet motive which clashes dissonantly against an unexpected VIb7 chord before it too comes to rest on the seventh of the chord. This is followed, at the words "and nothing to get hung about," by melodic motion within a rapid IV–V–VI progression and finally (after a two-beat measure of accompaniment alone), at the words "Strawberry Fields Forever," by a syncopated speech rhythm motive which concludes the phrase over a quick V–I cadence.

The verse that follows is, for the first four measures, based harmonically on the descending chromatic countermelody heard first in the introduction, and melodically on a declamatory line with several repeated notes (see ex. 46).

(Ex. 46   "Strawberry Fields Forever." Verse, meas. 1–4)

The last four measures of this section continue this melodic style over a reshuffling of the stereotyped IV–V7–I–vi pattern and a cadential formula.

But while the use of nonharmonic tones and an unexpected VI chord provide a somewhat disorienting effect, the uniquely ethereal properties of the song can be attributed largely to the accompanying instrumental and electronic texture, a texture unprecedented in its kaleidoscopic changes of tone color and density. The process used to accomplish such a feat is revealed in part by journalist Thomas Thompson's observation of the Beatles' recording session that produced "Strawberry Fields Forever":

After several all-night sessions, the recording was finally finished and John listened thoughtfully to the playback.

"It's not exactly what I had in mind when I wrote it," he said, and ordered an entirely new version. . . . Working with Martin, John produced a new score for three cellos and four trumpets. Still not satisfactory. Like layers on a cake, the tracks began to be laid down on one another. A rhythm track of Ringo's drums and percussion was added, then played backward and rerecorded and added again. Unsatisfied, they hit upon the idea of getting studio bystanders to pick up bongos, tambourines, conga drums and tympani and bang away, and this too went into the cake. Then George recorded a track on an old table harp he had found in a junk shop, and Paul added one more track on his mellotron [a computerized electric organ synthesizer]. In the end, this many layered tape was superimposed on the original that John had disliked—and the Beatles loved it.[2]

Other significant components of the song include the great variety of textures and effects gained by the use of conventional instruments alone (i.e., the cellos and trumpets). Cello glissandi alternate with sustained pitches in a sharply reduced texture and active lines which take on a significant melodic identity. Sharp, rhythmic trumpet interjections alternate with sustained chords which substitute for the bass and guitars. The synthesized sounds, while used sparingly, are not merely superficial; a synthesized percussion track (consisting mostly of rhythmic "sucking" sounds) completely replaces the conventional percussion track for long periods of time and is integral in defining the mysterious ethos of those sections. After a series of refrain-verse alternations, each of which exhibits its own unique coloring and textural identity, the coda represents the Beatles' most successful experiment with collage. Here, the synthesized flutes give way to a fragmentary, distorted guitar solo, repeated piano chords which conflict tonally with the continuing cello lines, and half-heard cries in the background. This conglomeration fades out and then back again as the flutes enter with a new motive, out of tempo with the percussion, the throbbing guitar, and the piano pitches which follow it. The "table harp" (evoking the chikari strings of a sitar) makes a final appearance, and a tape-manipulated voice intones the words "cranberry sauce" as the drum track fades and the song disappears.

Generally more straightforward in its melodic-harmonic character, McCartney's "Penny Lane" is a "sing along" song with a melody as memorable (and simple) as in any of the singles of this period. The verse begins guilelessly enough with a series of cascading phrases over the familiar I–vi–ii7–V7 progression (see ex. 47).

(Ex. 47   "Penny Lane." Verse, meas. 1–4)

But in the fourth measure the melody comes to rest on the seventh of a minor seventh chord built on tonic, and this is followed by an unusual diminished chord built on submediant (vi°) and a chromatic bVI before the phrase concludes conventionally on a V7.

The celebratory refrain is based on a simple four measure phrase which recalls the early Beatles in its direct appeal (see ex. 48).

(Ex. 48   "Penny Lane." Refrain, meas. 1–3)

This section is based (somewhat unusually) on the key of the subtonic (bVII), a key which is arrived at in a simple but effective manner as the subdominant chord of the original key serves as the dominant of the new key (i.e., V/bVII–bVII). The return to the original verse key is even more direct: the subdominant of the refrain key is followed immediately and unceremoniously by the dominant of the verse key as the lyrics return us to the narrative and the dominant takes us back to our original key.

While McCartney's lyrics lack the often obvious hallucinatory references of "Strawberry Fields Forever," they nevertheless manage to evoke a colorful and occasionally surrealistic collage of visual images from the Beatles' childhoods, most of them associated with the real "Penny Lane," a busy Liverpool street. The poignance of many of these images is greatly enhanced by McCartney's settings; while much of the song is guileless and predictable, the occasional harmonic nuances (especially in the verse) add a sophistication not apparent on a first hearing.

But while "Penny Lane" may match "Strawberry Fields Forever" in expressive word painting, it offers far less complexity of arrangement. Aside from the usual complement of guitars, piano, bass and drums, only flutes, brass, and clanging fire bells are included, and these are used in a rather conventional manner for the most part. The elegant Neo-Baroque trumpet solos (dictated by Paul) are a worthy exception to this, as are the snatches of electronic effects heard between the last two verses and within the song's brief fadeout coda. But, on the whole, "Penny Lane" is a much less revolutionary song than "Strawberry Fields Forever" even if more commercially successful. Still, the relatively sophisticated imagery exhibited by both songs and the innovative techniques demonstrated by "Strawberry Fields Forever" erased any doubts that the Beatles were determined to extend the creative boundaries of rock music. The group's next release was eagerly awaited. And, four months later when it was issued, the response was unparalleled in the history of popular music.

Sergeant Pepper's Lonely Hearts Club Band

Released in April, 1967, *Sergeant Pepper's Lonely Hearts Club Band* has generally been hailed as the peak achievement of the Beatles' career. Mellers labels the album "the single most decisive event in pop's brief history," suggesting that it offers not "a miscellany of songs" as had previous albums, but rather a "sequence of intimately related numbers, forming a whole and performed without a break."[3] This view of *Sergeant Pepper* has been shared, at least in part, by several commentators. Richard Poirier, editor of *Partisan Review,* describes the album in the following way:

> Under the aegis of an old-time concert given by the type of music-hall band with which Lennon's father, Alfred claims to have been associated, the songs, directly or by chance images, offer something like a review of contemporary English life, saved from folk-song generality by having each song resemble a dramatic monologue . . . Their arrangement is apparently haphazard, suggesting how the hippie and the historically pretentious, the genteel and the mod, the impoverished and the exotic, the Indian influence and the influence of technology are inextricably entangled into what is England.[4]

Peter Shrag of the *Saturday Review* suggests further that the album "declares that the conventional world of jobs, money, and status is blind, brutal, and destructive, that it is full of people who hide behind a wall of illusion." The album, he states, may be music, but it is also "literature and criticism, a kind of selective filtering back from one generation to another."[5]

In his study of *Sergeant Pepper* and the 1969 album *Abbey Road,* Dale Cockrell insists that thematic unity in the former is very much a self-conscious rather than an accidental achievement.[6] Cockrell's assertion is at least partially substantiated by Paul McCartney in his interview with Aldridge:

> We realized for the first time that some day, someone would actually be holding a thing they'd call "The Beatles' new LP" and that normally it would be nothing more. So the idea was to do a complete thing that you could make what you liked of; just a little magic presentation.[7]

The *Sergeant Pepper* album begins with what Mellers describes as a "public number."[8] Whereas *Revolver* began with disjointed instrumental, electronic, and speech sounds, *Sergeant Pepper* substitutes the tuning sounds of a complete orchestra and typical preconcert audience noise. The difference, of course, involves more than a choice of sonorities. The fragmented noises of *Revolver*, regardless of their seemingly random deployment, represent a self-consciously "avant-garde" gesture, while the orchestra and crowd sounds of *Sergeant Pepper* serve mainly to set the scene for the events to come, musical and otherwise. The opening of *Sergeant Pepper* thus eschews any artistic pretension and provides a "social" rather than "artistic" sound with which to begin the album.

The opening song itself, "Sergeant Pepper's Lonely Hearts Club Band," begins in a manner reminiscent of "Taxman" with its use of an intense, high-volume distorted guitar sound, hand tremolo effects, rhythmically reiterated pitches alternating with wide melodic leaps, sharp rhythm guitar chords, and an active, syncopated bass guitar. While Mellers correctly points out that the song "recalls Edwardian military music,"[9] it is just as clearly an evocation of the psychedelic style, as McCartney himself indicates in the Aldridge interview when he characterizes "Sergeant Pepper's Lonely Hearts Club Band" as "a bit of a brass band in a way but also a rock band because they got that San Francisco thing."[10] The San Francisco area was, of course, the home of many of the most successful proponents of the psychedelic style, although the most famous examples of this style (e.g., the second album of the Jefferson Airplane) had not yet been recorded at the time of *Sergeant Pepper*'s release.

The harmonic progression of the song's instrumental introduction is itself stylistically ambiguous in its II7–IVb7–Ib7 progression, but there can be no mistake about the harmonic identity of the verse section. The I–II–IV–I progression is completely unrelated to any military band or music hall style, but is an excellent example of the Beatles' pop-rock harmonic style, demonstrated in its maturity as early as 1964 by "Eight Days a Week" and continuing in songs such as "You Won't See Me" of 1965 and "Day Tripper" of 1966, all of which make use of an identical or a similar chord progression in some section.

The vocal melody of the verse consists of short phrases with many repeated notes. It may be interpreted either as the "reciting tone" style used by the announcer in an attempt to excite the prospective audience (. . . "Let me introduce to you . . . the one and only Billy Shears . . ."), or in terms of its traditional rhythm and blues identity, similar examples being found not only in the songs of Chuck Berry and Little Richard, but also McCartney's "I'm Down" among others. But it is the "side show" implications that seem to be the most important here, as Sergeant Pepper's band is introduced and allotted a five-measure solo section of patently old fashioned military band music.

The first part of the refrain that follows seems to return to the psychedelic rock style. The harsh, dissonant quality of the accompaniment, the pairing of bass and rhythm guitars on the first and third beats of the measure against solo fragments by the lead guitar, and the rhythmic pounding on a single distorted pitch are typical gestures in that style. But, while the harmonic progression begins with a minor third root movement that is distinctively rock-styled (i.e., I–bIII–IV–I), there are no blues implications or dissonances in the melody other than an added sixth sonority in the second measure of the section. Furthermore, the third and fourth measures alternate between IV and I with a V/V–V progression coinciding with another brief brass band segment in the second phrase. This shift from the "progressive" rock style to the "period" style continues in the second half of the refrain. The guitars and harmonized vocal return but both are toned down in intensity and the harmonic progression is even more conventional, eschewing the earlier minor third root relationship. The old fashioned quality of this section is confirmed by a clichéd cadence reiteration supplied by the wind band at the end of the last phrase. The second verse section that follows exhibits the strongest period flavor of all. The brass band accompanies in sustained pitches; the repeated note melody ("It's wonderful to be here, it's certainly a thrill") is delivered with a restrained, almost sedate vocal quality, and generally alternates between the third of the subdominant chord and its lower auxiliary (harmonized by a bVII7 chord), a stereotypical characteristic of the dated music hall style. Once again a secondary dominant chord plays an important role in the harmonic scheme, and the staccato articulation and clichéd brass countermelody all contribute to reinforce the dated quality of this section.

At this point the original verse section returns, complete with its psychedelic sound effects (an occurrence which is greeted enthusiastically by the crowd who seems equally enchanted with both musical styles). But just as this section served initially more as a vocal introduction than as a proper verse, it serves here as both a postlude and a transition to the next song, as the announcer presents "Billy Shears," the first featured member of Sergeant Pepper's Lonely Hearts Club Band.

"Sergeant Pepper" ends on a dominant chord with a descending scalewise bass line. This is followed by a series of ascending chords (vocal "cheers" with instrumental accompaniment) separated by a whole step (i.e., I–II–III), a pattern characterized by Cockrell as "an introductory formula associated with vaudeville and early popular music of the century."[11]

After the splashy introduction provided by the opening song, Billy Shears's contribution is a fairly modest one. A McCartney composition, "With a Little Help from My Friends" is sung by Ringo, the "nonsinger" of the group. Shears (like Ringo) is somewhat tentative in his approach and begins by seeking the audience's indulgence; he'll get by only with their patience and a little help from his friends.

Musically, the song is as simple and guileless as "Yellow Submarine," which also featured Ringo as vocalist. The repetitive melody stays within the range of a fifth for the entire eight measure verse over a harmonic progression of I–iii–ii–V7–I (with a descending scalewise bass line providing inversions for the second and third chords). This progression had appeared in early songs such as "Do You Want to Know a Secret?" and "I'm Happy Just to Dance with You," while Lennon's 1963 "Ask Me Why" anticipates "With a Little Help from My Friends" both melodically and harmonically to some extent. These and other similar examples are all ballads and the initial I–iii progression has, in fact, generally been associated with the ballad style in the Beatles' music. A less intense atmosphere prevails here as well, although the chord progression is aided in momentum by the descending bass line which begins it.

But while "With a Little Help from My Friends" is reminiscent of early Beatle songs in its simplicity for the first eight measures, the eight-measure refrain that begins in measure nine introduces a somewhat more sophisticated bVII–IV–I progression. While the subtonic chord (bVII) had occurred as early as 1965 in the Beatles' music (e.g., in "It's Only Love"), its popularity with the Beatles had increased dramatically in 1966 and 1967 and the chord had become one of their favorite "surprise" harmonies by the time of the *Revolver* album.

After joining with the soloist for the second appearance of the melodically repetitive refrain, the background vocals take the lead in a call and response relationship in the eight measure bridge (background:

"Do you need anybody?" Solo: "I need somebody to love"). Two new chords are introduced in the first two measures (vi7 and V7/V) along with a new melodic idea. The V7/V never resolves in the expected manner, however, and the soloist responds over a I–bVII–IV progression related to the refrain.

After the bridge, the song proceeds with a verse-refrain-bridge-refrain pattern and a unique coda in which the final bVII–IV–I progression is slowed to half speed and two striking chords (bVI and iv with an added sixth) are inserted before the final tonic chord.

But despite this and other subtle harmonic and textural devices, "With a Little Help from My Friends" does not seem to be modeled in any distinctive way after an archaic music hall style. It is, in fact, typical mature Beatle music in its incorporation of a surprise chord (bVII) in an otherwise conventional harmonic progression, and in its mixture of solo vocal-background vocal relationships. Nevertheless, the nature of the narrative dialogue and the simplicity of the melodic line do serve as a link of sorts to the show concept referred to earlier and, therefore, to the overall context of the album.

This partially musical and partially literary connection becomes considerably more tenuous in Lennon's "Lucy in the Sky with Diamonds." Like the previous song, its lyrics are at least partially narrative. But the context here is quite different; the simplicity of Billy Shears's appeal is replaced by a magical (or perhaps hallucinatory) text, reinforced by the exotic celesta sound of the opening organ melody. The basic melodic-harmonic ingredients of the song are not particularly exotic, however. Against the counterpoint of the organ melody, the first section of the verse exhibits a repetitive melody revolving around the third scale degree and based on a progression of I–Ib7–vi–bVI+–I–Ib7–vi–bVI generated by a descending bass pattern.

A similar nine-measure phrase pair follows, harmonically complicated by the introduction of a tamboura drone. After a single transitional measure, the twelve-measure second section of the verse begins in a key one half-step higher. The organ countermelody is eliminated here, but the music retains its mysterious quality through the use of a new filtered vocal sound, a synthesized chord effect (along with rhythm guitar chords), and the doubling of the melody by a legato lead guitar. The melody is even more repetitive than before, centering again around the third scale degree. The chord progression is generally conventional, based primarily on the tonic and dominant chords with V/V and VI also occurring. But the melodic-harmonic interaction is more remarkable.

Nonharmonic ninths and sixths abound to a degree extraordinary even for the Beatles' music, and the result is a "floating" quality which, along with the instrumentation, reinforces the dreamlike imagery ("Cellophane flowers of yellow and green / towering over your head"), while defying the momentum created by the chord progression and the increased activity of the bass guitar (see ex. 49).

(Ex. 49   "Lucy in the Sky with Diamonds." Bridge, meas. 3–7)

This floating effect is nullified completely by the first measure of the shouted refrain section. This six-measure section (in 4/4 meter) is so elementary and stereotyped in its repeated I–IV–V7 harmonies (a rare use of this clichéd progression by the Beatles), instrumental accompaniment and unison vocal, that it can only be understood as an "anonymous" rock gesture included for the purpose of inserting an element of "earthy reality" into an otherwise dreamlike experience. Under these conditions, it is clear that the more stereotyped and less inspired the gesture, the more suitable it would be for these purposes. And it is within this context that this most pedestrian of rock choruses should be heard.

Still, there are few hints of any music hall style in either section of the song and it seems that "Lucy in the Sky with Diamonds" is related to the *Sergeant Pepper* show concept more in terms of its magical narrative text than in any intrinsically musical manner.

The links to a music hall style are clearer in McCartney's "Getting Better." The frequently bouncy, repeated note melody makes a consistent use of the lower auxiliary in places—a characteristic often associated with older music hall styles—and generally resembles the melody of "With a Little Help from My Friends" in its simplicity and narrow range.

The harmonic materials are, on the whole, equally simple and straightforward. Nevertheless, the song shows a masterful use of subtle effects, notably a reiterated pedal point, unusual textural contrasts, and imaginative background vocal interjections.

The song's introduction contains what is perhaps its most striking gesture: staccato quarter note chords on the subdominant are offered by one guitar against a piercing pedal reiteration on the dominant note by another. This pedal-engendered conflict pervades almost the entire song and constitutes one of its most distinctive features. After a two-measure fragment taken from the vocal refrain, the momentum is established by the addition of bass and percussion and the eight-measure verse begins with an alternation of V–I (see ex. 50).

(Ex. 50   "Getting Better." Verse, meas. 1–4)

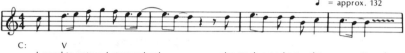

C: V
          I used to get mad at my school - ,   the teach-ers who taught me weren't cool -.

The accompaniment is more complicated. The reiterated dominant pedal is heard in both bass guitar (in alternating octaves) and high-pitched lead guitar in a sparse but detailed texture which includes a syncopated, undampened cymbal part, snare drum only on beat two of each measure, a brief clichéd guitar riff suggesting the tonic chord (more likely heard here as a subdominant in relationship to the dominant chord) and an active pattern of interjections supplied by the background vocals.

The ten-measure refrain exhibits a melody similar in type to that of the verse over a I–ii–iii–IV progression complicated by the continuing high-pitched pedal, a walking four-beat bass pattern, and the continued vocal echoes and responses.

The return of the verse features a fuller texture, achieved mostly by the dropping of the high-pitched pedal to a lower octave and a more active percussion part.

The second refrain lightens the texture once again, returning to the high-pitched pedal and more fragmented bass guitar activity. This time, however, the chorus is supplied with an additional eight-measure section which introduces a divided vocal harmony effect similar to that found in McCartney's "Paperback Writer."

The return of the verse demonstrates the most drastic change in texture yet. A tamboura drone is added to the pedal effect along with off-beat bongo drum taps. However, the first four measures proceed without the guitar and bass, producing a partially suspended momentum similar to that occurring in several of the *Revolver* songs and the singles of that period (e.g., Lennon's "Rain"). The momentum is reestablished with the addition of the guitars in the fifth measure and the active texture is fully restored. The final (repeated) refrain again sees a reduction in texture, however, and the fadeout coda of reiterated high-pitched guitar (and sitar) pedal and bongos evokes the opening measures, while lacking their dissonant intensity.

While most of the Beatles' songs in this period (and earlier) demonstrate an "additive" approach to texture (i.e., the gaining of momentum by a consistent increase in the density or activity of the accompaniment), "Getting Better" does not. As Cockrell points out, McCartney's manipulation of texture suggests rather a sort of arch form with the final section mirroring the opening introduction.[12] This unusual (although not unprecedented) approach is particularly successful here since the reiterated pedal which closes the song has contributed so much to its essence.

While "Getting Better" takes the form of a "confessional" address to the audience ("I used to be mad at my school / the teachers who taught me weren't cool") which turns out to be a love song ("it's getting better / since you've been mine"), McCartney's "Fixing a Hole" is more of a daydreaming novelty number with both whimsical and surreal overtones ("I'm fixing a hole where the rain gets in / and stops my mind from wandering"). Still, the two are related musically by their use of a casually bouncing, triplet-divided rhythm and other more subtle melodic-harmonic details.

After a two-measure harpsichord introduction that synopsizes the harmonic activity of the verse, "Fixing a Hole" again features an accompaniment of block chords played on the beat with cymbal filling in the shuffle rhythm and both anchored by a repeated tonic-dominant bass pattern. The verse melody resembles that of the previous song in its reliance on repeated notes as well as its use of a characteristic, rapidly ascending-descending phrase similar to one which began the verse in both "Getting Better" and "With a Little Help from My Friends." But, taken as a whole, this melody is much more sophisticated. It is greatly varied in its rhythm, types of motion, and contour, combining blues flats (both the third and the seventh degree) with affective lyricism and unusual changes in vocal quality (see ex. 51).

(Ex. 51   "Fixing a Hole." Verse, meas. 1–4)

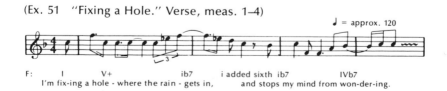

F: I   V+   ib7   i added sixth ib7   IVb7
     I'm fix-ing a hole - where the rain - gets in,   and stops my mind from won-der-ing.

Harmonically, the verse is simple but distinctive. Its progression of I–V+–ib7–i added sixth–ib7–IVb7–ib7–i added sixth is, like many of McCartney's, based initially on a chromatically descending line. The prominent augmented chord and the use of several conspicuous nonharmonic sevenths and ninths in the melody lend an unusual degree of poignance, while the continued tonic-dominant bass movement provides a pedallike effect beneath the changing chords.

The bridge section assumes a more traditional rock stance in its thickened texture, increased rhythmic activity, fuller vocal tone, repeated note melody, and use of I–IV (against I–V bass motion) and V/V–V progressions.

Each return of the verse presents an increasingly fuller texture, but the basic contrast between the two sections remains. In this alternation of a lyrical section with a more obviously rock-inspired section, the song parallels Lennon's "Lucy in the Sky with Diamonds." But in "Fixing a Hole" the lyrical verse is more varied, both melodically and harmonically, even if the rock-styled bridge is similarly stereotyped in both instances.

The next song, McCartney's "She's Leaving Home," is a sentimental Victorian ballad about a girl who, misunderstood and unloved, leaves the middle-class parental nest to search for a more meaningful and exciting life. There has been, since the album's release, some debate as to the merits of both lyrics and music of this song. In reference to the latter, Mellers has characterized the song as "a corny waltz,"[13] while composer-critic Ned Rorem has described it as "a mazurka equal in melancholy and melodic distinction to those of Chopin."[14] At any rate, it is, in its unrelieved lyricism, different from all other *Sergeant Pepper* songs discussed to this point. It is also more expansive melodically than any previous song, and exhibits a more balanced mixture of conjunct and triadic motion (see ex. 52).

(Ex. 52 "She's Leaving Home." Verse, meas. 1–5)

The leap of a seventh between the second and third measures of the repeated sixteen measure verse temporarily evokes the dramatic style of "Eleanor Rigby" (which displayed ascending leaps of an octave and a tenth in a similar context). In fact, the wide-ranging melody has little in common with the folklike simplicity of the tunes for "With a Little Help from My Friends" and "Getting Better" (other than the frequent repetition of phrases) while being more distinctive than Lennon's waltz melody in the verse of "Lucy in the Sky with Diamonds."

The harmony in "She's Leaving Home" is typical of the mature Beatles in its use of bVII (here with an added sixth) along with its emphasis on the minor supertonic (ii) and submediant (vi) chords. Also characteristic of the Beatles' harmonic usage in this period is the pedal effect of a sustained dominant note beneath a IV–V progression in the second half of the verse. The nineteen measure refrainlike bridge is less distinguished both melodically and harmonically. The divided vocal melody lines move almost completely by step, while the only mild surprise is a minor dominant which occurs unexpectedly at midphrase in the latter part of the bridge.

The sentimental "period" flavor of the song is greatly enhanced by the accompaniment. The song begins with romantic harp arpeggios and soon introduces a lyrical cello countermelody which closely matches the vocal melody in its elegiac style. A full string ensemble (arranged by Mike Leander) is subsequently added to the accompanying texture, although its function is generally that of providing lushly supportive harmony rather than the intense punctuating phrases supplied by the strings in "Eleanor Rigby."

The Victorian sentimentality of "She's Leaving Home" contrasts sharply with the next song, Lennon's "Being for the Benefit of Mr. Kite." This song is a salute to show business itself (in this case the circus) and perhaps the most obvious manifestation of the *Sergeant Pepper* show concept. The lyrics were inspired, at least in part, by an authentic circus poster that reads "Pablo Fanques Fair Presents the Hendersons for the Benefit of Mr. Kite" and also contains references to "men and horses, hoops and garters, lastly through a hogshead of real fire," all of which found their way into Lennon's lyrics.[15]

The circus atmosphere is established from the beginning of the song. The introduction presents synthesized wind band chords under an organ melody (which recurs somewhat modified in an instrumental ritornello) accompanied by marchlike percussion, including an unusual snare drum roll on the final chord of the introduction. When the fourteen measure main section begins, it features a descending "harmonium-sound" countermelody (played by a second organ and bass harmonica)[16] and off-beat chords, bass drum downbeats and cymbal offbeats, and a bass guitar which begins in strict rhythm but indulges in some soloistic fills at phrase ends. Vocal harmony is added in the second half of this section, and a two measure ritornello of organ melody recalling the introduction closes the section.

The three appearances of this fourteen measure vocal verse differ very little, but sufficient variety is provided by the two instrumental solo sections. In the first, the strict four-beat pulse of the verse is transformed into a quick waltz which presents an organ melody in emulation of an old fashioned calliope. Superimposed over this is a second rising and falling swirling organ part which functions more as a varied noise background than as counterpoint. This solo section comes to an end with a brief cadence figure which signals a return to the clear tonality of the vocal verse.

The second solo section appears after the third verse and concludes the song. It is again based on the harmony and accompaniment of the vocal verse although it makes a more extensive use of tape-manipulated instrumental sounds (described by producer's assistants Mal Evans and Neil Aspinal as "various organ recordings speeded up, slowed down, electronically distorted, played backwards, and dipped in a bottle of coke").[17]

Although it is clearly the instrumental and tape accompaniment that lends "Mr. Kite" its festive atmosphere, the melodic-harmonic content is of interest for its similarity to earlier works. Lennon's song demonstrates musical affinities with "Fixing a Hole" in its use of augmented chords, and resembles a great number of other Beatles' songs in its use of a descending scale line or passacaglia figure to generate the chord progression (see ex. 53).

(Ex. 53   "Being for the Benefit of Mr. Kite." Verse, meas. 1–4)

In terms of the *Sergeant Pepper* album, however, the most significant aspect of Lennon's song is the way in which it recapitulates the festive show atmosphere of the first song on the album and summarizes much of the jaunty music hall spirit which pervades many of the songs on side one by its incorporation of circus music effects, while simultaneously reinvoking the magical atmosphere of "Lucy in the Sky with Diamonds" by its use of electronic effects.

The second half of the program begins with Harrison's "Within You Without You," the second of his heavily Indian-influenced works. While this song has little musical connection with the songs of side one, its lyrics do relate to theirs to some extent in their preoccupation with hypocrisy and individual isolation (c.f. Shrag's comments quoted earlier). Even from a musical point of view, the song can at least be viewed as a sort of "exotic entertainment" not inconceivable in a turn-of-the-century British music hall.

"Within You Without You" begins with a rhythmically free section featuring sitar and tamboura drone, perhaps in emulation of the "alapa" of Hindustani classical music. Following this, the tabla enter followed by the vocal melody doubled by a dilruba (a fretted, long-necked Indian bowed lute). The dilruba is reinforced by (and sometimes alternated with) a battery of strings including three cellos and eight violins.

The vocal melody proceeds mostly in half notes while the dilruba and other strings weave countermelodies against it and fill phrase endings with melodic phrases which, in their extensive ornamentation, are idiomatic of Hindustani classical music. But except for some idiomatic glissandos, the vocal melody itself is almost completely devoid of ornamentation. Its reliance on the flatted seventh scale degree and its generally tonal implications combine with this lack of idiomatic ornamentation to give the melody a mostly western sound, despite its occasional metric freedom (measures of 5/4 and 3/4 meter are included), the accompanying drone and the presence of the dilruba (see ex. 54).

(Ex. 54 "Within You Without You." Verse, meas. 1–4)

♩ = approx. 126

We were talk - ing - a - bout the space be - (tween)

At any rate, the most remarkable aspect of this piece is its instrumental solo section in 5/8 meter. Here, an extensively ornamented version of the vocal melody is performed by dilruba and echoed or imitated by the sitar in a manner characteristic of the Hindustani tradition. Pizzicato strings are added to mark the 5/8 meter, and cellos are eventually added to the melody, which is also joined by sitar in the final measures of the second. Following this section, there is a break in the rhythm and a brief alapalike section is reintroduced in which cello and sitar exchange free soloistic fragments before the verse vocal melody begins.

The melodic concept embodied in the vocal melody of "Within You Without You" appears to be more western than Indian in nature, and the battery of string instruments which accompany the sitar and dilruba are not in keeping with the "purist" traditions of classical Indian music. Nevertheless, the work shows a closer kinship with classical Indian music than Harrison's earlier "Love You To" in its metric freedom and especially in its highly ornamented and idiomatic solo section.

But the *Sergeant Pepper* show audience seems not to be impressed by this exotic flight, for the final notes of "Within You Without You" are juxtaposed with a few seconds of embarrassed laughter suggesting that Harrison's mystical lecture on the essence of truth has not been fully appreciated. But the audience is soon placated by the more accessible selection that follows, McCartney's "When I'm Sixty-Four," a good natured but poignant look at the needs of old age.

If "Fixing a Hole" is, as Mellers, suggests, a "quintessential Beatle tune,"[18] then "When I'm Sixty-Four" is the quintessential *Sergeant Pepper* tune. For while the melodic-harmonic content of such songs as "Fixing a Hole," "With a Little Help from My Friends," and even "Being for the Benefit of Mr. Kite" can be perceived as compatible with an old fashioned music hall style, "When I'm Sixty-Four" must be considered a direct imitation on that style.[19]

The instrumentation of two B flat clarinets, bass clarinet, piano, bass guitar and snare drum brushstrokes in and of itself evokes an antiquated music hall style. Musical characteristics that similarly suggest an older "period" style include the shuffling syncopation of the introductory clarinet duet; the simple verse vocal melody, especially in its use of upper and lower auxiliary notes; and the breaks in accompaniment which reduce the texture to only bass and vocal soloist. The simple harmony is equally appropriate to an old fashioned popular style. Even the minor subdominant chord and the secondary dominants that occur in the latter part of the sixteen measure verse may be considered appropriate to a light-hearted (and sentimental) music hall style as well as to the Beatles' own.

The sixteen measure bridge is more ambiguous in its stylistic identity. The rhythmically reiterated chords in bass and piano is more of a rock

gesture, but the bouncy melody and descending clarinet countermelody suggest more an old fashioned tango. The clichéd syncopated
exchange between chimes, bass clarinet, and bass drum in the final two
measures of the section also hints at an older popular style. So despite
the rock characteristics glimpsed in the bridge, "When I'm Sixty-Four"
remains the clearest embodiment of the music hall style found on the
Sergeant Pepper album. It is the second (and perhaps most fully realized)
in a line of old-style musical parodies which begins with McCartney's
"Good Day Sunshine" and extends through the five remaining albums
released by the Beatles as a group. But "When I'm Sixty-Four" is the last
obviously "period" or music hall piece on the *Sergeant Pepper* album.
The four remaining songs (one of which is a reprise) each explore
somewhat different directions.

Immediately following "When I'm Sixty-Four" is "Lovely Rita,"
McCartney's novelty song about a parking meter maid. It is the first song
clearly in the rock idiom since the introduction, exhibiting rock-
influenced characteristics from the opening measures. The opening
sonority, provided by driving piano chords and acoustical rhythm
guitar, is maintained throughout the song, supplemented after the first
eight measures by bass guitar (in four-beat repeated note and walking
patterns) and accented off-beat percussion in the rock style. The eight
measure introduction, based on a standard progression of V–IV–I–V,
features a three-part repeated note vocal and recurs as a bridge to the
coda.

The verse exhibits a mostly pentatonic vocal melody over a progression which begins with a I–bVII–IV–I pattern (precedented in several
recent Beatles' songs) (see ex. 55).

(Ex. 55 "Lovely Rita." Verse, meas. 1–4)

The repeated three measure phrase that follows is distinguished only
by a series of secondary dominants which end on bIII and some
vocally-produced wire-brush sounds. After a one-measure interlude of
synthesized "whoops," the first four measure phrase is repeated (creating an unusual a b b a pattern) with the addition of a sequential,
harmonized vocal countermelody. This countermelody extends the

section with an unusual series of descending chords (V–IV–iii–ii) over a dominant pedal. The series concludes with a IV chord which is held for almost four beats before rising to the (consonant) dominant chord. Harmonized vocal interludes are by no means new to the Beatles at this point–several of McCartney's compositions had made use of them—but this is the first occurrence of descending parallel chords over a sustained pedal note, an idea which was to be developed extensively in subsequent Beatles' compositions.

Other noteworthy features of the song include sparse, syncopated drum solos of a type heard in "With a Little Help from My Friends," a piano solo which blends barrelhouse and stride styles as in "Good Day Sunshine" and some high-pitched, falling vocal "oohs" in thirds reminiscent of the early Beatles (e.g., "Thank You Girl").

But the most remarkable attribute of the song is almost certainly its coda. Punctuated by solo vocal interjections, the bass engages in sporadic syncopation along with the piano while the latter contributes some isolated melodic fragments. The seemingly random reiteration of bass and piano along with various noises and rhythmic amplified breathing effects may be intended to reproduce the disorienting collage effect of random street noises, certainly an appropriate gesture in a musical salute to a meter maid. The result, at any rate, is one of carefully choreographed confusion which is only partially resolved by the conclusion—a IV–bII progression in the piano followed by a falling glissando to the tonic pitch.

The style of "Lovely Rita" is basically rock-oriented, especially in its effects of vocal harmony and its energetic percussion accompaniment. Nevertheless, the song also contains elements which might be associated with the music hall (e.g., the piano solo and the "novelty" lyrics), and this stylistic mixture is typical of several *Sergeant Pepper* songs, most notably the title song itself.

The next song on the album, Lennon's "Good Morning Good Morning," has little to do with the music hall, although its preoccupation with alienation and communication does provide a link with one of the undercurrents of the *Sergeant Pepper* theme. The song also has the distinction of combining a motown-soul horn arrangement, psychedelic lead guitar solos, and a blues-influenced melody within a continuously shifting metric framework.

After an appropriate rooster "crow," the soul band influence is heard immediately in the opening measures of the refrainlike introduction. Brass and saxophone riffs and chords are punctuated by heavily accented rhythm guitar, bass guitar and percussion, the total sonority being comparable to the earlier "Got to Get You into My Life." A group vocal repeats a three-note motive five times during this section over a reiteration of I–IV. The introduction concludes with a measure of snare drum sixteenth notes—a gesture repeated several times throughout the song—and a single lead guitar pitch with rapid hand vibrato which previews the psychedelic style of the extended solo heard later.

Although the introduction is in the standard 4/4 meter, the verse is metrically flexible to a degree never before encountered in the Beatles' music, exhibiting changes of 5/4–3/4–4/4–5/4–4/4–3/4–4/4 in the space of eleven measures. This constant fluctuation has an unusually disruptive effect on momentum which is compounded by the extraordinary harmonic rhythm. The opening two measures of 5/4 meter, for example, exhibit an alternation of I and bVII chords in the following pattern: I (three beats)-bVII₍(five beats)-I (two beats; the last of which is replaced by cymbal and bass drum).

The melody itself is blues-influenced in its narrow range, extreme repetitiveness and extensive use of the 5–b7–1 scale pattern (e.g., in measures one and three) (see ex. 56).

(Ex. 56   "Good Morning Good Morning." Verse, meas. 1–2)

On the repeat of the verse, the original melody is cut off after the fourth measure (this time by a new horn riff) and replaced by a bridge section of four and one-half measures of declamatory melody of narrow range over an alternation of I and IV chords. This section is again cut off by snare drum sixteenth notes and the verse returns with brass-saxophone accompaniment throughout.

After the third appearance of the verse, the psychedelic lead guitar launches into a high intensity, distorted solo featuring rapid changes in register and exaggerated hand vibrato as in "Sergeant Pepper's Lonely Hearts Club Band." The solo also makes conspicuous use of a triplet pattern and a descending modal scale, complete with "exotic" half-step ornaments and turns reminiscent of the solo in "Taxman."

Following the solo, the verse returns exhibiting its fullest texture. Vocal harmony is added, and the lead guitar interjections continue the psychedelic atmosphere. To conclude the piece (and to link it with the next), the "Good Morning" refrain is repeated several times, accompanied by a collage of various animal noises which continue even as the music fades out.

While "Lovely Rita" consistently reinvoked a rock style for the first time since the introductory song, "Good Morning, Good Morning" specifically recalls the hard-edged psychedelic "San Francisco sound" of "Sergeant Pepper's Lonely Hearts Club Band." After the linking passage of animal sounds (in which the clucking of a chicken is transformed into the distorted notes of the lead guitar), the tempo is counted off and a heavy percussion introduction combines with surging crowd noises in an attempt to recapture the atmosphere which characterized the beginning of the album. And yet, despite the clamour of the crowd, the atmosphere is somehow different for this reprise (with new lyrics) of the refrain of the title song ("We're Sergeant Pepper's Lonely Hearts Club Band / We hope you have enjoyed the show. / Sergeant Pepper's one and only Lonely Hearts Club Band / We're sorry but it's time to go"). Although the opening sonority is similar to that of the song's first appearance, the tempo is quicker and the biting lead guitar riffs become more violent and more frequent, even replacing the two measure solo originally allotted to Sergeant Pepper's wind band. The lead guitar riffs become even more prominent after the key shifts up a whole step to the song's original key and the mood remains frantic until the final bars—a IV–I cadence over which the vocal soloist exclaims furiously. This is followed by an instrumental tag provided by hard-edged guitars and percussion and based on the I–bIII–IV–I progression which dominates the song.

As the show comes to its official conclusion, the reprise of "Sergeant Pepper's Lonely Hearts Club Band" reminds the listener that the title song encapsulates virtually every possible musical link occurring among the ten intervening songs on the album. Such links include the music hall simplicity of "With a Little Help from My Friends," "Getting Better," and "When I'm Sixty-Four"; the circus atmosphere of "Being for the Benefit of Mr. Kite" and, closely related to it, the magical atmosphere of "Lucy in the Sky with Diamonds," and the progressive or psychedelic rock style demonstrated in varying degrees by the last three songs.

But ultimately, the most significant connections among these songs are literary or thematic in nature. And it is certainly a literary rather than a musical thread that is continued in the final postscript (or encore) of a song, the Lennon-McCartney collaboration "A Day in the Life."

The softly strummed chords of an acoustical guitar introduce the song. The guitar is bolstered by piano and bass guitar in the final measures of this introduction, and this sonority, along with a soft conga drum accompaniment, is maintained throughout the first statement of the first of three distinct sections. This ten measure section, composed by Lennon, is once again constructed on harmonies based on a descending passacaglia or countermelody with the resulting progression of I–iii–vi–IV–vi–ii–(V). This pattern is particularly reminiscent of McCartney's "For No One," but Lennon had also made recent use of comparable patterns (e.g., in two other songs on *Sergeant Pepper*) and the idea is equally characteristic of his approach. This descending countermelody (not always implied by the active, syncopated bass part) is broken in the seventh measure. Here, the IV chord passes to bVII, at which point a new descending line generates a bVII–vi–vi7 progression for two and one-half measures. The last two measures are then repeated with the final chord replaced by IV–V.

Lennon's sensitive, breathy vocal delivers a lyrical, balanced melody which features an unusually expressive use of nonharmonic tones, notably the leaps to dissonant notes in the latter part of the first and fourth measures (see ex. 57).

(Ex. 57   "A Day in the Life." Verse, meas. 1–4)

G: I   iii   vi   IV   vi   ii
I read the news to-day oh - boy, -   a-bout a luck-y man who made the grade - .

As the section repeats, sparse, syncopated percussion fills are inserted into the vocal pauses, and the last three measures are replaced by three which exhibit a repeated half-step melodic movement between the third scale degree and its lower auxiliary, followed by an ascent to the tonic in the higher octave, a melodic highpoint reinforced by dramatic piano chords.

The third appearance of this section begins in a manner similar to the first (with the blurred seconds of the piano accompaniment more evident), with the melody rising to the same climactic high pitch. After reaching this climax a second time, the melody descends to the third scale degree and the half-step melodic motive heard earlier is transformed into a slow trill. Beneath this trill, the bass line ascends gradually before coming to rest on the sixth scale degree—the tonal center of the next section. At this point, there begins a gradual but massive crescendo of an ascending orchestral cluster along with various synthesized and taped traffic sounds. This dramatic effect builds for ten measures before dropping away suddenly, leaving only the reiteration of the new tonic by bass and piano and the soft ringing of an alarm clock with which the next section "wakes up."

Lennon's lyrics in this first section consist of a surrealistic compilation of bits from current newspapers combined with references to drug experiences: "I read the news today oh boy / About a lucky man who made the grade / And though the news was rather sad / Well, I just had to laugh. . . ."

The second section, composed by McCartney, was originally intended to be part of a separate song. Its lyrics unfold a rather mundane narrative, again concluding with an hallucinatory reference: "Woke up, got out of bed / Dragged a comb across my head / found my way downstairs and drank a cup / And looking up, I noticed I was late. . . ."

Musically, the second section is even more contrasting. The vocal melody consists of short phrases (at a tempo double that of the first section) over the new tonic chord for three measures. This is relieved in the fourth and fifth measures by a syncopated bass and piano figure which suggests a bVII chord against a pedal on the dominant (see ex. 58).

(Ex. 58   "A Day in the Life." Bridge, meas. 1–3)

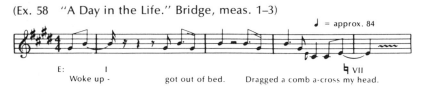

After seven measures of this new section, a one measure descending bass line is introduced. This descending line, and the piano syncopation above it, suggest the frantic activity referred to in the lyrics while providing a musical link back to the song's first section and, less emphatically, with the music hall style heard in earlier songs. The section comes to an abrupt conclusion at the words "Somebody spoke and I went into a dream." In the third section that follows, a distant echo effect is superimposed over wordless voices which present a sustained, rising and falling melody based harmonically on a progression of fifths. The vocal line is gradually obscured by the progressively louder orchestral unisons on the root of each chord in a striking and unique effect.

Following the last measures of the wordless melody, a two measure unison brass motive plunges the key down a minor third for the return of the first section. This section is unchanged except for increased percussion activity and new lyrics (e.g., "I heard the news today oh boy / Four thousand holes in Blackburn Lancashire"). It again concludes with a reiterated tonic pitch and piano and strings against an ascending line supplied by bass and orchestra. Once again this bass line leads into a crescendoing cluster of orchestral and taped sounds which, after another tension-filled buildup, resolves into a brief, high-pitched string chord followed by a low-pitched tonic chord sonority which requires more than half a minute to decay.

This striking resolution does little to knit together the three disparate sections of the song and the two unprecedented tape-instrumental links which connect them. But it does provide a "cosmic" gesture with which to conclude this most cosmic of all Sergeant Pepper songs. While the song's meaning is not clarified, its uniqueness is underlined in an extraordinarily graphic way.

Except for its use of passacaglia-derived harmony, the musical relationship of "A Day in the Life" to other songs on Sergeant Pepper is minimal. Literary or thematic parallels with other songs are possible, however, especially in its references to hallucinatory experiences and its generally surrealistic posture. And, of course, like every other song on Sergeant Pepper, "A Day in the Life" may be seen as representing one aspect of contemporary British life as seen through the eyes of the Beatles.

Still, it is not clear whether these or any other possible literary connections are truly relevant to the success of this song or of the album as a whole. Ultimately, Sergeant Pepper's Lonely Hearts Club Band warrants its position as a highpoint in the popular music of the 1960s not so much for any specific devices of literary or musical unity, but for the originality and inventiveness of its songs taken individually. While the impression of a unified form or "gestalt" unquestionably exists, it has less bearing on the significance of the album than do the individual merits of each song. And the songs of Sergeant Pepper are unique and meritorious, not merely because of their melodic, harmonic, or rhythmic content (they are not all extraordinarily sophisticated in this respect), but because they consistently demonstrate a freedom from (and a transcending of) the limiting conventions and formulas of dance-oriented rock. Albums as early as Rubber Soul had obviously taken steps in this direction, but Sergeant Pepper represents the ultimate step beyond which the Beatles declined to advance.

Post-Pepper
Singles and Albums

Slightly more than a month after the release of *Sergeant Pepper's Lonely Hearts Club Band*, the Beatles offered a new single release featuring Lennon's "All You Need Is Love" and "Baby, You're a Rich Man," a Lennon-McCartney collaboration. Not surprisingly, these songs demonstrate more of a kinship with the striking and extroverted qualities of the earlier singles "Strawberry Fields Forever" and "Penny Lane" than with the more subtle "chamber music" concept that characterizes so much of the *Sergeant Pepper* album.

"Baby, You're a Rich Man" makes use of the same sort of unusual instrumental and electronic effects that had distinguished "Strawberry Fields Forever," for example, the scratching of muffled guitar strings, synthesized block chord effects, and an exotic melody produced by an electronic instrument in emulation of an Indian "shah'nai" (a double-reed oboelike instrument). The melodic, harmonic, and rhythmic elements of the song are, however, much simpler and more straightforward than in "Strawberry Fields Forever." While its particular pattern of stepwise motion and leaps is an unusual one for the Beatles, the verse melody remains securely within the harmonic implications of the simple accompaniment (see ex. 59).

(Ex. 59 "Baby, You're a Rich Man." Verse, meas. 1–3)

The refrain is unusually repetitive melodically (and contains some ascending figures similar to those heard in the verse), while the har-

141

monic structure is similar to the verse in its use of a restricted vocabulary.

Composed as a "sing along" song for the international television program "Our World," Lennon's "All You Need Is Love" is almost equally conventional in its melodic-harmonic content. In regard to its use of rhythm, the song is a bit more sophisticated, especially in its metrical fluctuations between 4/4 and 3/4 and its use of free, declamatory speech-rhythm within that fluctuation (see ex. 60).

(Ex. 60   "All You Need Is Love." Verse, meas. 1–4)

The accompanying instrumental arrangement, while considerably less ambitious than in "Strawberry Fields Forever," has its distinctive features. These include a brass band version of the "Marseillaise" (the French National Anthem) as an introduction; harpsichord chords and active cello counterpoint; an occasionally heterophonic doubling of the chorus vocal by the lead guitar; and a clichéd brass band countermelody similar to that found in "Penny Lane."

But the most distinctive feature of the song—apart from its simplistic repetition and frequent meter changes—comes in the extended coda section. The coda is no mere avant-garde token as in "Penny Lane," but rather the Beatles' most well-developed exercise in "concrete" or colage music to that point. Such extramusical sounds as cowboy-style "whoops" are combined with various musical sounds such as a decorative Baroque-style trumpet fragment, snatches of a big band version of "In the Mood" (contributed by George Martin) and "Greensleeves" (both in the "wrong" key) and a faint echo of the refrain of "She Loves You," suggesting that "All You Need Is Love" may itself be a parody of the "love generation" then emerging.

Four months after the release of "All You Need Is Love" and "Baby, You're a Rich Man," the Beatles' final single of the year was issued, containing McCartney's "Hello, Goodbye" and Lennon's "I Am the Walrus." While the two previous singles had held the top spot on the American charts only briefly, "Hello, Goodbye" remained there for three weeks while "I Am the Walrus" rose no higher than number fifty-six.

The difference in the success of these two sides clearly reflects their stylistic differences. "Hello, Goodbye" continues the lighter style of "All You Need Is Love" and "Penny Lane" while presenting a less problematic sense of continuity. Lennon's "I Am the Walrus," on the other hand, is a more intense and serious work, replete with the dissonant string glissandos and plummeting cello lines of "Strawberry Fields Forever." Even more than Lennon's earlier single, "I Am the Walrus" is tonally ambiguous, its repeated note melody intoned over a unique chord progression (see ex. 61).

(Ex. 61   "I Am the Walrus." Verse, meas. 1–3)

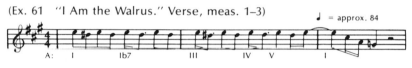

While both sides of the previous single had demonstrated a certain amount of ambiguity in their "flower-power" lyrics, "I Am the Walrus" exhibits what is perhaps Lennon's most "abstract" stream-of-consciousness imagery:

Sitting on a cornflake, waiting for the van to come.
Corporation tee shirt, stupid bloody Tuesday,
Man you been a naughty boy, you let your face grow long.
I am the eggman. They are the eggmen. I am the walrus.
Goo goo g' joob.

With its combination of unusual instrumental and melodic-harmonic effects and its singular text, "I Am the Walrus" is the last clearly "progressive" or experimental recording released by the Beatles (except for a concrete music or collage piece composed by Lennon for a later album and Harrison's Indian-influenced excursions). McCartney's side of the single, "Hello, Goodbye," plainly illustrates the trend toward greater simplicity that the Beatles are to embrace for the remainder of the group's career.

Magical Mystery Tour

Even before the release of "Hello, Goodbye" and "I Am the Walrus," the Beatles had begun work on *Magical Mystery Tour,* an hour long color film made for television. The film, put together without the aid of manager Epstein who had died earlier in August, was loosely conceived as a "hallucinatory adventure" in which the Beatles and a group of carefully chosen actors toured the English countryside in a bus "filming whatever happened to happen, and occasionally staging premeditated happenings along the way."[1] While the film was far from being a critical success, the soundtrack album, released in late November in the United States and early December in England, was quite successful, remaining in the American charts for more than a year. The British version of *Magical Mystery Tour* was released as a pair of extended play records and contained six songs from the film (including "I Am the Walrus"), while the American version was an LP album which also contained five of the Beatles' most current single releases.

None of the five new songs recorded for the soundtrack is particularly innovative. The title song, composed by McCartney, is largely a reworking of "Sergeant Pepper's Lonely Hearts Club Band" without the vitality or variety of the original. "Flying" is a charmingly simple instrumental (the first in five years) for guitars, drums, and mellotron solo attributed jointly to all four of the Beatles. McCartney's "Your Mother Should Know" is a poignantly bouncy period piece in the manner of "When I'm Sixty-Four."

The single most popular song on the soundtrack (as determined by the number of "cover" recordings made of it) is McCartney's "The Fool on the Hill," a lyrical ballad that celebrates the wisdom of innocence. Musically, the song is innocent as well. While well unified from a motivic point of view, the song is as elegantly simple as any composed by McCartney (see ex. 62).

(Ex. 62   "The Fool on the Hill." Verse, meas. 1–4)

The refrain adds a bit more harmonic complexity with its temporary change to the minor mode and an unexpected chromatic mediant progression (bVII–II). While the instrumental arrangement shows, in its use of flute, recorders, and harmonica, that the Beatles are not entirely through with such surprises, the song as a whole remains one of the best examples of the naive style which the Beatles were to exploit more and more after *Sergeant Pepper.*

Harrison's "Blue Jay Way," named after his place of residence during his visit to Los Angeles in the summer of that year, is the third of his heavily Indian-influenced songs and the first in which he also liberally incorporates electronic effects. The song is dominated by two brief musical ideas, both of which unfold over a sustained tone provided by an organ. While the instruments used are exclusively western (including a cello which provides prominent countermelodies), the piece achieves an unusually exotic—if not exactly Indian—effect by its use of unusual interval patterns and sharp dissonances sustained against the pedal.

Despite its great popularity and the individual merit of some of its songs, The *Magical Mystery Tour* soundtrack can only be seen as a "holding action." For the first time since 1964, the album, with the exception of "I Am the Walrus," represents no clear expansion of the Beatles' style, nor does it exhibit any increased sophistication in their use of studio techniques.

The Singles of 1968

While the *Magical Mystery Tour* album represented a retrenchment of sorts for the Beatles, the four had actively been seeking new frontiers in other areas throughout much of 1967. Together they opened the Apple Boutique, a mod fashion clothing store and precursor of the short-lived Apple Corporation launched in 1968 for the purpose of encouraging artistic activity in various areas.[2] Earlier they had become enamored with the transcendental meditation techniques of the Maharishi, and this interest led them, in February of 1968, to begin a three-month course in India with their guru.[3] Only Lennon and Harrison came close to finishing their course and it is difficult to pinpoint what, if any, musical influences may be attributable to their relatively brief infatuation with the Maharishi, since Harrison's enthusiasm for Indian music was already well established by this time and the other Beatles had been exposed to Indian mysticism via Leary's writings more than a year earlier.

The Beatles' first single release of 1968 is the first (and last) to feature an Indian-influenced Harrison composition. "The Inner Light," released as the "B" side of McCartney's "Lady Madonna" in March, makes use of classical Indian musicians imported from Bombay and what is perhaps Harrison's most distinctive and carefully shaped melody in this style. While the Indian-derived drone remains prominent as in "Love You To," "Within You Without You," and "Blue Jay Way," the clear harmonic implications of the melody makes the song more accessible to western ears than those earlier efforts. Nevertheless, the song climbed no higher than number ninety-six on the *Billboard* charts, the poorest showing of any Beatles' song released as a single.

While the lyrics of "The Inner Light" continue to reflect Harrison's interest in Eastern mysticism, there is little in McCartney's "Lady Madonna"—musically or textually—to suggest such a concern. While the lyrics contain some rather cryptic allusions ("Friday night arrives without a suitcase / Sunday morning creeping like a nun / Monday's child has learned to tie his shoelace / See how they run"), the music draws heavily on the rhythm and blues tradition, the first released song to do so since the *Revolver* album. Accompanied by pounding piano and prominent rhythm and blues sax riffs and delivered in McCartney's husky "Presley" voice, the song exudes raw energy and excitement to an extent not found in either the elaborately arranged psychedelic singles or the more subtle *Sergeant Pepper* songs. "Lady Madonna" is not without some subtleties of its own, however. While the verse is dominated harmonically by an alternation of I and IV, phrase endings exhibit an unexpected use of a bVI–bVII–I progression (first heard as early as "P.S. I Love You" in 1962). The bridge introduces a shift to a new key and a little more harmonic variety including a sustained 4–3 suspension resolution which sets up a return to the original key. Still, as a whole, the song is more straightforward and conventional than the songs composed for *Sergeant Pepper,* at least in its exploitation of standard rock formulas.

Rhythm and blues influence is prominent on the "B" side of the Beatles' next single as well. Lennon's "Revolution," released along with McCartney's "Hey Jude" in late August as the Beatles' first recording for the newly formed Apple Corporation, exploits the Chuck Berry influenced eighth note accompaniment heard in several of the Beatles' earlier rhythm and blues covers, along with heavily distorted lead guitar riffs. As in "Lady Madonna," the song relies primarily on an alternation of I and IV chords for the first part of the verse. The last four measures introduce some new secondary dominant chords, but the refrain returns to the I–IV alternation. The repeated note melody makes some use of flat thirds and flat sevenths while its contour generally follows the underlying chord tones. This intense, blues-based song is probably most notable for its lyrics, however. It is the first clearly political statement by the Beatles and, somewhat surprisingly given their ultra-liberal reputation, it makes a "counter-revolutionary" statement ("But when you talk about destruction, / Don't you know that you can count me out.")

While "Revolution" turned out to be an unusually popular "B" side, the "A" side, McCartney's "Hey Jude," became one of the greatest Beatles' hits of all time. It remained on top of the *Billboard* charts for nine weeks, an accomplishment approached only by "I Want to Hold Your Hand" in 1964.

Like "Fool on the Hill," the song is a model of lyrical simplicity. As in many other Beatles' compositions of this period, the harmonic vocabulary is limited to tonic, subdominant, and dominant in the eight measure verse. The melody shows a skillful balance of stepwise motion and leaps and demonstrates one particularly poignant feature a leap from the dominant seventh of the V7 chord to a nonharmonic eleventh of that chord at the words "a sad song" (see ex. 63).

(Ex. 63 "Hey Jude." Verse, meas. 1–4)

The twelve and one-half measure bridge section is equally straightforward. Even more motivically unified than the verse, it displays a little more harmonic variety in its inclusion of a secondary dominant and a submediant chord (see ex. 64).

(Ex. 64 "Hey Jude." Bridge, meas. 1–5)

After a standard verse-verse-bridge-verse-bridge-verse pattern (with vocal harmony in thirds added on the final verse), a long coda is introduced, based on a repeated, four measure unison vocal phrase over a I–bVII–IV–I progression (see ex. 65).

(Ex. 65   "Hey Jude." Coda, meas. 1–4)

This phrase is repeated again and again (supplemented by vocal chorus), spinning out the song to an unprecedented seven minutes in length. Eventually, the basic piano-acoustical guitar accompaniment sonority is reinforced by a full orchestra in a manner reminiscent of "She's Leaving Home." The multiple repetitions of this phrase, enlivened by soloist McCartney's furious exclamations, take on an almost hypnotic quality which some commentators have compared to the chanting of a mantra—the only remaining vestige of the Beatles' concern with transcendental meditation.

Yellow Submarine

July 17, 1968, saw the world premier of *Yellow Submarine*, a feature length, psychedelic pop art cartoon based loosely on the Beatles' 1966 single and "Sergeant Pepper's Lonely Hearts Club Band," but with little involvement on the Beatles' part otherwise. While the soundtrack album was not released until January, 1969, the four new songs it contained had all been recorded by January, 1968. (The album also contained "Yellow Submarine," "All You Need Is Love," and several instrumentals composed by George Martin.) One of these, McCartney's "All Together Now," suggests the repetitive chant of a children's game song ("One, two, three, four / can I have a little more?"). Harrison's "It's All Too Much," probably composed in June, 1967, reflects its earlier origin in its combination of electronic effects (mostly guitar feedback), elaborate effects of orchestration (e.g., some Baroque-styled trumpet fanfares) and elements of Indian influence (e.g., the use of a drone and some sharp dissonances against it, and the use of the bass guitar in emulation of the mridangam drum). Harrison's "Only a Northern Song," composed hurriedly in January, 1968, to satisfy the demands of King Features, the film's producers, contains self-disparaging lyrics ("If you're listening to this song / you may think the chords are going wrong / but they're not / he just wrote it like that"), and a parodistic use of the sort of electronic and pretaped special effects which had played an integral part in *Sergeant Pepper* and *Revolver*.

Finally, Lennon's "Hey Bulldog," also recorded in January, 1968, is a rhythm and blues-influenced pop-rock song which begins with a recurring blues riff but features a certain amount of harmonic variety, especially in its chromatic bridge section.

While none of these four songs constitutes a significant contribution to the Beatles' work, the *Yellow Submarine* album was nevertheless a popular one, and the film itself spawned the "second great wave of Beatle novelties."[4]

Solo Albums in 1968

Two solo albums were released in this period: Harrison's *Wonderwall,* the soundtrack for a film directed by Joe Massot which premiered at the 1968 Cannes Film Festival; and Lennon's *Unfinished Music No. 1—Two Virgins,* coproduced with Yoko Ono, an avant-garde, New York based artist who was to have increasing influence on John, marrying him a year later.

Harrison's album features rather conventional rock and rockabilly instrumentals, many of which are ostinato-based, side by side with improvisations with classical Indian musicians. Despite its lack of stylistic focus, *Wonderwall* managed to climb to number forty-nine in the American *Billboard* charts. The Lennon-Ono album fared less well, rising no higher than 174. The album, recorded in a single evening, consisted mostly of nature sounds (e.g., birds from outside Lennon's window) and various vocally produced noises. While the album was not particularly exceptional from the standpoint of the serious avant-garde, its seemingly haphazard sounds seemed strange even to those Beatle fans who had managed to assimilate electronically reinforced textures and collage effects in smaller doses.

The Beatles (*The White Album*)

In late November, Apple Records released *The Beatles,* a double album (two 33⅓ records) in a simple, all-white cover which came almost immediately to be known as "the White Album." Despite its relatively high price tag (double albums being rare at this point), the album sold briskly and remained on the *Billboard* charts for a total of sixty-five weeks.

   The album contains a total of thirty-one songs, most of which are officially attributed to Lennon and McCartney jointly with four attributed to Harrison and one (for the first time) to Ringo. There is little in this collection of songs to suggest either literary or musical unity, however. Aside from a frequent preoccupation with satire and irony of various kinds, the album fails to demonstrate any particular theme or conceptual reference point.

   The songs composed by McCartney represent a case in point. Four are moderate tempo ballads with acoustical guitar accompaniment reminiscent of the popular folk style of 1964 and 1965. "I Will" makes prominent use of the common I–vi–ii–V progression, a cliché which seldom occurs conspicuously in the earlier style. (Two exceptions to this are the 1963 "Bad to Me," composed for Billy J. Kramer, and "This Boy," another 1963 composition which was considerably enriched by nonharmonic tones in the Beatles' version.) An interesting comparison can be made between "I Will" and McCartney's "I'll Follow the Sun" of 1964. While "I Will" has been referred to as a "virtual remake" of the earlier song,[5] the differences between the two are as instructive as their similarities. "I'll Follow the Sun" was composed in a period when the Beatles were more or less consciously striving for novelty, or at least the avoidance of clichés, and the opening chord progression is an unusual V7–IVb7–I–IIb7. In contrast to this, "I Will," composed almost a year after *Sergeant Pepper,* the Beatles' greatest experimental triumph, demonstrates more interest in the graceful manipulation of clichés than in the invention of novel features (see ex. 66).

(Ex. 66   "I Will." Verse, Meas. 1–4)   ♩ = approx. 102

F: I   vi   ii   V7   I   vi   iii   V7/IV
Who   knows how long I've loved you, - you   know I love you   still, -

   Like "Blackbird," McCartney's "Mother Nature's Son" is an even more simplified example of the popular folk style. It surpasses even the songs of *Rubber Soul* in its musical naivete (see ex. 67).

(Ex. 67   "Mother Nature's Son." Verse, meas. 1–4)   ♩ = approx. 90

D: I   IV   I
Born a   poor young coun-try   boy - ,

While McCartney has been most noted for lyrical compositions, his rhythm and blues influenced songs have also achieved considerable public attention, especially "Lady Madonna" and the 1965 hit "I'm Down." McCartney makes four rhythm and blues influenced contributions to the "White Album". "Back in the USSR" is a salute to Chuck Berry with vocal effects reminiscent of the Beach Boys. "Birthday," composed with Lennon, is an even more primitive rhythm and blues chant with a surprising key shift in the bridge. In "Why Don't We Do It in the Road?", McCartney modifies his husky "Presley voice" to achieve the effect of a country blues shouter, while the simple accompaniment of guitar, piano, bass, and drums is played by McCartney himself with the help of multiple tracking. The musical style is less surprising than the song's crudely sexual theme; which makes an unusually graphic contrast with the sentimental "I Will" which follows it on the album.

McCartney's "Helter Skelter" is probably best known for the part it played in the murder trial of Charles Manson, where it was claimed that the song provided the inspiration for some of Manson's acts.[6] From a musical point of view, the song pays homage to the then emerging progressive British blues style, a post-psychedelic style characterized by high volume lead and bass guitars displaying great virtuosity. McCartney's husky but frantic voice is applied to a repeated note, blues-based melody harmonized with the traditional blues chords enlivened by some unexpected chromatic mediants.

The three final McCartney songs are all musical parodies of one sort or another. "Honey Pie" nostalgically evokes the popular style of the 1920s, complete with sentimental, out-of-tempo introduction, megaphone effects, a "sweet" big band accompaniment, and novelty chords (as in the verse progression of I–bVI–V/ii–V/V–V–I). ("Wild Honey Pie," a short, mostly instrumental fragment, is unrelated to this song.) "Martha My Dear," supposedly dedicated to McCartney's sheep dog, is also a period piece of sorts but shows much more originality harmonically, rhythmically, and in its use of orchestral effects. "Ob-la-di, Ob-la-da" is a West Indian novelty number which masterfully reproduces the style of a Jamaican night club singer. Finally, McCartney's "Rocky Racoon" is a western ballad spoof with a suitably simple and repetitive verse after a narrated introduction.

Of the thirteen original songs composed by Lennon, seven are slow or moderate tempo ballads of one sort or another. Three are relatively intense rock ballads, similar in type to the uptown rhythm and blues songs composed by Lennon in 1963 and 1964. "I'm So Tired" is based largely on a I–vi–ii–V progression like McCartney's "I Will" (and Lennon's earlier "This Boy"), but a greater tension and restlessness (in keeping with the song's lyrics) is provided by Lennon's unusual use of nonharmonic tones (see ex. 68).

(Ex. 68   "I'm So Tired." Verse, meas. 1–4)

The ironic "Happiness Is a Warm Gun" is one of Lennon's most fragmented and discontinuous songs. The refrain, the largest single section of the piece, is based on a I–vi–IV–V progression closely related to the verse progression in "I'm So Tired," while the verse exploits the ii, iii, and vi chords almost exclusively. "Sexy Sadie," Lennon's satirical portrait of the Maharishi, makes use of the sort of melismas heard in the earlier uptown rhythm and blues songs[7] along with a bridge chord progression of I–ii7–iii7–IV recalling McCartney's "Here, There and Everywhere" and Lennon's "If I Fell."

Among the more lyrical songs composed by Lennon is "Dear Prudence," which uses a verse chord progression based on a descending chromatic line beneath a rather fragmented, mostly pentatonic melody. The verse of "Cry Baby Cry" is built on a similar chromatic chord progression and also exhibits a series of short melodic phrases. Both of these songs retain some aspects of the more aggressive style of accompaniment associated with rock ballads. Only two of Lennon's ballads, "Julia" and "Good Night," demonstrate the sort of sustained lyricism associated with most of McCartney's ballads. Dominated by Lennon's acoustical guitar, "Julia" is a delicate evocation of the mother he hardly knew, the first of the sometimes painfully autobiographical songs concerning his mother which Lennon was to compose. "Julia" makes use of an unusually narrow ranged melody but one which again shows Lennon's subtle use of nonharmonic tones.

Lennon's "Good Night," sung by Ringo, is in some respects his most intriguing composition on the album. Accompanied by a lush orchestral texture in an extraordinarily commercial arrangement and reeking with

sentimental minor seventh dissonances, it would appear to be a quintessential McCartney ballad (see ex. 69).

(Ex. 69 "Good Night." Verse, meas. 1–4)

In many respects, this song is the ultimate Beatles' parody and sums
up the entire album as it concludes it. Here, Lennon shows himself to be
equal to McCartney as a conjurer of the commercial ballad style just as
McCartney showed himself to be a master of a wide range of styles in his
ten contributions to the album.

Lennon's more rock-styled songs on the album are not of great significance from a musical point of view. "Revolution 1" is a slower tempo,
subdued version of the single release which hints at a more revolutionary political stance.[8] "Glass Onion" is a conventional medium tempo
rock song notable only for its references to earlier songs ("Well here's
another clue for you all / the Walrus was Paul"), and a rather cursory use
of a string quartet. "Everybody's Got Something to Hide Except Me and
My Monkey" is even more rudimentary in its harmonic vocabulary and
extensive melodic repetition, although demonstrating one of the highest energy levels of any Lennon composition on the album. "Yer Blues"
is another homage to the progressive British blues style with particular
reference to Eric Clapton, the virtuoso lead guitarist of the popular trio
"Cream." "The Continuing Story of Bungalow Bill" is, like "Rocky
Racoon," a parody of a folk ballad which concerns an American tiger
hunter Lennon met in India.[9] Musically, it is somewhat less fragmented
than "Happiness Is a Warm Gun" and shows more harmonic variety,
although its lyrics lack the picturesque and imaginative turns of phrase
which characterized "Happiness." Lennon's final piece, "Revolution
9," represents his last independent avant-garde gesture. The piece is an
eight minute exercise in concrete music described by Lennon as

    . . . an unconscious picture of what I actually think will happen when it
happens: that was just like a drawing of revolution. All the thing was made
with loops. I had about thirty loops going, fed them all into one basic
track. I was getting classical tapes, going upstairs and chopping them up,
making it backwards and things like that, to get the end effects. One thing
was an engineer's testing tape and it would come on with a voice saying

"This is EMI Test Series #9." I just cut up whatever he said and I'd number nine it.[10]

While the political symbolism may be a bit heavy-handed from time to time and the techniques of musical organization less subtle than in comparable works of "serious" composers, the piece is put together with skill and a sensitivity to texture. And when "Revolution 9" fades into "Good Night," the final song on the album, the juxtaposition of the two serves as a dramatic symbol of the distance which the Beatles had traversed in their seven year recording career.

Harrison's four contributions to the album show his abandonment of the classical Indian influence which had dominated his output for almost two years. "While My Guitar Gently Weeps" is a plaintively lyrical lament based harmonically on a chromatically descending line similar to those employed so frequently by both McCartney and Lennon. "Long, Long, Long" exhibits an elegantly simple waltz melody in the verse with a more overtly rock-styled bridge recalling the early Beatles in its use of vocal harmony. The song is followed by a few seconds of rasping, grating mechanical sounds along with ethereal organ sounds and vocal wails suggesting that Harrison too was reluctant to surrender all the trappings of the Beatles' experimental period. "Savoy Truffles" features Lennonesque stream of consciousness lyrics within a conventional hard rock context, while "Piggies" contributes the most obvious satire on the album in its attack on the corporate establishment (among others) set elegantly for harpsichord and string ensemble.

Finally, Ringo's "Don't Pass Me By," the first song attributed solely to him, is an attractive and cheerful rockabilly song complete with bluegrass-style fiddle and calliopelike organ accompaniment. Like so many others on the "White Album," the song is perfectly idiomatic and representative of its style, yet distinguishable as a Beatles' composition by its sensitivity to detail and its subtle deviations from the listener's expectations.

Singles of 1969

The Beatles' double album was followed in January, 1969, by the release of the soundtrack from Yellow Submarine and, in April, the release of a new Beatles' single featuring McCartney's "Get Back" as the "A" side and Lennon's "Don't Let Me Down" as the "B" side. "Get Back" rose quickly to the top position on the Billboard charts and remained there for five weeks, the last Beatles' single to be so successful. ("Don't Let Me Down" rose only to number thirty-five.)

Like the singles immediately before it and most of the songs on *The Beatles,* both sides show the group's continuing interest in a relatively simple style which draws in an obvious way on the rhythm and blues tradition. "Get Back," featuring guest artist Billy Preston on electric piano and Lennon on lead guitar, is a highly refined rhythm and blues song which exhibits a typical repeated note melody complete with blues flats and an alternation of I and IV chords (see ex. 70).

(Ex. 70 "Get Back." Verse, meas. 1–4)

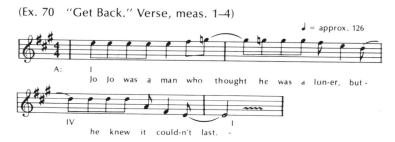

Emotionally, Lennon's soul-influenced plea "Don't Let Me Down" contrasts dramatically with the almost abstract "coolness" of "Get Back." The musical materials, however, are equally basic; a pair of melodic phrases repeated several times over a ii7–I (occasionally with added major seventh) progression dominate the piece.

In late May, the Beatles released "The Ballad of John and Yoko," a country-tinged blues ballad narrating the misadventures of Lennon and Yoko Ono in their much publicized quest for peace in Vietnam. The song rose no higher than number eight on the *Billboard* charts, the poorest showing for any Beatles' "A" side since the flood of releases in 1964 (although the song did make it to the top position in the British *Melody Maker* charts). The "B" side, Harrison's lackluster "Old Brown Shoe," fared much worse, failing completely to break into the "Hot 100" singles chart. Only two additional singles were to be released by the Beatles as a group and these will be discussed in connection with the albums from which they were taken.

Solo Albums of 1969

While Harrison and McCartney were both very active in this period as record producers for various artists associated with Apple Records, four solo albums were also released, two by Zapple Records, a supposedly lower-priced subsidiary of Apple. Lennon and Yoko Ono released *Unfinished Music No. 2: Life with the Lions* in May, another album of avant-garde effects heavily influenced by Yoko Ono. Released on the same day was Harrison's *Electronic Sound,* containing a surprisingly fluent pair of electronic pieces whose authorship has been questioned.[11]

Later in the year, Lennon and Yoko Ono teamed up again with the newly formed Plastic Ono Band to record and release "Give Peace a Chance" backed by Yoko Ono's "Remember Love," and a hard rock song, "Cold Turkey," the first song attributed to Lennon alone, backed by "Don't Worry Kyoto (Mommy's Only Looking for a Hand in the Snow)" by Yoko Ono.

Another experimental album, *The Wedding Album,* was offered at about the same time (i.e., late October) by Lennon and his bride, while Lennon returned to conventional rock with the album *The Plastic Ono Band—Live Peace in Toronto* which contained Lennon's versions of older rock songs such as "Blue Suede Shoes" and "Dizzy Miss Lizzy," and some of his recent singles along with a couple of selections by Yoko Ono.

Let It Be

In February, 1970, Apple Records released the album *Hey Jude* (also known as *The Beatles Again*), a collection of recent hits and a couple of songs from 1964 and 1965. But the last new album-length contributions by the group had already been recorded (if not released) by the middle of 1969. Although not released until May, 1970, the film *Let It Be,* directed by Michael Lindsay-Hogg, documented the making of a Beatles' album in the studio in January, 1969. The soundtrack album, also released in May, 1970, contains eleven versions of songs different from those heard on the soundtrack and a single Harrison composition ("I, Me, Mine") recorded almost a year later.[12] While the original session was produced by George Martin, as had all Beatle recordings since 1963, the final version of the album was produced, with the permission of John Lennon, by Phil Spector, an American producer famous for his commercial arrangements of rhythm and blues songs. Spector's lush orchestrations were tagged on to some of the Beatles' original studio efforts with results which were less than pleasing to McCartney and many critics.[13]

Most of the songs on the album are, like "Get Back" (which appears in a different version here), reconstructions of an earlier rhythm and blues style. Lennon's "One After 909" may date back as early as 1959,[14] and the Beatles' version of the folk standard "Maggie Mae" suggests their early skiffle period. Other songs which demonstrate fidelity to an earlier rhythm and blues style include Lennon's "I Dig a Pony" and the Lennon-McCartney collaboration "I've Got a Feeling." Both employ a relatively simple harmonic vocabulary (although the former suggests the uptown rhythm and blues style in its use of minor chords) but use a bVII chord in the refrain in a manner which recalls Beatles' compositions from 1966 and 1967. Related to these two songs is Lennon's "Dig It," a Dylanesque chant over a repeated I–IV–V–IV–I progression, and Harrison's "For You Blue," a less intense (and somewhat tongue-in-cheek) folk blues with slide guitar contributions by Lennon. Also folklike in the simplicity of its acoustical guitar accompaniment and duet texture is McCartney's "Two of Us." While the bridge section shows more harmonic sophistication, the verse demonstrates some of the same pristine folk qualities—melodic and harmonic—as many of the songs on *Rubber Soul*.

Four songs on the album are ballads of one kind or another. Lennon's "Across the Universe," composed in the first flushes of enthusiasm for transcendental mediation, is his most lyrical contribution to the album, although less harmonically adventurous than other earlier ballads. The song also features an elaborate, over-dubbed background arrangement involving an orchestral and vocal "wall of sound" of the sort long associated with producer Phil Spector. Harrison's "I, Me, Mine," recorded in January, 1970, shows something of a split personality. Its verse is a triple meter, minor key lament which exhibits a poignant use of nonharmonic tones, while its shouted refrain in 4/4 time strongly evokes an intense rhythm and blues style.

The two best known ballads from the album are both by McCartney. Before the album's release, "Let It Be" had been released as a single (in a remixed version) backed by Lennon's "You Know My Name (Look Up the Number)," and had done well in both the American and British charts. The song is a gospel-influenced ballad based on a chord progression similar to that found in the composer's earlier "For No One" (see ex. 71).

(Ex. 71 "Let It Be." Verse, meas. 1–4)

Finally, McCartney's "The Long and Winding Road" was released with the album in May, 1970, backed by Harrison's "For You Blue." This single, released only in America and the last to be released by the Beatles as a group (except for reissues of songs recorded earlier), was slightly less successful than "Let It Be" in the American charts but still managed to hold the top position for two weeks. An example of McCartney's mature, harmonically sophisticated "adult" ballad style, the song was over-dubbed with Spector's most elaborate commercial arrangement, one which was both a surprise and a source of irritation for McCartney.

Abbey Road

The release of the *Let It Be* soundtrack was delayed for more than a year after the initial recording session and, in the meantime, the Beatles returned to the recording studio in the summer of 1969 for what was to be their final group effort. The documentary film had made clear the many tensions that had come to exist among the four Beatles, and increasingly each of them seemed more involved with his individual career than with the group's welfare. Although two new Beatles' albums were to appear in 1970 (*Hey Jude* and *Let It Be*), the group was by then moribund and squabbling. Five solo albums were released that year—with varying degrees of success—as the Beatles set out to establish themselves independently.

But while the Beatles were no more by 1970, they had a final offering to make in 1969 and it was a significant one.

Side one of *Abbey Road* begins with Lennon's "Come Together," an archetypical blues song with a verse melody based primarily on the first, flat third, and flat seventh scale degrees. The melody is, in fact, so close to Chuck Berry's "You Can't Catch Me" for the first several measures that litigation was brought by Berry's publisher.[15] The familiar Berry-influenced eighth note accompanying chords are also in evidence along with a distinctive bass ostinato, one of several provided by McCartney for this album. Harmonically, the song remains faithful to the standard blues progression with a minor tonic chord replacing the conventional major tonic and a brief move to the relative minor for the refrain. While the basic materials of the song are far from complex, the Beatles' arrangement is much more concerned with subtle effects (e.g., fluctuations in texture and dynamics) than was the case for most of the rhythm and blues-influenced songs on the *Let It Be* album.

The rhythm and blues-influenced style is heard twice more on side one. McCartney's "Oh! Darling" is a parody of Little Richard's pleading ballad style, with an unexpected chromatic mediant relationship in the bridge representing the only graphic deviation from that style.

Lennon's "I Want You (She's So Heavy)" also draws heavily on the rhythm and blues tradition, and has been characterized as "the weightiest slab of 'heavy metal' the Beatles ever quarried. . . ."[16] The song, which expresses John's Love for Yoko Ono, is as intense as any composed by Lennon, surpassing even "Don't Let Me Down" in directness of expression. The verse melody is once again archetypically blueslike, this time doubled heterophonically by Lennon on lead guitar (see ex. 72).

(Ex. 72 "I Want You." Verse, meas. 1–4)

The initial ten and one-half phrase group stays on tonic for the first six measures but is enlivened harmonically by some mediant relationships in measures seven and eight. The blueslike melody is then repeated over subdominant harmony, ending up on an abrasive Vb9/V chord and some virtuoso bass fills. The simple refrain ("She's so heavy") is heard over a much repeated chord sequence of I–V7/V–VI–V which eventually serves as a lengthy coda to this unusually long piece.

As in "Come Together," the musical materials are in some repects as primitive as any on the backward-looking *Let It Be* album. But the intensity level and the attention to detail, especially in regard to matched vocal and guitar articulation and inventive bass guitar contributions, once again distinguish this song from the more superficial reconstructions heard on that album.

Two "novelty" songs are also included on side one: Ringo's "Octopus's Garden," a moderate tempo pop-rock fantasy based on the venerable I–vi–IV–V cliché, and McCartney's "Maxwell's Silver Hammer," another example of his lighthearted music hall style. "Maxwell's Silver Hammer" features, as an added attraction, some playful synthesizer solos and riffs by Harrison. Here the electronic instrument is used more like an exotic organ than as a producer of novel instrumental textures as in many of the Beatles' more inventive singles of 1967 or Harrison's relatively sophisticated *Electric Sound* album. This use of the synthesizer may be seen as symptomatic of the *Abbey Road* album as a whole; it is not experimental in the same sense as *Revolver, Sergeant Pepper,* or even *Rubber Soul,* yet it is as refined and attractive an album as any created by the Beatles.

Two compositions by Harrison are included. "Something," on side one, was released as a single (backed by Lennon's "Come Together") and eventually became the Beatles' third best-selling single in America after "Hey Jude" and "I Want to Hold Your Hand." This is the only real "adult" commercial ballad Harrison ever composed with the Beatles, although his "I, Me, Mine" on the *Let It Be* album also shows some characteristics of that genre. "Something" was "covered" by numerous adult ballad singers, receiving almost as much attention in this respect as McCartney's "Yesterday."

The instrumental sonority is based upon the standard guitars, organ, and drums complement, but is reinforced by lush, if restrained, string accompaniment arranged by producer George Martin. While the verse melody displays the limited range and repeated notes appropriate to Harrison's limited vocal capabilities, it is as lyrical and appealing as any composed by the Beatles. Other notable commercial ballad characteristics include a prominent use of major seventh chords and, in the last two measures of the verse, a contrasting melodic idea over a descending chromatic line in the harmony similar to those found in McCartney's "Michelle" and "All My Loving" among several other songs by both Lennon and McCartney (the result of which is an equally typical progression of vi–bVI+–I 6/4–#vi°). This familiar device had been hinted at in Harrison's "While My Guitar Gently Weeps," but never before had the composer used it in the same context as his two colleagues.

After a two measure transitional link featuring an unusual IV–bVI–V progression, the more rock-styled bridge occurs in a new key (on the sixth scale degree). Here the more conventional progression of I–

iii–vi–I–IV–bVII–I occurs, generated once again by a descending bass line in the manner of McCartney's "For No One" and "Let It Be."

Compared to the extravagant lushness of "Something," Harrison's "Here Comes the Sun," which opens side two of the album, is almost folklike in its simplicity. The song is introduced by an acoustical guitar riff which displays the main melodic material of the verse. The verse melody consistently exploits the first, second, and third scale degrees with the entire sixteen-measure melody covering a range of only six notes. Despite these restrictions, the melody makes an expressive use of nonharmonic tones, including one leap to a dissonant major seventh. The verse is harmonized largely by I–IV–V7 with a single V7/V used with great effect.

The syncopated refrain introduces the bIII and bVII chords briefly for harmonic variety, while both a subtle string accompaniment and a clever use of synthesizer fills and solos add color and texture. But basically the materials are as simple and beguiling as any used by Harrison in his compositional career with the Beatles.

While Lennon's love ballad "Because" is not, as he suggests, Beethoven's "Moonlight" Sonata (Op. 27, No. 2 in c# minor) played backwards,[17] the song does resemble the first movement of Beethoven's work in some harmonic aspects (especially the use of the Neapolitan or bII chord), its arpeggiated texture, and some aspects of the melodic rhythm.

More importantly, the song makes a singular effect as the result of a skillful manipulation of a relatively small number of unusual harmonic devices. After a stark harpsichord introduction which capsulizes the harmonic movement of the verse, the first phrase of the ten measure verse melody is introduced in three-part harmony over a slowly unfolding progression of I–ii07–V7 (see ex. 73).

(Ex. 73 "Because." Verse, meas. 1–4)   ♩ = approx. 78

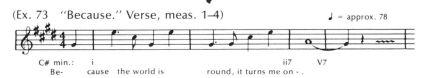

C# min.:   i   ii7   V7
Be-   cause the world is   round, it turns me on - .

The second phrase moves to the major submediant (a comparable event occurring in Beethoven's work as well). A ninth chord on the submediant is expressed by the vocal harmony in the third measure of the second phrase, an unusual gesture if only for its resolution within the submediant chord itself. The last phrase, which served also as a vocal introduction to the verse, begins with a tonally ambiguous bVI chord followed by an unexpected bii⁰ chord which lends a Beethovenian sense of mysterious urgency.

The brief, four measure bridge section dispels much of this intensity by its use of major subdominant and dominant seventh chords, but a more somber mood returns with the verse, and the final verse section of synthesizer melody with harmonized vocal accompaniment concludes the song on an unusually serious note.

The next song, McCartney's "You Never Give Me Your Money," begins what has been referred to as a "pop symphony," an attempt made by McCartney and George Martin to link an entire sequence of songs both thematically and formally.[18] This "symphony" or suite includes a total of eight songs or fragments of songs played with little or no break between them. Neither the literary nor the musical links are as clear as in *Sergeant Pepper,* but a sense of continuity has seemed almost unavoidable to most commentators:

> The ensuing sequence resembles a dream not so much in the subject matter of the individual segments . . . but in the almost hallucinatory way one musical/lyrical setting unfolds into another.[19]

"You Never Give Me Your Money" is itself a composite with four distinct sections and two connecting links. The initial eight measure section is a lament concerning the Beatles' sometimes painful financial disputes with Apple Records. The surprisingly poignant effect of this section is primarily due to the three-part vocal harmony which contributes numerous nonharmonic sevenths and ninths over a basic progression of vi7–ii–V7–I–IV–ii–V/vi–vi. Other sections are slightly less sophisticated harmonically but exhibit more rhythmic interest, for example, the second four measure section with its boogie-woogie bass under a sequential melody and a series of secondary dominant chords.

The soft murmuring of crickets serves as a transition to the next song, Lennon's "Sun King." After an introduction of lush guitar chords and "pseudo-Aztec" drumming,[20] this Latin ballad introduces a vocal verse sung in an imaginary Spanish-sounding language and abounding with ninth, eleventh, and added sixth chords in the tight, three-part vocal harmony which also characterized "Because."

A brief percussion bridge launches into Lennon's "Mean Mr. Mustard," the first of three consecutive uptempo fragments all under two minutes in length. The song is conventional, blues-influenced pop-rock and describes a character as colorful (if less attractive) as some encountered on *Sergeant Pepper.*

This is immediately followed, at an even faster tempo, by Lennon's "Polythene Pam," composed, like the previous song, during Lennon's visit to India and concerning "a mythical Liverpool scrubber dressed up in his jackboots and kilt."[21] Based largely on repeated chord patterns of bIII–IV–I and bVI–bVII–I, the song features extraordinarily active syncopation by both drums and guitar, making it one of the most exciting on the album. A descending bass line provides a link to McCartney's "She Came in Through the Bathroom Window," another uptempo song about another whimsical and colorful character. The complex rhythmic accompaniment continues along with a subtle use of vocal fills as in the previous song. The verse presents a blues-based melody over a I–IV alternation, while the bridge moves first to vi and then to bIII by way of secondary dominants.

After a brief pause, McCartney's slower tempo "Golden Slumbers" is heard. With its delicate melody and poignant nonharmonic tones, the song is almost as nostalgia-filled as the traditional tune on which it is based, despite some solid, rocklike gestures in the percussion accompaniment. "Golden Slumbers" passes directly into McCartney's moderate tempo "Carry That Weight," basically a chanted four measure refrain over an alternation of I and V7. After eight measures, there is an eight measure recapitulation of the delicate first section of "You Never Give Me Your Money" with slightly modified lyrics. This is in turn followed by eight more measures of the "Carry That Weight" refrain accompanied by a full, orchestral sonority with grandiose effect.

This is followed immediately by McCartney's uptempo "The End." This is introduced by a brief group vocal ("Oh yeah! All right! Are you gonna be in my dreams—tonight?") followed by a rare drum solo and a series of hard-edged repeated chords alternating Ib7 and IVb7 over which Harrison, McCartney, and Lennon trade two measure lead guitar solos in an unusual and exciting display of raw virtuosity. The final section of the song is a lyrically drooping, harmonized melody with the message "And in the end, the love you take is equal to the love you make." The final chord sequence of bIII–IV–I recalls not only "Polythene Pam" but also the harmonies which closed their last epic, *Sergeant Pepper's Lonely Hearts Club Band.*

But, perhaps in an attempt to deescalate the seriousness and sentimentality of their final recorded statement, the Beatles were to play one last surprise. After a pause of several seconds, a final, unlisted song is presented—McCartney's "Her Majesty," a good-natured music hall ditty accompanied by acoustical guitar ("Her majesty's a pretty nice girl but she doesn't have a lot to say"). As on side one, this final song is cut off in mid-note and the album ends "in progress."

But, of course, no more progress was to be made, even if more Beatles' releases were to follow. And while the album contributed no specific innovations or personal breakthroughs, its technical excellence and polish, as well as its intrinsic musical interest, made it phenomenally successful. Its sales of more than five million ranked it as the top-selling Beatles' album of all time, surpassing even *Sergeant Pepper* by more than two million as of 1978.[22] The question of whether this most successful album is also the Beatles' greatest is not so simply determined.

Style Characteristics: 1967–1969

Form

The major changes that take place in this period are concerned with composite forms, that is, large forms that are made up of smaller, generally self-contained units. The most obvious examples of this are, of course, the integrated album concept of *Sergeant Pepper's Lonely Hearts Club Band* and the suite on side two of *Abbey Road*, both of which have been discussed.

On a smaller scale, composite songs are also encountered for the first time in the Beatles' repertoire. For example, the Lennon-McCartney collaboration "A Day in the Life" was originally conceived of as two separate songs which were combined only for the purposes of the album. Lennon's "Happiness Is a Warm Gun" combines widely ranging and seemingly unrelated sections which may or may not have been conceived independently, as does McCartney's "You Never Give Me Your Money" on the *Abbey Road* album.

Melodic Characteristics

While no new melody types are introduced in this period, certain melody types do seem to be closely associated with specific albums. Music hall simplicity, repetitiveness, and narrowness of range characterize many of the songs on *Sergeant Pepper,* while strongly blues-influenced melodies occur in several of the songs on the backward-looking *Let It Be* album. The encyclopedic *The Beatles* album (the "White Album") is too diverse to be neatly characterized, although blues-influenced melodies are found with relative frequency while music hall tunes are somewhat scarce ("Honey Pie" and "Ob-la-di, Ob-la-da" being two notable exceptions). Similarly, *Magical Mystery Tour* demonstates little melodic homogeneity, although two of the singles contained on the American version—Lennon's "I Am the Walrus" and "Strawberry Fields Forever"—exhibit far less tonal focus than the typical Beatles' melody.

Nonharmonic tones continue to contribute to the distinctiveness of many of the Beatles' melodies but, on the whole, decline somewhat in significance and frequency of occurrence. While such songs as "Lucy in the Sky with Diamonds," "A Day in the Life," "I'm So Tired," (from *The Beatles*) and "Because" (from *Abbey Road*) demonstrate a striking use of nonharmonic tones, several of the songs on each of the four major albums issued in this period are relatively unadventurous in this regard.

Harmony

Although *Sergeant Pepper* seems, in many respects, to represent a retrenchment in harmonic experimentation comparable to *Rubber Soul,* the refinements of previously established characteristics which it exhibits are worthy of note.

Harmonic elements of lesser importance which recur here include the mediant root progressions found in "Sergeant Pepper's Lonely Hearts Club Band," "She's Leaving Home," and "Lucy in the Sky with Diamonds"; the augmented chords so significant to the harmonic identity of "Fixing a Hole" and "Being for the Benefit of Mr. Kite"; and the period-flavored harmonies of "When I'm Sixty-Four," anticipated in "Good Day Sunshine" from the *Revolver* album.

While the use of the subtonic chord (bVII) was a major element in many of the songs of 1966, that chord is encountered in a significant context only in "Good Morning Good Morning" and "With a Little Help from My Friends."

The two most important devices found in *Sergeant Pepper* are the ostinato-derived harmonies and the pedal effects, both of which are used here with the greatest frequency, variety, and sophistication encountered in any group of songs in the Beatles' career. The pedal (or drone) is incorporated into songs as diverse as "Lucy in the Sky with Diamonds," "Getting Better," "Lovely Rita," and "Within You Without You," and there is a suggestion of a pedal effect in "Fixing a Hole." Ostinato-derived harmonies are manifest most clearly in "Being for the Benefit of Mr. Kite" (generated by an inner harmonium line rather than the bass), "Lucy in the Sky with Diamonds," and "A Day in the Life," as well as in "With a Little Help from My Friends" and parts of "She's Leaving Home."

The *Magical Mystery Tour* album is even less conspicuous for its harmonic experimentation with only "I Am the Walrus" and "Strawberry Fields Forever" showing any real sophistication. *The Beatles* album similarly offers relatively few examples of striking harmonic effects, although songs such as Lennon's "Julia" do demonstrate some unusual chord choices. Predictably, the *Let It Be* album is generally unadventurous in its use of harmony, and the final *Abbey Road* album contains only a few songs which contain novel harmonic gestures (e.g., "Something" and "Because").

Rhythm and Meter

The *Sergeant Pepper* period contains the Beatles' most notable attempts at introducing metric and rhythmic complexity into their songs. Most remarkable are the sectional meter changes in "Lucy in the Sky with Diamonds" and "Being for the Benefit of Mr. Kite" and the small scale metric fluctuations and rhythmic variety of "All You Need Is Love," "Good Morning Good Morning" and "Love You To." Subsequent albums and singles fail to show a comparable interest in metric or rhythmic experimentation.

Instrumental and Vocal Arrangements

Once again, the *Sergeant Pepper* album and surrounding singles (e.g., "Strawberry Fields Forever" and "I Am the Walrus") contain the most sophisticated examples of instrumental and vocal arrangements, especially in regard to electronic and concrete music effects. Concrete sounds contribute significantly to the identities of four songs: "Sergeant Pepper's Lonely Hearts Club Band," "A Day in the Life," "Good Morning Good Morning," and "Strawberry Fields Forever." A less sophisticated usage is found in "Being for the Benefit of Mr. Kite" giving the general effect of a "super-calliope."

Subsequent albums neglect these devices almost completely, a significant exception being "Revolution 9," Lennon's massive tape collage piece on *The Beatles*. Even the more elaborate instrumental arrangements (e.g., those which make an unusual use of strings, trumpets, etc.) are generally avoided in later albums.

Lyrics

Just as the musical styles demonstrated by the albums and singles in this period vary greatly, so too does the nature of the Beatles' lyrics. The significance of the lyrics on the Sergeant Pepper album has been discussed at some length. The Magical Mystery Tour album lacks the thematic focus of Sergeant Pepper, and its lyrics generally display that diffuseness. However, certain of the singles included on that album (e.g., "Strawberry Fields Forever" and "Penny Lane") stand out as powerful evocations of the Beatles' childhoods, while others show an unusual talent for surreal, stream-of-consciousness lyrics which were unique in their period (e.g., "I Am the Walrus").

The lyrics on The Beatles album range even more widely. Several scathing satires are included (exhibiting varying degrees of subtlety) alongside of maudlin love ballads, although many of these exhibit satirical elements as well.

Neither Let It Be nor Abbey Road demonstrates this remarkable range. The lyrics on Let It Be deal with conventional themes for the most part, although occasional obscure or surreal turns of phrase (e.g., as in "Get Back") lend them a degree of sophistication. In its use of frankly autobiographical lyrics, Abbey Road continues a trend established in The Beatles, although a larger and more complex context is provided for some of the songs by their inclusion in the pop suite on side two of the album.

The Beatles
in Perspective

In this final chapter, three matters remain for us to consider: what does the evolution of the Beatles' music look like in broadest outline?; what was the Beatles' compositional method?; and, what has been their influence on the popular music of the mid and late 1960s?

Outline

In this survey of the Beatles' music from 1962–1969, we have followed their stylistic development through many stages. The first was their eclectic and derivative apprenticeship period of the first two British albums in 1963. Here, the Beatles seemed content to refine the many models available to them rather than to concern themselves with originality of conception.

In the period of their early maturity, the 1964 albums *A Hard Day's Night* and *Beatles for Sale* demonstrated the Beatles' emergence as producers of largely original, nonderivative pop songs which surpassed those of their contemporaries in attention to detail and novelty of effect.

The release of the *Help!* album in August of 1965 (and the surrounding singles) showed the Beatles' complete mastery of the pop-rock tradition and the beginning of a significant expansion of musical and literary resources.

Having left behind the dance-oriented pop-rock style, the *Rubber Soul* album of December, 1965, marked the Beatles' entrance into the ranks of innovative composers. The earlier stylistic borrowings had been replaced largely by a variety of original and coherent new styles related only marginally to the typical popular music product of the period.

The release of *Revolver, Sergeant Pepper's Lonely Hearts Club Band,* and the accompanying singles in 1966 and 1967 manifested the Beatles' full maturity as innovative composers and recording artists, capable of transcending the most sophisticated rock styles of the day with considerable success. The expansion of resources was complete at this point, and the Beatles in this period demanded to be experienced as composers of a new, popular contemporary music rather than as the most exalted among pop composers working within the prevailing social-dance conventions.

But this high point of experimentation endured for only a brief period. Apparently convinced that their innovative approach could be sustained no longer and beset by internal disagreements as to artistic direction, the group began to turn away from experimentation as early as the *Magical Mystery Tour* album of November, 1967. By the release of *The Beatles* (the "White Album") in November, 1968, the return to more conventional styles was almost complete, although the Beatles' virtuosity in remaking well-worn genres in their own image was never more evident.

While the final singles and albums were as commercially successful as ever for the Beatles, only *Abbey Road* seemed to challenge the boundaries of popular music as had the group's unique achievements of 1966 and 1967.

Compositional Process

Songwriting

According to biographer Davies, Lennon's first attempts at songwriting involved "elaborating and adapting other peoples' words and tunes to his own devices."[1] Spurred on by McCartney, both began to compose original songs, often basing them around a newly learned chord. These early songs (Davies suggests that over one hundred were composed before 1963) were reportedly written in a sol-fa syllable notation.[2]

From the earliest stages, three of the Beatles composed both separately and in collaboration, with both Lennon and McCartney contributing words and music to their joint compositions.

Davies states that, in composing, McCartney usually begins with the tune (and probably the accompanying chords).[3] This view is substantiated in McCartney's discussion of "Yesterday":

I woke up one morning and went to the piano. And I just, you know, started playing it. And this tune came. Because that's what happens you know, they just come. But I couldn't think of any words for it so originally I called it 'Scrambled Egg.' For a couple of mornings that was what it was called. Then I thought of 'Yesterday' and the words started to come and we had a song.[4]

According to Davies, Lennon starts with the lyrics or "a piece of rhythm" to which words are fitted. These rhythms are often combined with small melodic fragments.[5] Harrison's composing methods are not well documented, but Davies does provide one example in which the melody was written before the lyrics.[6]

Lennon and McCartney report making use of both guitar and piano in their songwriting. Shepherd refers to McCartney's use of piano in this connection as early as 1964,[7] but it is possible that Lennon's piano competency dates from a later period. In the 1968 *Rolling Stone* interview, Lennon comments on the advantages of composing with piano:

> Most of this session for the *Magical Mystery Tour* album has been written on guitar 'cause we were in India writing and only had our guitars there. They have a different feel about them. I missed the piano a bit because you just write differently. My piano playing is even worse than me guitar. I hardly know what the chords are, so it's good to have a slightly limited palette. . .[8]

Recording Process

While the Beatles' earliest compositions were "written, worked out, and perfected"[9] while touring, they soon graduated to making "demonstration" tapes of their own songs for presentation to the rest of the group and to lay the groundwork for the final recording. Lennon describes his use of tape recorders in the 1970 *Rolling Stone* interview:

> . . . I used to write upstairs where I had about ten Brunell tape recorders all linked up; I still have them. I'd mastered them over the period of a year or two—I could never make a rock and roll record but I could make some far out stuff on it.[10]

While this practice of making demonstration tapes was probably continued in at least some cases as long as the Beatles remained as a group, many of the latter compositions were worked out almost completely in the studio. In 1968, Harrison remarked: "Nobody knows what the tunes sound like till we've recorded them, then listened to them afterwards."[11]

One example of this trial and error method was described in connection with "Strawberry Fields Forever," and it is clear from that description and others provided by Hunter Davies and George Martin that the

Beatles' recording process in the later years, while flexible, was never haphazard.[12]

While this final (recording) stage of the compositional process seems to have become increasingly sophisticated through 1967 (i.e., in its use of the studio-as-instrument), that sophistication is not maintained after the release of Sergeant Pepper and the singles surrounding it. Just as the basic musical ideas employed by the Beatles become generally less complex, so too does the recording process which transforms them into completed works. A minimum of multiple tracking is required for the songs on The Beatles, Let It Be, Yellow Submarine, and Abbey Road. The process of demonstrating a new song and determining its arrangement is shown in the film Let It Be no longer to involve a carefully prepared demonstration tape or an elaborate trial and error method—often requiring the complete resources of the studio and the technical assistance of producer George Martin—but instead to be merely a matter of calling out chords to the accompanying Beatles. (Martin's role in the final Abbey Road album was almost certainly more substantial, however.) It is interesting to note that while the sophistication of the recording process varies from album to album, the initial songwriting process apparently does not. All extant Beatles' manuscripts contain no musical notation other than occasional chord symbols,[13] and even McCartney's music lessons appear not to have had any effect on his method of songwriting.

Individual Styles

Even when the Beatles composed independently, their songs often reflected a common reliance on specific compositional techniques. The use of chromatically descending countermelodies to generate chord progressions occurs in both Lennon and McCartney compositions over a period of five years and even Harrison makes use of the idea in some of his later songs. Similarly, pedal effects and ostinatos occur with great frequency from 1965–1967 in the songs of Lennon, McCartney, and Harrison. Harmonic vocabularies are also held in common to some extent during a given time period (e.g., the use of the I–bVII–IV progression) as are certain melodic mannerisms (e.g., the use of the dissonant fourth scale degree). This is not to suggest that no compositional differences existed among the Beatles when working independently. Lennon's pentatonically oriented uptown rhythm and blues style was unique among the Beatles in the early years, as was McCartney's harmonically sophisticated adult commercial ballad style in 1964 and

1965. Harrison's early pop-rock style showed a very personal harmonic sense (manifest most clearly in his use of minor chords), and his later Indian-influenced compositions between 1966 and 1968 were individual in the extreme.

Nevertheless, all attributions of stylistic characteristics should be seen in terms of tendencies rather than absolutes. McCartney did try his hand at the uptown style (though basing his attempt on a different model), and some of Lennon's early rock ballads make more than occasional use of commercial ballad characteristics. Furthermore, Lennon's "Good Night" on *The Beatles* album shows a keen understanding of the commercial ballad, none the less because the song is a parody like so many others on the album. And the success of Harrison's "Something" (from the *Abbey Road* album) as a commercial ballad is ably demonstrated by the number of covers by "adult" singers which it generated.

The three composing Beatles also seemed to show a comparable enthusiasm for experimentation with avant-garde effects in 1966 and 1967. It is true that Lennon's singles "Strawberry Fields Forever" and "I Am the Walrus" are somewhat more adventurous (musically and textually) than McCartney's in this period, and Lennon's "Revolution 9" is the last truly avant-garde gesture made by the Beatles. But it is also true that Lennon's eventual rejection of avant-garde elements was absolute while McCartney retained sufficient interest in experimentation to produce his pop suite on *Abbey Road.*

Both McCartney and Lennon also showed (particularly in the post-Pepper period) a desire to return to their rhythm and blues roots. Even Harrison offered a return to a relatively pure blues style in his "For You Blue" on the *Let It Be* album. And Harrison's Indian-influenced compositions are paralleled to some extent by Lennon's "Tomorrow Never Knows" on the *Revolver* album.

So while tendencies may be observed in the Beatles' compositional choices, rigid categories are not likely to be helpful in trying to come to terms with their music. This is equally true in regard to the Beatles' lyrics. For example, while Lennon's lyrics often tend to suggest a more bitterly sarcastic posture than McCartney's or Harrison's in 1964 and 1965, the latter Beatles show a well developed and even occasionally acrid sense of irony in their later compositions.

Finally, the obvious fact of the Beatles' "group identity" should not be underestimated as a factor in controlling the quality and even the homogeneity of the Beatles' output. While it is true that the Beatles were presented more as soloists than as group members on *The Beatles* album, and little unanimity of spirit existed by the time of the *Abbey Road* album, a certain amount of corporate "editing" (and perhaps self-editing as well) was inevitable simply because all of the music was to be released under the group's name. The absence of this collective censorship is clearly evident in the extreme postures taken in the solo albums released immediately before and after the Beatles' breakup.

The Influence of the Beatles

There is no question that the Beatles' success, as measured both in terms of record sales and critical acclaim, has far outdistanced that of their closest competitors in the 1960s (e.g., the Rolling Stones, Bob Dylan, and the Beach Boys). However, the question of the Beatles' influence on their contemporaries is one which evokes a certain amount of controversy. It is generally assumed that the Beatles were the most innovative of the rock-based groups of the 1960s, as suggested here by ethnomusicologist Henrietta Yurchenco:

Without question, they have extended the popular music language of our time. . . . Though a number of folk-rock groups have been musically experimental in the past few years, no other has shown the wild inventiveness of the Beatles.[14]

This supremacy is not universally acknowledged, however.

And while only an imbecile would debate that they set trends just like ringin' a bell, it's become clear in retrospect that only very rarely did they deserve credit as innovators: in most cases they only showed a mass audience a refined version of a lick they'd heard somebody else fooling around with.[15]

The problem is further complicated by the fact that not all innovations are influential, just as it is not necessary to be innovative to have influence. Even the most minor of the Beatles' stylistic deviations from the pop-rock conventions of the day may be considered innovations of a sort, but relatively few of these minor deviations can be said to have had much effect on the music of the Beatles' contemporaries. The following discussion will, therefore, concentrate on those aspects of the Beatles' musical style which have had the most influence on the popular music of the mid and late 1960s, whether original or not.

The Beatles' influence on others in their early stages seems to have been minimal. The American popular market was, in January, 1964 (as it had been for several years), extremely eclectic. When the Beatles' "I Want to Hold Your Hand" reached number one on the *Billboard* charts (February 1, 1964), it had been preceded in that position by "There! I've Said It Again," a ballad recorded by Bobby Vinton, and "Dominique," a folk song performed in French by "the Singing Nun." The Beatles held the first position on the charts for fourteen weeks after that date before being deposed by Louis Armstrong's recording of the show tune "Hello Dolly."

During this early period of Beatle domination (in which the Beatles controlled as many as six of the top ten positions nationwide), other established rock performers continued to achieve success with the styles they had relied on in the past. In the week of March 28, in which Beatles' singles filled the first four positions on the *Billboard* charts, "Dawn," by the Four Seasons (a vocal group reminiscent of the black vocal group style of the 1950s), held the fifth position, and the Beach Boys "Fun Fun Fun," a tuneful uptempo song, was number six. The Beach Boys retained their more restrained style with notable success in the months and years to come, although their next single, "I Get Around," bears some melodic resemblance to the Beatles' "Can't Buy Me Love" released three months earlier. The more polished and commercial style of the Four Seasons was maintained despite a diminishing rate of success in their subsequent releases, none of which rose to number one for a period of three years.

Most of the other major successes of the year are equally untouched by the Beatles' influence. The Supremes, a motown trio, experienced their first triumphs in the wake of the Beatles, and English groups such as the Animals (who possessed the number one record for three weeks in the latter part of the year—"The House of the Rising Sun") and the Rolling Stones demonstrated heavily blues-based styles which bore little resemblance to the Beatles'.

As early as May, 1963, the Beatles had been accompanied on the British charts by Gerry and the Pacemakers with "How Do You Do It?" (a song originally offered to the Beatles) and "I Like It." Both of these songs are in the tuneful pop-rock style of "Please Please Me," released some months earlier (even sharing some instrumental characteristics with the Beatles' song), but lack the intensity and originality of harmony which characterized the Beatles' recordings.

By 1964, two other groups incorporating vocal harmony similar to the Beatles, the Searchers and the Hollies, had begun to make their mark on the British charts. Both worked in the pop-rock style of Gerry and the

Pacemakers, but again without the intensity and harmonic variety associated with comparable releases by the Beatles.

However, two English groups prominent in the American and British charts do demonstrate the influence of the Beatles in this period: the Dave Clark Five, whose "Glad All Over" echoes the call and response style of the Beatles (a more refined and mannered version of which is, of course, exhibited also by motown groups such as the Supremes), and employs an alternating chord pattern similar to one found in two of the Beatles' earlier singles; and Manfred Mann, whose "Do Wah Diddy Diddy" also incorporates aspects of the Beatles' vocal style in a composition not unlike Lennon's early uptown style songs.

In 1965, the Beatles' domination of the American popular market was shared with the Supremes, who recorded four national hits (only one less than the Beatles in this period), and various other motown-style performers. The one week reign of the Beatles' "Ticket to Ride" as the top-rated song nationally was ended in May by the Beach Boys with "Help Me Rhonda," a song typical of their generally unchanging style bearing no trace of Beatle influence.

The simplistic, lighthearted pop-rock style continued to be represented in the releases of the British groups Freddy and the Dreamers and Herman's Hermits as well as the American Gary Lewis and the Playboys, among others. Several other singers and groups recorded in a more distinctively original pop-rock style in this period (e.g., the Kinks), but most of these are equally unrelated to the increasingly sophisticated Beatles' style in any significant way. One possible exception to this is the work of the American group, the Beau Brummels, whose "Laugh Laugh" displays unusually chromatic harmony in a sequential context similar to those appearing in earlier Beatles' songs such as "I'll Follow the Sun," and "Things We Said Today," and some appearing subsequently on the *Help!* album.

A second example of relatively sophisticated harmony similar to the Beatles' is found in the pop-rock songs recorded by British singer Petula Clark. Her 1965 recording of "Downtown" shows a use of minor chords that parallels the uptown style of Lennon, while her 1965 recording of "I Know a Place" contains harmonic surprises and sudden modulations which are precedented in this style only in the Beatles' recordings.

A more ambiguous situation exists in respect to the uptempo country and western and folk-rock songs which appeared on the popular music charts for the first time in 1965. Country and western ballads by such singers as Johnny Tillotson, Gene Pitney, and Jim Reeves (especially popular in England in the early 1960s) had occasionally penetrated the popular charts before that year, but few of the uptempo country-flavored or rockabilly recordings had made much impact in America since the early Presley era (i.e., 1955–1960). This situation begins to change in early 1965 as the Beatles released an extended play 45 rpm record containing two Carl Perkins rockabilly tunes ("Honey Don't" and "Everybody's Trying to Be My Baby") and an original country-influenced song, "I'm a Loser." In the same month, the Beatles released another country and western influenced single, "I Don't Want to Spoil the Party." All four of these had been released several months earlier in England (on *Beatles for Sale*) and had received some air-play in the United States at that time. By March, 1965, Buck Owens, a successful performer in the country and western field for several years, and Jack Jones, a commercial pop singer, had both achieved great success with uptempo country and western influenced songs ("Tiger by the Tail" and "The Race Is On") closely related in style to the Beatles' earlier country-styled recordings. While Owens had previously recorded in the rockabilly style (with limited success in the pop market), Jones's release was completely alien to the commercial ballad style for which he was generally known. None of these country and western influenced songs, including those composed and performed by the Beatles, can be considered particularly innovative. But it is likely that the Beatles' success in this idiom, while not influential from a stylistic point of view, nevertheless provided (for the first time in years) an atmosphere in which other rockabilly or country and western influenced songs could achieve widespread success even in the popular market.

The folk-rock synthesis that emerged in 1965 had less to do with the Beatles' accomplishments. The more commercial popular folk style continued to flourish, and a more intense and "serious" folk style was to be found in the music of the Byrds, whose June, 1965, recording of Bob Dylan's "Mr. Tambourine Man" is often credited with starting the folk-rock movement. This style was continued and expanded by other recorded versions of Dylan material (e.g., the Turtles' "It Ain't Me Babe") and overt imitations of the Dylan style, such as Barry McGuire's "Eve of Destruction."

The Beatles' singles of 1965 were unconnected with any aspect of the folk-rock style, and most of their popular folk song examples had appeared almost a year earlier on British albums. The *Help!* album contained one folk-influenced song, however. "You've Got to Hide Your Love Away" clearly evokes Dylan's early acoustical style and is often offered as evidence of his influence.

The folk and country and western influenced songs on *Rubber Soul* (released later in 1965) have little in common with the then popular versions of those styles, although the difference in this case involves a contrasting approach rather than the level of sophistication demonstrated. The rockabilly style of Lennon's earlier songs has been replaced on *Rubber Soul* by the bluegrass style of McCartney's "I've Just Seen a Face," a song devoid of concessions to the rock audience. The popular folk song style has similarly been replaced by the more "purist" approach evident in Lennon's "Norwegian Wood" and "Girl," both of which lack the energy level and emphasis on rhythm associated with the emerging folk-rock style.

The sitar heard on "Norwegian Wood" represented the first recorded use of that instrument by a rock group, although it had been used in a decidedly commercial manner on the soundtrack of *Help!* which was recorded as early as February, 1965. The first use of the instrument is sometimes attributed to the Byrds who, according to rock critic Lillian Roxon, used it in their 1966 release "Eight Miles High" after supposedly having introduced Harrison to the instrument prior to the recording of *Rubber Soul.*[16] The British group the Yardbirds have also been credited with this innovation,[17] although Roxon states that only the "sitar sound" was used by the Yardbirds in 1965, achieved by the use of feedback.[18] While the instrument quickly became very popular after 1965, it was generally used in a non-Indian melodic fashion comparable to Harrison's use in "Norwegian Wood." No idiomatic usage of the sitar comparable to Harrison's on *Revolver* and *Sergeant Pepper* was made by any pop group until 1968 when folk singer Richie Havens incorporated the sitar (and the "electric sitar") in his album *Somethin' Else Again.*

Possible offshoots of Harrison's experimentation with Eastern music include the pseudo oriental effects found in the recordings of Country Joe and the Fish (e.g., "Eastern Jam" on the 1967 album *I-Feel-Like-I'm-Fixin'-to-Die*), and the Indian-influenced gestures of "East-West" from the August, 1966, album *East-West* by the Paul Butterfield Blues Band.

Mention should be made at this point of the use of amplifier feedback as an innovative device. Feedback is created by a reamplification of a sound signal, and the result of feedback is a sustained, penetrating tone which is capable of distorting a pitch while sometimes adding higher overtones to it. The effect is easily, often accidentally produced, and as such hardly qualifies as a discovery of major importance on the part of any individual or group. The Beatles' "I Feel Fine," released in late 1964, had made use of feedback on its opening pitch, a sustained dominant which was modified in tone color by the touch of a metal object (or fingernail).

Roxon[19] and Gillett[20] state that the Yardbirds had used feedback in live performances prior to the Beatles' recording, although their first recorded use of it ("I'm a Man") occurs almost a year after the Beatles' single. Roxon also suggests that the British group the Who was at least "the first to popularize the creative use of feedback" if not the first to experiment with it.[21]

Whether or not the use of feedback was a recording innovation for the Beatles, it simply represented one more unique and earcatching sound gesture and was not repeated in subsequent recordings, being replaced eventually in the later albums by tape effects and the electronic filtering of the guitar sound (as in "I'm Only Sleeping").

One of the most influential innovations of 1965 for the Beatles was the neo-Classical string ensemble accompaniment featured on "Yesterday," which was first released on the British *Help!* album in August, 1965. As previously stated, the use of string accompaniment would not in itself distinguish any pop or rock recording in 1965, but the Beatles' juxtaposition of the neo-Classical accompaniment with the popular ballad style achieved an effect unprecedented in popular music. The only possible antecedents for this accomplishment to have achieved popular success occur in the recordings of British popular folk singer Marianne Faithful. Her 1964 recording of Mick Jagger's "As Tears Go By" had featured the accompaniment of a string orchestra which included some isolated Baroque style mannerisms, and was backed by a version of "Greensleeves" with a comparable arrangement. Subsequent recordings also incorporated the string orchestra, although again without extensive references to any neo-Classical style. While these examples represent possible antecedents for the Beatles' innovation, they remain mere tokens and lack the distinctive identity which marks the Beatles' synthesis of styles.

Following the Beatles' tremendous success with "Yesterday," the popular charts were filled with various emulations of the Baroque-rock or Classical-rock styles. In December, 1965, the Rolling Stones recorded a version of "As Tears Go By" which stressed the Baroque implications hinted at in Marianne Faithful's version and, in 1966, recorded "Lady Jane" which featured a neo-Classical instrumental sound obtained by the use of a dulcimer and acoustical guitar as well as a harpsichord.

A number of rock groups incorporated "classical" gestures into their music in the mid and late 1960s and the impact of the Beatles' experiments on the commercial music market was considerable. Within months of the release of "Yesterday" as an American single, several pop albums incorporating similar stylistic gestures were released. One of the most interesting of these was *The Baroque Beatles Book,* a collection of Baroque idiom arrangements of the Beatles' songs by musicologist Joshua Rifkin.

The Beatles' influence in the years 1966–1968 can be summarized in four categories: specific imitations of the Beatles' compositional or performing style (e.g., vocal arrangements); the development of the psychedelic guitar style; the use of electronic or concrete music effects; and the concept of album unity.

In regard to the first of these categories, several groups which patterned themselves closely on the Beatles for all or part of their performing careers may be noted. The most obvious of these include the Knickerbockers whose 1966 hit "Lies" evoked the early Beatles' style of "Please Please Me" in its vocal sonorities and instrumental mannerisms; the Monkees, a group put together to star in a 1966 television series based generally on the type of exploits found in the film *A Hard Day's Night,* whose first single, "Last Train to Clarksville," closely resembled the Beatles' "Paperback Writer" released just two months earlier; and the Australian Bee Gees whose "New York Mining Disaster" of 1967 also recalled the vocal harmony (and accent) of the early Beatles (although this style may well have been developed independently of the Beatles).

Influence of a less specific nature can be heard occasionally in the music of more independent groups such as the Lovin' Spoonful. Alan Dister, in *Les Beatles,* states that the leader-composer of the Lovin' Spoonful, John Sebastian, was influenced in this period by both the tranquil themes of McCartney and the hard rock style of Lennon.[22] The Lovin' Spoonful's January, 1966, recording of "Day Dream" is similar in its old-style harmonies to Lennon's earlier "I Call Your Name," and precedes McCartney's piano period piece "Good Day Sunshine" by several months, while Sebastian's "Summer in the City" of June, 1966, is one of few songs in this period to share the intensity of such Lennon compositions as "You Can't Do That."

Harrison's psychedelic lead guitar style, first heard in "Taxman" although electronically anticipated in effect in "I'm Only Sleeping," seems to have had a significant influence on some other guitarists almost immediately. Guitar distortion and feedback effects had of course been used prior to the release of *Revolver,* but they had generally been used to ornament conventional blues-derived solos or, as in the Rolling Stones' "Satisfaction" of July, 1965, for repeating accompaniment riffs. Harrison's comparatively original style in "Taxman," though not completely devoid of blues characteristics, represented a welcome alternative to the series of blues clichés which had marked most "serious" solos up to that point. Jimi Hendrix (of the Jimi Hendrix Experience) showed traces of the emerging new psychedelic style in his first album *Are You Experienced?,* and the British group Cream (whose lead guitarist was Eric Clapton, formerly of the Yardbirds) provided a mature example of the psychedelic style in its December, 1967, recording of "Sunshine of Your Love," a song which bears some harmonic resemblance to "Sergeant Pepper's Lonely Hearts Club Band."

The psychedelic style, in its many manifestations, was to become an identifying characteristic for a number of groups in the late 1960s, while the Beatles returned to it only once after the *Sergeant Pepper* album for an obvious parody of the then advanced and mannered British psychedelic style in "Yer Blues" (on *The Beatles*). Regardless of his minor role in its subsequent development, Harrison's Indian-influenced version of the psychedelic style on *Revolver* must be considered one of the first recorded examples of a new guitar style which eventually came to define an important genre of rock in the late 1960s.

Aside from their incorporation of neo-Classical accompaniments of various sorts, the Beatles' use of electronic and tape effects constituted their most easily imitated innovation. Only two months after the release of *Sergeant Pepper,* the first album of the Jimi Hendrix Experience demonstrated an extensive use of concrete music effects in its "Third Stone from the Sun." The use of sound effects was not, of course, new to the rock tradition. Songs about cars and motorcycles had often incorporated these noises into the recording. The Beatles' taped effects, however, were offered not as programmatic gimmicks but as extensions of the traditional rock sonorities, capable of being assimilated into the overall context. It is with this intention that Hendrix also incorporated them into his first album. A less extensive but more publicized use of electronic effects also occurred in the Rolling Stones' album, *Their Satanic Majesties Request,* released five months after *Sergeant Pepper.*

By 1967, a superficial use of electronic effects was widespread

among psychedelic bands such as the Electric Prunes, whose hit "I Had
Too Much to Dream" demonstrated simplistic sound modulation and
tremolo effects.

By 1968, a more pretentious use of electronic effects as well as
orchestral accompaniment began to occur. The Moody Blues' 1968
album *The Days of Future Passed* made extensive use of both electronic
and elaborate orchestral effects, a trend to be continued into the 1970s
by various groups. By this time, even rhythm and blues groups such as
the Electric Flag found a place for concrete collage effects as in
"Another Country" from the first album.

Mention should be made in this connection of Frank Zappa and the
Mothers of Invention who incorporated electronic effects into parts of
their first album, *Freak Out,* which was released simultaneously with
Revolver (August, 1966). The effects were used in a satirical context in
this album, but not without an obvious "art consciousness" which also
characterized their use in the Beatles' music. Zappa's use of electronic
effects and other such avant-garde gestures represented an accomplishment roughly parallel to that of the Beatles, although Zappa's
recording career began later than theirs and lacked their earliest period
of artistic innocence. Still, the widespread use of electronic effects by
rock groups in the late 1960s and early 1970s seemed in most instances
to be an extension of the Beatles' approach rather than Zappa's often
tongue-in-cheek attempts.

The most difficult problem of assessing influence exists in regard to
the question of album unity. There is no question that, by the late 1960s,
the old rock concept of a string of unrelated songs had begun to give way
in many cases to a more thoughtful formulation and ordering of album
content. An example of this can be seen in the production of the *Rubber
Soul* album as early as 1965. This is the first album that owes its identity
completely to the Beatles themselves rather than to their advisors.
Nevertheless, there seems to have been no achievement comparable to
Sergeant Pepper's Lonely Hearts Club Band prior to its release in June,
1967. We have seen that the concept of album unity on *Sergeant Pepper*
was predominantly a literary one, although certain interrelationships in
musical style were also noted. This predominantly literary unification of
a large form is also demonstrated to a certain extent in an album
released in the same month by the Who. Their album, *Happy Jack,*
contained an extended song titled "A Quick One While He's Away"
which Roxon describes as a "complicated twelve minute rock opera"[23]
and which Gabree describes as containing a "sequential story line" and

"several distinct musical statements,"[24] although no interrelationship between these sections is claimed. However, the work is distinct from the Beatles' effort, not only in its comparative brevity and its sequential, operalike story line, but also in its conventional rock music idiom. This idiom is maintained by the Who even in their most ambitious rock "opera" of 1969, *Tommy,* as demonstrated by the commercial success of several singles drawn from that album.

In the months following the release of *Sergeant Pepper,* several overt attempts to achieve a comparable album unity were made. In September, 1967, Chad and Jeremy, who had previously worked in a folk-flavored pop-rock style, included on one side of their new album *Of Cabbages and Kings* a five-part "Progress Suite" which featured both vocal and instrumental sections. In the next month, two more ambitious recordings were released: the Electric Prunes' *Mass in f Minor* and Van Dyke Park's *Song Cycle.* The latter is described as being "rich in allusions to Beethoven, Debussy, Mahler, and, most of all, the American Charles Ives," and yet sounding like "Broadway Show Tunes written in a country-style idiom."[25] This Broadway-country combination is referred to in most descriptions of Park's music, and his predominantly commercial (as opposed to rock-based) idiom makes any direct comparison with *Sergeant Pepper* difficult, regardless of the loose literary-based unity common to both albums.

A second potential influence attributable to *Sergeant Pepper* is that of its fantasy-oriented atmosphere. As Dister suggests, the unworldly, psychedelic atmosphere evoked by the music and lyrics of the Beatles' album had an immediate influence on groups such as Cream, the Jimi Hendrix Experience, and the Moody Blues.[26] The two 1968 albums of the Moody Blues, *Days of Future Passed* and *In Search of the Lost Chord* are prime examples of the new preoccupation with fantasy—a preoccupation which, aided by the increasing demand for "hallucinatory" experiences, was to extend into the 1970s. Even the rhythm and blues-oriented Rolling Stones, in *Their Satanic Majesty's Request* of 1967, became involved in an attempt to permeate an entire album with a unifying psychedelic atmosphere.

In connection with album unity, Frank Zappa and the Mothers of Invention must again be considered as innovators on a level with, though distinct from, the Beatles. Both *Freak Out* and *We're Only in It for the Money* (a parody of *Sergeant Pepper* in some respects, released in January, 1968) showed signs of musical as well as literary interrelations within an extended section of more than one album side. The intention seemingly expressed in both works was that of evoking a carefully choreographed confusion by a free association of ideas which aid in reinforcing the satirical implications of the album.

Although there is little connection between Zappa's efforts in this area and the Beatles' (the most significant manifestations of Zappa's influence occur some years later), the two groups have in common a disdain for conventionality which separates them from many subsequent efforts in this direction. Most of the earliest musical reactions to *Sergeant Pepper* remained basically within the social-dance or popular-folk conventions of the mainstream pop style of the late 1960s. Not until the end of that decade and the early part of the next did the sort of art consciousness embodied by the Beatles and Zappa begin to manifest itself in a comparable expansion of the traditional rock context in the work of others.[27]

It should be emphasized at this point that these influences must be considered merely probable in most instances, unless specific documentation of indebtedness exists. And, of course, this is rarely the case in the competitive commercial market of popular music which so esteems the pretense, if not the product, of originality. It is also true in many cases that influence is more correctly expressed in terms of providing an environment in which certain types of experimentation will be accepted, than in terms of specific and concrete examples of imitation. This is undoubtedly the case in regard to the Beatles' relationship to subsequent experiments in album unity. Arnold Shaw quotes Van Dyke Parks to the effect that while the Beatles did not influence him directly, they "helped to create the recording climate" in which he could mature.[28]

In terms of specific innovations which have proven to be influential, there can be no doubt that the Beatles were at least as influential as any recording rock group in the 1960s. However, the popular music of this period remained extremely diversified, and large areas within it remained untouched by the innovations of the Beatles or any of the other experimental forces of the time. In short, it is not altogether appropriate to speak of the Beatles' influence in terms of a revolutionary impact. As comparatively widespread and potent as the group's influence was in the 1960s, most of the popular music produced in the 1970s and early 1980s shows relatively little trace of it.

This is not to suggest that those who originally heralded the Beatles as revolutionaries in the world of popular music were incorrect. The degree to which the Beatles' music differed from their contemporaries' between 1964 and 1967 justified their claims of a revolutionary new approach to popular music. It can be seen in retrospect that the heralders of the Beatles erred not in their appraisal of the group's distinctiveness and merit, but in their analysis of the nature of popular music and its susceptibility to authentic revolutions of any kind.

In view of this, it seems correct to suggest that is is not in terms of innovation or influence alone that the Beatles' success must be measured. One of the most frequently cited examples of an acknowledged master credited with few influential innovations is W. A. Mozart. Composer-critic Ned Rorem has argued that the Beatles' originality lies not in their innovations but in their superiority to their contemporaries, a superiority which is

finally as elusive as Mozart's to Clementi: both spoke skillfully the same tonal language, but only Mozart spoke it with the added magic of genius. Who will define such magic?[29]

Rorem defines it himself to some extent in his discussion of the "unexpected" in the Beatles' music. Although certainly no objective measurement of merit, the determination of surprises and deviations within the conventions of a musical style nevertheless helps to provide an indication of the significance of the music. As has often been suggested, stylistic deviations from the norm are not, in themselves, necessarily meritorious, but it is difficult to conceive of great music, or at least "outstanding music," without them.[30] While it has been demonstrated in this study that the Beatles' musical style, like Mozart's, most certainly contains much that is conventional, their distinctiveness and ultimately their superiority must be judged, like Mozart's, on the basis of their subtle stylistic deviations from that convention as much as by the impact of their major innovations. It is within this context that the Beatles' superiority is most apparent; no other group or figure in the popular music of the 1960s approached the Beatles in consistency and significance of original characteristics, and no other group or figure in that period succeeded in matching the great quantity of distinctive and exciting music produced by the Beatles in a career that was all too brief.

Notes and References

Chapter One

1. The most trustworthy source for this information remains Hunter Davies, *The Beatles* (London, 1969; rev. edition, New York).
2. Ibid., p. 108.
3. Ibid., p. 114.
4. Ibid., p. 152.

Chapter Two

1. Jann Wenner, *Lennon Remembers* (San Francisco, 1971), p. 184.
2. Bill Harry, ed., *Mersey Beat: The Beginnings of the Beatles* (New York, 1977), p. 29.
3. Ibid., p. 43.
4. Charlie Gillett, *The Sound of the City: The Rise of Rock and Roll* (New York, 1970), p. 305.
5. Miles, comp., and Pearce Marchbank, ed., *Beatles in Their Own Words* (New York, 1978), p. 22.
6. Davies, *The Beatles*, p. 40.
7. Ibid., p. 106.
8. "Life-Lines of the Beatles," *New Musical Express*, February 15, 1963.
9. Arnold Shaw, *The Rock Revolution*, Paperback Library (New York, 1971), p. 103.
10. Gillett, *Sound of the City*, p. 123.
11. Gillett uses this term to describe more or less the same repertoire, although he defines it differently (*The Sound of the City*, p. 220).
12. Harry, *Mersey Beat*, p. 49.
13. Wenner, *Lennon Remembers*, p. 70.
14. "Life-Lines of the Beatles" for all references to the Beatles' poll choices.
15. Harry Castleman and Walter J. Podrazik, *All Together Now* (New York, 1975).
16. See Terence J. O'Grady, "The Ballad Style in the Early Music of the Beatles," *College Music Symposium,* 19, no. 1 (Spring 1979):221–30.
17. There are also six cuts on the record accompanied by the Titans rather than the Beatles.

18. These songs are compared in O'Grady, "Ballad Style," p. 224.
19. Harry, *Mersey Beat,* p. 52.
20. Davies, *The Beatles,* p. 148.

Chapter Three

1. Davies, *The Beatles,* p. 175.
2. Gillett, *Sound of the City,* p. 309.
3. According to Davies (p. 176), Ringo plays maracas on the released version.
4. Davies, *The Beatles,* p. 178.
5. For a more extensive comparison, see O'Grady, "Ballad Style," pp. 221–30.
6. Davies, *The Beatles,* p. 105.
7. Ibid., p. 147.
8. See O'Grady, "Ballad Style," for further comparison.
9. These were substituted for "Love Me Do" and "P.S. I Love You" in later releases of the album at the request of Capitol Records.
10. Davies, *The Beatles,* p. 200.
11. Lawrence Gushee, professor of musicology at the University of Illinois—Urbana, has suggested to me that this "novelty chord" of the popular music of the 1920s derives from the still older stereotyped progression of I–i°7–I since it is basically an augmentation of the middle chord (a flat sixth root is added and the seventh is eliminated) and generally functions in the same manner.

Chapter Four

1. Wilfrid Mellers, *The Twilight of the Gods: The Music of the Beatles* (New York, 1973), p. 45.
2. Carl Belz, *The Story of Rock,* 2d ed. (New York, 1972), p. 133.
3. For example, see Mellers, *Twilight,* pp. 28–31.
4. See O'Grady, "Ballad Style," pp. 221–30.
5. Billy Shepherd, *The True Story of the Beatles* (New York, 1964), p. 157.
6. Quoted in Nicholas Schaffner, *The Beatles Forever* (New York, 1978), p. 39.
7. Rolling Stone Editors, *The Rolling Stone Interviews,* Paperback Library (New York: Coronet Communications, 1971), p. 199.

Chapter Five

1. Schaffner, *Beatles Forever,* p. 46.
2. Ibid., p. 47.
3. Ibid., p. 42.

4. See O'Grady, "Ballad Style."

5. In Wenner, *Lennon Remembers*, p. 83, John states in connection with *Rubber Soul* that "We were just getting better, technically and musically. . . . We finally took over the studio."

6. Mellers, *Twilight*, p. 58.

7. Wenner, *Lennon Remembers*, p. 128.

8. Mellers, *Twilight*, p. 59.

Chapter Six

1. Schaffner, *Beatles Forever*, p. 64.

2. Ibid., p. 55.

3. Ibid., p. 57.

4. Davies, *The Beatles*, p. 247.

5. Rolling Stone Editors, *Rolling Stone Interviews*, pp. 191–92.

6. Mellers, *Twilight*, p. 69.

7. Schaffner attributes this solo to McCartney (p. 63).

8. George Melly, *Revolt into Style: The Pop Arts* (New York, 1971), p. 85.

9. See, for example, Alan Keesee's "Indian Influence on the Beatles" in Edward E. Davies, ed., *The Beatles Book* (New York, 1968).

10. The fact that Harrison was aware that his songs constituted at best a compromise with the classical Indian tradition is made clear by his discussion of his Indian-influenced songs in Davies's biography, pp. 346–51.

11. Miles, and Marchbank, *Beatles in Own Words*, p. 84.

12. Ibid., p. 85.

13. Rolling Stone Editors, *Rolling Stone Interviews*, p. 196.

14. Mellers, *Twilight*, p. 182.

Chapter Seven

1. Mellers, *Twilight*, p. 84.

2. Thomas Thompson, "The New Far-Out Beatles," *Life*, 62, no. 24 (June 16, 1967):101–06.

3. Mellers, *Twilight*, pp. 86–87.

4. Richard Poirier, "Learning from the Beatles," in Jonathan Eisen, ed., *The Age of Rock: Sounds of the American Cultural Revolution*, Vintage Books (New York, 1969), p. 177 (reprinted from *Partisan Review*, Fall, 1967).

5. Peter Shrag, cited in Julius Fast, *The Beatles: The Real Story* (New York: Bantam Books, 1964), p. 4.

6. Dale Cockrell, "The Beatles: *Sergeant Pepper's Lonely Hearts Club Band* and *Abbey Road*, Side Two: Unification within the Rock Recording" (Master's Thesis, University of Illinois-Urbana, 1973), p. 77.

7. Alan Aldridge, "Beatles Not All That Turned On" in Eisen, *The Age of Rock*, p. 77.

8. Mellers, *Twilight*, p. 87.

9. Ibid.

10. Aldridge, *Beatles Not All*, p. 140.

11. Cockrell, *Beatles and Sergeant Pepper's*, p. 47.

12. Ibid., p. 53.

13. Mellers, *Twilight*, p. 92.

14. Ned Rorem, "The Music of the Beatles" in Eisen, *The Age of Rock*, p. 156.

15. Aldridge, *Beatles Not All*, p. 142.

16. Castleman and Podrazik, *All Together Now*, p. 158.

17. Schaffner, *Beatles Forever*, p. 79.

18. Mellers, *Twilight*, p. 94.

19. The song was composed by McCartney as early as 1960 according to Davies (*The Beatles*, p. 313) but it is unlikely that it was then conceived in the complex arrangement in which it is here presented.

Chapter Eight

1. Schaffner, *Beatles Forever*, p. 90.

2. For a further explanation of Apple's activities, see Peter McCabe and Robert D. Schonfeld, *Apple to the Core: The Unmaking of the Beatles* (New York, 1972).

3. The details of this encounter are related in Davies, *The Beatles*, and Schaffner's *Beatles Forever*.

4. Schaffner, *Beatles Forever*, p. 100.

5. Ibid., p. 114.

6. Ibid., p. 115.

7. These melismas are used somewhat less predictably here than in the earlier style and contribute to the urgency of the song by suggesting asymmetrical and elided phrase patterns. I am indebted to Mr. Daniel Dorff for bringing to my attention the subtlety of the middle level phrase structure which characterizes much of *The Beatles* album.

8. In the slower album version, the lyrics read "count me out—in" which, according to Lennon, showed the dual nature of his position. Quoted in Wenner, *Lennon Remembers*, p. 131.

9. Schaffner, *Beatles Forever*, p. 114.

10. Wenner, *Lennon Remembers*, p. 32.

11. Schaffner, *Beatles Forever*, pp. 118–19.

12. Castleman and Podrazik, *All Together Now*, p. 89.

13. Schaffner, *Beatles Forever*, p. 138.

14. Davies, *The Beatles*, p. 72.

15. Schaffner, *Beatles Forever*, p. 175.

16. Ibid., p. 125.

17. Mellers, *Twilight,* p. 116.
18. Schaffner, *Beatles Forever,* p. 124.
19. Ibid., p. 126.
20. Mellers, *Twilight,* p. 120.
21. Miles and Marchbank, *Beatles in Own Words,* p. 102.
22. Schaffner, *Beatles Forever,* p. 126.

Chapter Nine

1. Davies, *The Beatles,* p. 42.
2. Ibid., p. 282.
3. Ibid., p. 298.
4. Alan Aldridge, ed., *The Beatles' Illustrated Lyrics,* Delacourt Press (New York, 1969), p. 101.
5. Davies, *The Beatles,* p. 298.
6. Ibid., p. 348.
7. Billy Shepherd, *The True Story of the Beatles* (New York, 1964), p. 78.
8. Rolling Stone Editors, *Rolling Stone Interviews,* p. 220.
9. Davies, *The Beatles,* p. 282.
10. Wenner, *Lennon Remembers,* p. 128.
11. Davies, *The Beatles,* p. 283.
12. Davies also describes the recording sessions for "With a Little Help from My Friends," "Getting Better," and "Magical Mystery Tour," in his chapter "The Beatles and Their Music," pp. 281–307. See also George Martin, *All You Need is Ears,* New York: St. Martin's Press, 1979, pp. 199–219.
13. Evidence of this can be seen in those Beatles' manuscripts reproduced in Davies's biography as well as those held by the University of Illinois-Urbana Music Library. All of these manuscripts contain only the texts of the songs with chord symbols occasionally indicated above the words.
14. Cited in Julius Fast, *The Beatles: The Real Story* (New York: Bantam Books, 1964), p. 224.
15. John Mendelsohn, "Nine Ways of Looking at the Beatles 1963–1973," *Stereo Review,* February, 1973, pp. 56–63.
16. Lillian Roxon, *Rock Encyclopedia* (New York: Grosset & Dunlap, 1971), p. 79.
17. Gillett, *Sound of the City,* p. 314.
18. Roxon, *Rock Encyclopedia,* p. 454.
19. Ibid., p. 181.
20. Gillett, *Sound of the City,* p. 314.
21. Roxon, *Rock Encyclopedia,* p. 527.
22. Alain Dister, *Les Beatles* (Paris, 1972), p. 138.
23. Roxon, *Rock Encyclopedia,* p. 528.

24. John Gabree, *The World of Rock* (Greenwich, Conn.: Fawcett Publications, 1968), p. 147.

25. Shaw, *Rock Revolution,* p. 180.

26. Dister, *Les Beatles,* p. 147.

27. Zappa and others are discussed in this connection in Tom Phillips, "The Album as Art Form: One Year after Sergeant Pepper," *Jazz and Pop,* 7 (May, 1968):35–36.

28. Shaw, *Rock Revolution,* p. 181.

29. Ned Rorem, "The Music of the Beatles," in Eisen, *The Age of Rock,* p. 155.

30. This position is based on the views of musicologist Leonard B. Meyer of the University of Chicago among others. His theories in this regard are put forth with great skill in *Emotion and Meaning in Music* (Chicago: University of Chicago Press, 1956), *Music, the Arts, and Ideas* (Chicago: University of Chicago Press, 1967), and *Explaining Music* (Berkeley: University of California Press, 1973).

Selected Discography

I. Major British and American Beatles' Albums: 1963–1970
(All compositions by Lennon-McCartney unless otherwise indicated)

Abbey Road.   Apple PCS 7088, Apple SO 383.
   Come Together
   Something (Harrison)
   Maxwell's Silver Hammer
   Oh! Darling
   Octopus's Garden (Starkey)
   I Want You (She's So Heavy)
   Here Comes the Sun (Harrison)
   Because
   You Never Give Me Your Money
   Sun King
   Mean Mr. Mustard
   Polythene Pam
   She Came in Through the Bathroom Window
   Golden Slumbers
   Carry That Weight
   The End
   Her Majesty

The Beatles.   (The White Album) (2 L.P.s). Apple PCS 7067/8, Apple SWBO 101.
   Back in the U.S.S.R.
   Dear Prudence
   Glass Onion
   Ob-La-Di, Ob-La-Da
   Wild Honey Pie
   The Continuing Story of Bungalow Bill

   While My Guitar Gently Weeps (Harrison)
   Happiness Is a Warm Gun
   Martha My Dear
   I'm So Tired
   Blackbird
   Piggies (Harrison)
   Rocky Racoon
   Don't Pass Me By (Starkey)
   Why Don't We Do It in the Road
   I Will
   Julia
   Birthday
   Yer Blues
   Mother Nature's Son
   Everybody's Got Something to Hide Except Me and My Monkey
   Sexy Sadie
   Helter Skelter
   Long, Long, Long (Harrison)
   Revolution
   Honey Pie
   Savoy Truffle (Harrison)
   Cry Baby Cry
   Revolution 9
   Good Night

Beatles For Sale.   Parlophone PCS 3062.
   No Reply
   I'm a Loser

Baby's in Black
Rock and Roll Music (Berry)
I'll Follow the Sun
Mr. Moonlight (Johnson)
Kansas City—Hey-Hey-Hey-
Hey! (Lieber-Stoller)
(Penniman)
Eight Days a Week
Words of Love (Holly)
Honey Don't (Perkins)
Every Little Thing
I Don't Want to Spoil the Party
What You're Doing
Everybody's Trying to Be My
Baby (Perkins)

The Beatles' Second Album.
Capitol ST 2080.
Roll Over Beethoven (Berry)
Thank You Girl
You Really Got a Hold on Me
(Robinson)
Devil in Her Heart (Drapkin)
Money (Gordy-Bradford)
You Can't Do That
Long Tall Sally (Penniman)
I Call Your Name
Please Mr. Postman
(Holland-Bateman-Gordy)
I'll Get You
She Loves You

Beatles VI. Capitol ST 2358.
Kansas City—Hey-Hey-Hey-
Hey! (Lieber-Stoller)
(Penniman)
Eight Days a Week
You Like Me Too Much
(Harrison)
Bad Boy (Williams)
I Don't Want to Spoil the Party
Words of Love (Holly)
What You're Doing
Yes It Is
Dizzy Miss Lizzy (Williams)

Tell Me What You See
Every Little Thing

Beatles '65. Capitol ST 2228.
No Reply
I'm a Loser
Baby's in Black
Rock and Roll Music (Berry)
I'll Follow the Sun
Mr. Moonlight (Johnson)
Honey Don't (Perkins)
I'll Be Back
She's a Woman
I Feel Fine
Everybody's Trying to Be My
Baby (Perkins)

*The Beatles With Tony Sheridan and
Their Guests.* MGM SE 4215.
(Additional material by Tony
Sheridan and other artists)
My Bonnie (Pratt)
Cry for a Shadow
(Lennon-Harrison)
The Saints (Public Domain)
Why? (Sheridan-Crompton)

The Early Beatles. Capitol ST 2309.
Love Me Do
Twist and Shout
(Russell-Medley)
Anna (Go to Him) (Alexander)
Chains (Goffin-King)
Boys (Dixon-Farrell)
Ask Me Why
Please Please Me
P.S. I Love You
Baby It's You
(David-Bacharach-Williams)
A Taste of Honey
(Marlow-Scott)
Do You Want to Know a Secret?

A Hard Day's Night. Parlophone
PCS 3058.
A Hard Day's Night

I Should Have Known Better
If I Fell
I'm Happy Just to Dance with
  You
And I Love Her
Tell Me Why
Can't Buy Me Love
Anytime at All
I'll Cry Instead
Things We Said Today
When I Get Home
You Can't Do That
I'll Be Back

A Hard Day's Night.   United Artists
Uas 6636.
(Additional material by George
Martin and Orchestra)
  A Hard Day's Night
  Tell Me Why
  I'll Cry Instead
  I'm Happy Just to Dance with
    You
  I Should Have Known Better
  If I Fell
  And I Love Her
  Can't Buy Me Love

Help!.   Parlophone PCS 3071.
  Help!
  The Night Before
  You've Got to Hide Your Love
    Away
  I Need You (Harrison)
  Another Girl
  You're Gonna Lose That Girl
  Ticket to Ride
  Act Naturally
    (Russell-Morrison)
  It's Only Love
  You Like Me Too Much
    (Harrison)
  Tell Me What You See
  I've Just Seen a Face
  Yesterday
  Dizzy Miss Lizzy (Williams)

Help!.   Capitol SMAS 2386.
  (Additional material by George
  Martin and Orchestra)
  Help!
  The Night Before
  You've Got to Hide Your Love
    Away
  I Need You (Harrison)
  Another Girl
  Ticket to Ride
  You're Gonna Lose That Girl

Hey Jude (Also called *The Beatles
Again*).   Apple SW 385/So 385.
  Can't Buy Me Love
  I Should Have Known Better
  Paperback Writer
  Rain
  Lady Madonna
  Revolution
  Hey Jude
  Old Brown Shoe (Harrison)
  Don't Let Me Down
  The Ballad of John and Yoko

In the Beginning (circa 1960).
  Polydor 24–4504.
  (Additional material by Tony
  Sheridan and other artists)
    Ain't She Sweet (Yellen-Ager)
    Cry for a Shadow
      (Lennon-Harrison)
    My Bonnie (Pratt)
    If You Love Me, Baby
      (Singleton-Hall)
    Sweet Georgia Brown
      (Bernie-Pinkard-Casey)
    The Saints (Public Domain)
    Why? (Sheridan-Crompton)
    Nobody's Child (Foree-Coben)

Introducing the Beatles.   Vee Jay
VJLP 1062.
  I Saw Her Standing There
  Misery
  Anna (Go to Him) (Alexander)

Chains (Goffin-King)
Boys (Dixon-Farrell)
Love Me Do*
P.S. I Love You*
Baby It's You
    (David-Bacharach-Williams)
Do You Want to Know a Secret?
A Taste of Honey
    (Marlow-Scott)
Twist and Shout
    (Russell-Medley)
*(These were replaced by "Ask
Me Why" and "Please Please
Me" in a later version of this
album.)

Let It Be.   Apple PXS 1, Red Apple
34001.
Two of Us
I Dig a Pony
Across the Universe
I Me Mine (Harrison)
Dig It (Lennon-McCartney-
    Harrison-Starkey)
Let It Be
Maggie Mae (Public Domain)
I've Got a Feeling
One After 909
The Long and Winding Road
For You Blue (Harrison)
Get Back

Magical Mystery Tour.   Capitol
SMAL 2835.
Magical Mystery Tour
The Fool on the Hill
Flying (Lennon-McCartney-
    Harrison-Starkey)
Blue Jay Way (Harrison)
Your Mother Should Know
I Am the Walrus
Hello Goodbye
Strawberry Fields Forever
Penny Lane
Baby, You're a Rich Man
All You Need Is Love

Meet the Beatles!.   Capitol ST
2047.
I Want to Hold Your Hand
I Saw Her Standing There
This Boy
It Won't Be Long
All I've Got to Do
Don't Bother Me (Harrison)
Little Child
Till There Was You (Willson)
Hold Me Tight
I Wanna Be Your Man
Not a Second Time

Please Please Me.   Parlophone
PCS 3402.
I Saw Her Standing There
Misery
Anna (Go to Him) (Alexander)
Chains (Goffin-King)
Boys (Dixon-Farrell)
Ask Me Why
Please Please Me
Love Me Do
P.S. I Love You
Baby It's You
    (David-Bacharach-Williams)
Do You Want to Know a Secret?
A Taste of Honey
    (Marlow-Scott)
There's a Place
Twist and Shout
    (Russell-Medley)

Revolver.   Parlophone PCS 7009.
Taxman (Harrison)
Eleanor Rigby
I'm Only Sleeping
Love You To (Harrison)
Here, There and Everywhere
Yellow Submarine
She Said She Said
Good Day Sunshine
And Your Bird Can Sing
For No One
Dr. Robert

I Want to Tell You (Harrison)
Got to Get You into My Life
Tomorrow Never Knows

Revolver.   Capitol ST 2576.
Taxman (Harrison)
Eleanor Rigby
Love You To (Harrison)
Here, There and Everywhere
Yellow Submarine
She Said She Said
Good Day Sunshine
For No One
I Want to Tell You (Harrison)
Got to Get You into My Life
Tomorrow Never Knows

Rubber Soul.   Parlophone PCS
3075.
Drive My Car
Norwegian Wood
You Won't See Me
Nowhere Man
Think for Yourself (Harrison)
The Word
Michelle
What Goes on? (Lennon-
McCartney-Starkey)
Girl
I'm Looking Through You
In My Life
Wait
If I Needed Someone
(Harrison)
Run for Your Life

Rubber Soul.   Capitol ST 2442.
I've Just Seen a Face
Norwegian Wood
You Won't See Me
Think for Yourself (Harrison)
The Word
Michelle
It's Only Love
Girl
I'm Looking Through You

In My Life
Wait
Run for Your Life

Sergeant Pepper's Lonely Hearts
Club Band.   Parlophone PCS
7027, Capitol SMAS 2653.
Sergeant Pepper's Lonely
Hearts Club Band
With a Little Help from My
Friends
Lucy in the Sky with Diamonds
Getting Better
Fixing a Hole
She's Leaving Home
Being for the Benefit of Mr.
Kite
Within You Without You
(Harrison)
When I'm Sixty-Four
Lovely Rita
Good Morning Good Morning
Sergeant Pepper's Lonely
Hearts Club Band (reprise)
A Day in the Life

Something New.   Capitol ST 2108.
I'll Cry Instead
Things We Said Today
Anytime at All
When I Get Home
Slow Down (Williams)
Matchbox (Perkins)
Tell Me Why
And I Love Her
I'm Happy Just to Dance with
You
If I Fell
Komm, Gib Mir Deine Hand

With the Beatles.   Parlophone PCS
3045.
It Won't Be Long
All I've Got to Do
All My Loving
Don't Bother Me (Harrison)

Little Child
Till There Was You (Willson)
Please Mr. Postman
  (Holland-Bateman-Gordy)
Roll Over Beethoven (Berry)
Hold Me Tight
I Wanna Be Your Man
Devil in Her Heart (Drapkin)
Not a Second Time
Money (Gordy-Bradford)

Yellow Submarine.   Apple PCS
7070, Apple SW 153.
(Additional material by George
Martin and Orchestra)
  Yellow Submarine
  Only a Northern Song
    (Harrison)
  All Together Now

Hey Bulldog
It's All Too Much (Harrison)
All You Need Is Love

Yesterday . . . and Today.   Capitol
ST 2553.
  Drive My Car
  I'm Only Sleeping
  Nowhere Man
  Dr. Robert
  Yesterday
  Act Naturally
    (Russell-Morrison)
  And Your Bird Can Sing
  If I Needed Someone
    (Harrison)
  We Can Work It Out
  What Goes On? (Lennon-
    McCartney-Starkey)
  Day Tripper

II. British and American Extended Play Releases (45 rpm)
(All compositions by Lennon-McCartney unless otherwise indicated)

All My Loving.   Parlophone GEP
8891.
  All My Loving
  Ask Me Why
  Money (Gordy-Bradford)
  P.S. I Love You

The Beatles.   Vee Jay VJEP 1–903.
  Misery
  A Taste of Honey
    (Marlow-Scott)
  Ask Me Why
  Anna (Go to Him) (Alexander)

The Beatles (No. 1).   Parlophone
GEP 8883.
  I Saw Her Standing There
  Misery
  Anna (Go to Him) (Alexander)
  Chains (Goffin-King)

Beatles for Sale.   Parlophone GEP
8931.
  No Reply
  I'm a Loser
  Rock and Roll Music (Berry)
  Eight Days a Week

Beatles for Sale (No. 2).
Parlophone GEP 8938.
  I'll Follow the Sun
  Baby's in Black
  Words of Love (Holly)
  I Don't Want to Spoil the Party

The Beatles' Hits.   Parlophone
GEP 8880.
  From Me to You
  Thank You Girl
  Please Please Me
  Love Me Do

The Beatles' Million Sellers.
Parlophone GEP 9846.
  She Loves You
  I Want to Hold Your Hand
  Can't Buy Me Love
  I Feel Fine

Extracts from the Film "A Hard Day's Night." Parlophone GEP 8920.
  I Should Have Known Better
  If I Fell
  Tell Me Why
  And I Love Her

Extracts from the Film "A Hard Day's Night" (No. 2). Parlophone GEP 8924.
  Anytime at All
  I'll Cry Instead
  Things We Said Today
  When I Get Home

Four By the Beatles. Capitol EAP 2121.
  Roll Over Beethoven (Berry)
  All My Loving
  This Boy
  Please Mr. Postman
    (Holland-Bateman-Gordy)

4 By the Beatles. Capitol R 5356.
  Honey Don't (Perkins)
  I'm a Loser
  Mr. Moonlight (Johnson)
  Everybody's Trying to Be My Baby (Perkins)

Magical Mystery Tour (2 E.P.'s).
Parlophone SMMT 1/2.
  Magical Mystery Tour
  Your Mother Should Know
  I Am the Walrus
  The Fool on the Hill
  Flying
  Blue Jay Way (Harrison)

Nowhere Man. Parlophone GEP 8952.
  Nowhere Man
  Drive My Car
  Michelle
  It's Only Love

Twist and Shout. Parlophone GEP 8882.
  Twist and Shout
    (Russell-Medley)
  A Taste of Honey
    (Marlow-Scott)
  Do You Want to Know a Secret?
  There's a Place

Yesterday. Parlophone GEP 8948.
  Yesterday
  Act Naturally
    (Russell-Morrison)
  You Like Me Too Much
    (Harrison)
  It's Only Love

III. Beatles' Compositions for Others through 1970
(All compositions by Lennon-McCartney unless otherwise indicated. Only compositions not recorded by the Beatles included.)

"Badge." (By George Harrison and Eric Clapton) Atco SD 7001, Polydor 583–053. Recorded by Cream.

"Bad to Me." Parlophone R 5049, Liberty 55626. Recorded by Billy J. Kramer with the Dakotas.

"Catcall." (By Paul McCartney) Marmalade 598–005. Recorded by the Chris Barber Band.

"Come and Get It." (By Paul McCartney) Apple 20, Apple 1815. Recorded by Badfinger.

"From a Window." Parlophone R 5156. Recorded by Billy J. Kramer with the Dakotas.

"Goodbye." Apple 10, Apple 1806. Recorded by Mary Hopkin.

"Hello Little Girl." Parlophone R 5056, Atco 6280. Recorded by the Foremost.

"I Don't Want to See You Again." Columbia DB 7356, Capitol 5272. Recorded by Peter and Gordon.

"I'll Be On My Way." Parlophone 523, Liberty 55586. Recorded by Billy J. Kramer with the Dakotas.

"I'll Keep You Satisfied." Parlophone R 5073, Liberty 55643. Recorded by Billy J. Kramer with the Dakotas.

"I'm in Love." Parlophone R 5078; Atco 6285. Recorded by the Fourmost.

"It's for You." Parlophone R 5162, Capitol 5228. Recorded by Cilla Black.

"Like Dreamers Do." Decca F 11916, London 9681. Recorded by the Applejacks.

"Love of the Loved." Parlophone R 5065. Recorded by Cilla Black.

"Nobody I Know." Columbia 8348 (EP). Recorded by Peter and Gordon.

"One and One Is Two." Phillips BF 1335. Recorded by the Strangers with Mike Shannon.

"Sour Milk Sea." (By George Harrison) Apple 1802, Apple 3. Recorded by Jackie Lomax.

"Step Inside Love." Parlophone R 5674, Bell 726. Recorded by Cilla Black.

"That Means a Lot." Liberty 55806. Recorded by P.J. Proby.

"Thingumybob." Apple 1800 and Apple 4. Recorded by John Foster and Sons Ltd. Black Dyke Mills Band.

"Tip of My Tongue." Piccadilly 7N 35137. Recorded by Tommy Quickly.

"Woman." (By Paul McCartney as Bernard Webb) Capitol 5579; Columbia DB 7834. Recorded by Peter and Gordon.

"A World without Love." Columbia DB 7225, Capitol 5175. Recorded by Peter and Gordon.

Selected Bibliography

This brief bibliography will make no attempt to reflect the massive amount of material on the Beatles which has accumulated in the last twenty years. Instead, it will focus on the few books which most effectively document the Beatles' lives and careers from 1962 to 1970 as well as those books and articles which make a substantial contribution to the analysis or evaluation of the Beatles' music.

Primary Sources

Aldridge, Alan, ed. *The Beatles' Illustrated Lyrics.* Delacourt Press. New York: Dell Publishing Co., 1969.

Golson, G. Barry, ed. *The Playboy Interview with John Lennon and Yoko Ono.* New York: Playboy Press, 1981.

Harry, Bill, ed. *Mersey Beat: The Beginnings of the Beatles.* New York: Omnibus Press, 1977.

Lennon, John. *In His Own Write & A Spaniard in the Works.* Signet Books. New York: New American Library, 1965.

Miles, comp., and Marchbank, Pearce, ed. *Beatles in Their Own Words.* New York: Omnibus Press, 1977.

Rolling Stone Editors. *The Rolling Stone Interviews.* Paperback Library. New York: Coronet Communications, 1971.

Wenner, Jann. *Lennon Remembers.* San Francisco: Straight Arrow Books, 1971.

Secondary Sources

Belz, Carl. *The Story of Rock.* 2d ed. New York: Harper & Row, 1972. One of the most intelligent of the histories of popular music in the 1960s and early 1970s, providing both a cultural context and useful stylistic information.

Castleman, Harry, and Podrazik, Walter. *All Together Now.* New York: Ballantine Books, 1975. The most complete and accurate Beatles' discography available.

Cockrell, Dale. "The Beatles: *Sergeant Pepper's Lonely Hearts Club Band* and *Abbey Road,* Side Two: Unification within the Rock Recording." Master's Thesis, University of Illinois, Urbana, 1973. A useful study of large scale album unity in two of the Beatles' most famous albums.

Davies, Edward E. *The Beatles Book.* New York: Cowles Education Corporation, 1968. A collection of essays on the Beatles' music including Alan Keesee's "Indian Influence on the Beatles."

Davies, Hunter. *The Beatles.* London: Mayflower Books, 1969 (revised edition, New York: Dell Publishing, Co., 1978). The most trustworthy source for biographical information on the Beatles, also containing some interesting remarks on the Beatles' compositional method.

Dister, Alain. *Les Beatles.* Paris: Edition Albin Michel, 1972. Particularly useful for its discussion of influences on the Beatles in their middle period.

Eisen, Jonathan, ed. *The Age of Rock: Sounds of the American Revolution.* Vintage Books. New York: Random House, 1969. Notable for essays on the Beatles by Richard Poirier and Ned Rorem among others.

Gillett, Charlie. *The Sound of the City: The Rise of Rock and Roll.* New York: Outerbridge & Dienstfrey, 1970. Valuable for its thorough analysis of rhythm and blues and early rock styles in the 1950s.

McCabe, Peter, and Schonfeld, Robert D. *Apple to the Core: The Unmaking of the Beatles.* New York: Pocket Books, 1970. An account of the business activities of the Beatles' Apple Corporation.

Martin, George. *All You Need Is Ears.* New York: St. Martin's Press, 1979. Useful for its descriptions of the Beatles' later recording sessions from producer Martin's point of view.

Mellers, Wilfrid. *The Twilight of the Gods: The Music of the Beatles.* New York: Viking Press, 1973. Provides imaginative technical analysis for some of the Beatles' music as well as a colorful view of their role as myth-makers in the 1960s.

Melly, George. *Revolt into Style: The Pop Arts.* New York: Doubleday and Co., 1971. An insightful analysis of the pop scene in London of the mid- and late 1960's.

Norman, Phillip. *Shout! The Beatles in Their Generation.* New York: Simon and Schuster, 1981. Provides some interesting new biographical detail, especially regarding the years 1968–70.

O'Grady, Terence J. "The Ballad Style in the Early Music of the Beatles." *College Music Symposium* 19, no. 1 (Spring, 1979). Discusses influences on the Beatles' early ballad style.

————. "*Rubber Soul* and the Social Dance Tradition." *Ethnomusicology* 23, no. 1 (January, 1979). Discusses the ways in which the *Rubber Soul* album transcends the social-dance conventions of the mid- 1960s.

Phillips, Tom. "The Album as Art Form: One Year after Sergeant Pepper." *Jazz and Pop* 7 (May, 1968). Surveys albums released within a year after *Sergeant Pepper* which demonstrate large-scale unity or integration.

Schaffner, Nicholas. *The Beatles Forever.* New York: McGraw-Hill, 1978. An excellent survey of the Beatles and musical and social development from 1964 to 1978.

Shaw, Arnold. *The Rock Revolution.* Paperback Library. New York: Coronet Communications, 1971. A useful study of rock in the 1960s with particular emphasis on the cultural climate and the business aspects of the recording industry.

Shepherd, Billy. *The True Story of the Beatles.* New York: Bantam Books, 1964. An interesting view of the Beatles' early successes.

Index

Copyright Acknowledgments